SPORTS AND GAMES
OF THE RENAISSANCE

Recent Titles in
Sports and Games Through History

Sports and Games of the Ancients
Steve Craig

Sports and Games of Medieval Cultures
Sally Wilkins

Sports and Games of the 18th and 19th Centuries
Robert Crego

SPORTS AND GAMES OF THE RENAISSANCE

Andrew Leibs

Sports and Games Through History

Greenwood Press
Westport, Connecticut · London

Library of Congress Cataloging-in-Publication Data

Leibs, Andrew.
　　Sports and games of the Renaissance / Andrew Leibs.
　　　　p.　　cm. — (Sports and games through history)
　　Includes bibliographical references and index.
　　ISBN 0–313–32772–6
　　1. Sports—History.　　2. Games—History. I. Title. II. Series.
　GV576.L43　2004
　796'.094'09024—dc22　　　　2004012230

British Library Cataloguing in Publication Data is available.

Library of Congress Catalog Card Number: 2004012230
ISBN: 0–313–32772–6

First published in 2004

Greenwood Press, 88 Post Road West, Westport, CT 06881
An imprint of Greenwood Publishing Group, Inc.
www.greenwood.com

Printed in the United States of America

The paper used in this book complies with the
Permanent Paper Standard issued by the National
Information Standards Organization (Z39.48–1984).

10　9　8　7　6　5　4　3　2　1

R
796. 1
LEI

This book is dedicated to
Makenzie Bouffard
Champion checkers player and my
Dog Eat Dog and *Fear Factor*–watching friend

▦ CONTENTS

▦ SERIES FOREWORD

I am pleased to introduce Greenwood Publishing's *Sports and Games Through History*. I feel this series offers readers the greatest geographical breadth and historical depth of any study on the games we play, how we play them, and what they tell us about the variations and the resounding similarities of the world's cultures.

The series explores sports, games, and physical activities during five periods: ancient times (776 B.C. to A.D. 476), from the first ancient Olympiad to the Fall of Rome; the Middle Ages (A.D. 476 to 1450), the start of the Dark Ages to the invention of printing; the Renaissance (1450 to 1649), printing to the start of the Modern Age; the 18th and 19th centuries (1700 to 1896), Colonial America to the first modern Olympiad; and the 20th century (1896 to 1999—the end of the "American Century" in sports).

The world's seven major regions (Africa, Asia, Europe, Latin America, the Middle East, North America, and Oceania) are all represented, though one of the series' great discoveries is how often sports and games cross geographic boundaries and historical time lines.

In his volume that opens the series, Steve Craig notes that some sports, such as archery and wrestling, are indigenous to every culture in the ancient world. From the pyramids of Egypt to the ruins of Rome, antiquity is strewn with references to, and artifacts from, what look like many modern sports and games, though the lack of written rules and accounts for most of these leaves our knowledge entombed in a netherworld of speculation.

One of the strengths of the series is that essential equipment and the rules of play are provided, wherever possible, for each sport and game, so that students can recreate an activity as well as read about it.

Along with the simultaneous development of sports around the world, the shaping powers of military and cultural imperialism are driving forces by the series' fourth volume on the 18th and 19th centuries. Bob Crego's book demonstrates the inexorable influence of Great Britain, both for the games it carried across its empire (the World Cup is awarded in soccer, not baseball), as well as the native games and traditions it banned while building colonies.

Above all, sports and games from all cultures offer insights that help us understand our own culture. One sees casinos on reservations differently after reading Sally Wilkins's book on the Middle Ages, where we learn about the vital role that games of chance played in the spiritual and emotional lives of most Native American tribes.

The series provides a global context on how sports and games have evolved. Almost without exception, every modern sport has antecedents that predate Christianity, though we see how technology and economic realities in each period covered in this series have shaped their development. The 1,000-year run of the ancient Olympics, the rise of chivalry, the ages of exploration and cultural imperialism, codification—all of these events elevated sports in the 20th century into industry as well as saw them become an indispensable aspect of daily life.

One of the best things to take into the reading of this series is your own knowledge and love of the sports and games you play, watch, and follow. The ensuing pages offer many adventures in learning where these came from and provide ideas on how to have the most fun as you explore the universe of play.

▦ ACKNOWLEDGMENTS

I wish to thank the many people who aided in the research of this book, especially New Hampshire writer Alan Ammann, who contributed a great deal to the games portion of the manuscript. I am also indebted to Carolyn Marvin, former head of adult services at the William-Fogg Library in Eliot, Maine, for her unparalleled ability to deliver research materials and superior editing skills.

I would also like to thank Steve Craig, Bob Crego, and Sally Wilkins for their outstanding contributions to Greenwood's Sports and Games Through History. The success of their books was an ongoing inspiration. In addition, I am most appreciative of editor Rob Kirkpatrick of Greenwood Press for his great feedback and development of this project.

⠿ CHRONOLOGY OF SPORTS AND GAMES DURING THE RENAISSANCE

1347–51	Black Death or Plague, which would eventually kill 75 million people, ravages Europe
1351	Tennis becomes an open-air game in England
1358	Bonifacio Rotario climbs the Rochemelon in the Alps
1377	Playing cards supplant dice as Germany's most popular game
1386–1400	Geoffrey Chaucer writes *Canterbury Tales*
1397	Founding of the Medici Bank
1400	The dice game hazard is widespread in England and Europe
1415	Battle of Agincourt
1416	Drift nets used for first time in fishing
1427	Portuguese reach the Azores
1429	Joan of Arc leads France to break English siege of Orleans; burned at stake in 1431
1429	Earliest mention of billiards
1434	Cosimo de Medici established rule in Florence
1440	Johann Gutenberg invents printing with movable type
1453	Constantinople falls to the Turks ending the Byzantine Empire; end of the Hundred Years War between France and England
1455	Gutenberg Bible printed
1455–85	Wars of the Roses ending with Henry VII defeating Richard III at the Battle of Bosworth Field, and establishing the Tudor dynasty
1465	Edward IV forbids "hustling of stones" and other "bowling-like" sports
1467	Scottish parliament prohibits "fute-ball and golfe"
1474	Archery and arquebus shooting competitions held in Geneva

1478	Spanish Inquisition persecutes Jews, Muslims, and heretics
1480	Leonardo da Vinci invents parachute
1487	Bartholomew Diaz sails around Cape of Good Hope
1490	Founding of Aldus Manutius's press in Venice
1492	Christopher Columbus reaches the West Indies; a form of lacrosse (baggataway) played by Iroquois in lower Ontario and upper New York State
1495–97	Leonardo da Vinci paints *The Last Supper*
1496	Oldest surviving tennis court built in Paris
1498	Vasco da Gama reaches India
1500	Spanish explorers discover tlachtli ball in Mexico; state academy for go formed in Japan; first cesarean section performed
1501	Card games gain great popularity throughout Europe
1501–4	Michelangelo sculpts statue of David
1502	Leonardo da Vinci paints the *Mona Lisa;* first watch is made
1508–12	Michelangelo paints ceiling of Sistine Chapel in Rome
1509	Europeans launch African slave trade
1512	Copernicus writes that the Earth revolves around the Sun (published in 1543)
1513	Henry VIII outshoots the crack shots in his Yeoman of the Guard in Calais, "He cleft the mark in the middle and surpassed them all." *The Prince* by Machiavelli published
1516	*Book of the Courtier* written by Baldassare Castiglione, published in Italy in 1528 and in England in 1561; *Utopia* written by Thomas More
1517	Luther posts his 95 Theses in Wittenberg; coffee introduced in Europe
1519	Charles of Spain becomes Emperor Charles V; Leonardo da Vinci dies; Magellan's five ships set sail around the world, one completes circumnavigation in 1521; Cortez brings Arabian horses to North America
1520	Henry VIII orders construction of bowling lanes at Whitehall; earliest references to tobogganing
1519–21	Cortez conquers the Aztecs
1526	Card game pique first played
1529	Turks besiege Vienna; first reference to the card game whist
1531	Sir Thomas Elyot publishes *The Book of the Governor* in England. "By exercise, the health of a man is preserved and his strength increased"
1534	Henry VIII of England breaks with Roman Catholic Church; completes his covered tennis play (court) at Hampton Court, linked by a gallery to Wolsey's earlier constructed court.
1535	Jacques Cartier sails up the St. Lawrence River
1540	Hernando de Soto discovers the Mississippi River

1545	Roger Ascham publishes his archery treatise *Toxophilus*
1549	Court jesters first appear in Europe
1550	Billiards played for the first time in Italy; first written reference to game that would become cricket
1551	First licensing of alehouses and taverns in England and Wales
1561	Modern chess-playing techniques developed in Spain by Ruy Lopez
1564	William Shakespeare born
1568	Bottled beer invented in London
1577–80	Francis Drake sails around the world
1582	Gregorian calendar reform
1585	Sir Walter Raleigh founds first English colony in Virginia
1588	Spanish Armada defeated by England; Drake plays bowls on Plymouth Hoe prior to battle
1592	Galileo invents the thermometer
1595	England abandons use of bow as war weapon in favor of musket
1599	George Silver's fencing treatise *Paradoxes of Defence* is published
1600	Pato played in Argentina; flintlock invented
1600–1603	Japan organizes swimming nationally, including an imperial edict that mandates its teaching in schools
1605	Newmarket becomes center of horse racing in England
1608	Royal Blackheath Golf Club founded in London; French found Quebec
1609	Henry Hudson sails up the Hudson River
1609	Starving Jamestown colonists observed lawn bowling
1609	Johann Kepler suggests explanation of planetary movement
1610	Galileo observes three bright stars near Jupiter; few days later, he figures there are four satellites of Jupiter
1610–11	Lodovico delle Colombe publishes *Against the Earth's Motion* against Galileo's celestial discoveries
1611	King James Bible published
1613	The Globe Theater burns down; John Dennys's *The Secrets of Angling* published
1618	King James I declaration on "Lawful sports to be used" issued. Known as the King's Book of Sports, it banned football, but legalized post-mass sporting activities on Sunday
1620	Last major jousting tournament held in England; Oliver Cromwell denounced for participating in cricket match
1621	On Christmas Day at Plymouth Plantation, William Bradford confiscates implements for pitching the bar and playing stool ball from newly arrived sporting Englishmen who'd refused to work on Christmas

1630	"Invention" of cribbage ascribed to Sir John Suckling
1635	Speed limit on horse-drawn coaches in London set at 3 m.p.h.
1643	First account of Native American football matches
1665	First horse races held in New York
1666	Cricket Club founded at St. Albans Hertfordshire, England

▦ INTRODUCTION

This book examines sports and games played around the world during the Renaissance, which, for the purposes of this volume, spans the years between the mid-15th and mid-17th centuries.

The Renaissance is one of the most dynamic periods in world history, encompassing a time when human culture escaped the mental and geographic lockdown of the Middle Ages into what we think of as our modern age. This period is characterized as an eruption of discovery and advancement in art, science, exploration, and commerce—an age during which life shimmered with the possibilities for expression, achievement, and joy on Earth, as was seen in the classic cultures of antiquity. As Bertrand Russell says in his *History of Philosophy,* "The long centuries of asceticism were forgotten in a riot of art and poetry and pleasure...old terrors ceased to be terrifying and the new liberty of the spirit was found intoxicating."

That's how the story goes, anyhow. Backing up assertions about the period's genesis, geographic and chronological parameters, or meaning creates difficulties. For one thing, many terms we use to discuss the period, including Renaissance (which means "rebirth") and feudalism (the land-based economy of the Middle Ages), were not coined until hundreds of years later. For another, the notion that a Renaissance occurred was not even conceptualized until 1860 when Jakob Burckhardt published *The Civilization of the Renaissance in Italy.* The Renaissance is, as Wallace Ferguson said, "the most intractable problem child of historiography."

On the other hand, something palpably new was at hand: within a hundred years, from the mid-15th to the mid-16th centuries, printing was invented; the New World discovered; the globe circumnavigated; the true course of celestial movements quantified; many of the greatest works in art and literature created; and the foundations laid for modern politics and philosophy.

Despite the vast number of innovations in art, science, and commerce, the Renaissance produced almost no new sports and games. It was, however, a significant period in sports history during which increased leisure time and an explosion in popularity of many pastimes led to their refinement and systemization. Sports and games invented in antiquity and developed during the Middle Ages became a more entrenched part of daily life. Through growing application in new urban areas and at court, pastimes assumed their modern shape.

In the Middle Ages, for example, annual football (soccer) matches between neighboring towns easily degenerated into melees. By the end of the 16th century, the game pitted teams of equal number, had developed man-to-man defenses, and had instituted roughness penalties. Playing cards invented in the 14th century exploded in popularity at the start of the 16th, with primero and one & thirty (forerunners of modern blackjack and poker) played throughout Europe. In Japan, during the stability of the Edo Period, warriors internalized their knowledge of ancient fighting techniques to create martial arts systems such as karate. Codification of most sports would come in the 19th century, but by the Renaissance, a consensus had seemed to form on how most sports are played.

Of all the technological advances of the Renaissance, one that had a major influence on sports was printing: movable type created an unparalleled ability to share and promote ideas across continents. At last the elaborate (and even secret, as many believed) techniques of fencing could be laid out in a book. Printing meant access to the rules for chess and other games, promoting fair, consistent play. It also meant calendars for counting the days until the next sports-filled feast day, not to mention playing cards, game boards printed on paper sheets such as "goose," and books that, for the first time, promoted the cultivation of the complete human being: well educated, appreciative of art, knowledgeable in the ways of politics, and physically capable.

The longing among young, ambitious men to attain a physical ideal both in bodily perfection and athletic skill prompted Baldassare Castiglione—in his *Book of the Courtier* (1528)—to quantify the necessary traits: the courtier should be "well-built and shapely of limb," and partake of "all bodily exercises (swimming, running, leaping) that befit a man of war." Similarly, Sir Thomas Elyot's *Book of the Governor* (1531) called activities such as running, swimming, and hunting exercises that made "the spirit of a man more strong and valiant." Both Baldassare and Elyot cited archery, fencing, and tennis as sports befitting gentlemen of rank, and as a result, these sports became immensely popular. These works—among the first "self-help" books in publishing history—exerted a great influence on a growing reading public, an influence that readers of modern exercise and diet books will readily understand.

Of all the innovations introduced during the Renaissance, the one that fused technology with a new awareness most definitively was an ever-growing consciousness of time. When the only means of measuring time other than the sun and seasons is the tolling of a church bell, it is easy to view life as an inexorable plod toward the next world. During the Renaissance, man learned how to measure the minutes in a day, and began to sense the shape of history, that they stood in a new age, separated from a golden past by centuries of stifling mediocrity and political repression. Clocks appeared in 1354; the first watches in 1500. In 1582, the solar year was standardized by the adoption of the Gregorian calendar in Spain. The ability to mark the passage of days on printed calendars led not only to the custom of celebrating birthdays, but added levels of certitude and optimism to the cycles of life.

When you can measure time, you can separate what time is yours and plan how to spend it. Leisure time is built into life. When you can mark off the days to a Shrove Tuesday football game or Morris dance on a calendar, the memories of previous feast-day revels can heighten anticipation and even inspire preparation for future events.

Though the Renaissance had its epicenter in Europe, its energy caused tremors that would be felt around the world. This was the age of exploration: Columbus, da Gama, and Magellan opened up new worlds far beyond the Mediterranean Sea, changed man's perception of the size and boundaries of the Earth, and painted the first broad strokes for humanity's embryonic image of globalization.

Exploration had a profound impact on sports. Spanish conquistadors brought back an amazing new substance called rubber used to make balls for a Mesoamerican game that would prove to be one of the oldest and most socially entrenched team sports in history. French and English explorers discovered kayaks and birch-bark canoes, and were astounded with their strength, lightness, and design. In addition to lacrosse sticks and bandy-type games similar to those played in England, settlers in the New World discovered cultures in which sports and games transcended pastime to become the center of a cosmology.

Ocean trade and colonization also led to the slave trade. In its way, this heinous institution, as Arthur Ashe notes in his book *A Hard Road to Glory,* would contribute to the development of some of the world's greatest athletes. By seizing the fittest African men and women they could find, and with the attrition that occurred during the arduous sea journey, slave traders inadvertently transplanted members of a culture that prized endurance and physical prowess to a land that would be built on their strength. And though it would take centuries for the nation to give them the opportunity to compete as athletes, when those days came in the 20th century, African Americans became the world's most accomplished athletes in numerous sports.

Exploration also opened the vastness of the Pacific Ocean and gave Europeans their first cursory knowledge of secluded nations such as Japan, and the tens of thousands of islands between the Strait of Magellan and the Indian Ocean, including Easter Island, Polynesia, and Australia. In Oceania, as in much of the world, the playing of traditional sports and games (boomerang throwing, surfing, kite flying, martial arts) invented thousands of years in the past continued unchanged, and their exoticism would eventually be carried to new lands and inspire new practitioners.

Following the Renaissance, the next great leap in sports evolution followed the industrial revolution in the mid-19th century. Urbanization, a growing working class with yet more leisure time, and class consciousness among the elite led to the further organization and codification of the rules of many modern sports, including baseball, cricket, and boxing. Sports as business both mythically and economically entwined in the human psyche would follow in the 20th century, but we see in the Renaissance the beginnings of sports shift from occasional pastime to quantified activity made more accessible through technology, transformed from diversion into human necessity.

▦ AFRICA

INTRODUCTION

The Renaissance, which began in Europe in the 14th century, ushered in the age of exploration, and this had a profound effect on the myriad complex cultures on the African continent. The same period that saw Dutch, English, French, and Spanish traders establish colonies in North America also witnessed the beginning of a reprehensible chapter in human history, the African slave trade.

Slavery was by no means a European invention. Enslavement had, for centuries, been a fact of life among tribes throughout Africa, a known consequence of war. But the buying and selling of human beings, the uprooting to a world thousands of miles away, and the brutality inflicted was a world-altering level of dehumanization for millions of Africans. And as the slave trade became more established, the colonization of Africa itself by European nations began.

Africa is an immense continent with vastly different cultures; hundreds of languages were spoken, and a broad range of economies had been established throughout sub-Saharan regions. The northeast regions, including Egypt, were a world apart in terms of culture: the triumph of Islam and long-established trade routes made Egypt, built on the Nile, and the Near East more connected to Europe and Asia than the agrarian cultures further south.

The regions from which slaves were taken were located in West Africa and included the Ivory Coast to western Nigeria and the Niger Delta, Angola, the lower Congo, and Gambia. It was here that Europeans encountered African games and rituals. For the most part, the majesty of the African warrior athlete, the finely tuned communal structures, and cultural and religious intricacies of the invaded lands were lost on the Europeans, who sought only to man their plantations.

However despicable the institution of slavery was, its practice dispersed African culture throughout the New World, which would have a profound effect on the worldwide development of sports. As Arthur Ashe notes in *A Hard Road to Glory,* "It made undeniable economic sense to the slave traders to capture the fittest they could find. Once in America, the Africans' love of physical expression combined with a new set of highly organized sports—and little chance for success elsewhere—to produce the greatest athletes the world had yet seen" (8).

Throughout most of Africa, sports and leisure activities were woven into everyday tasks. As George Godia notes (Wagner 267–68) in an essay about sports in Kenya:

> Traditional physical exercises were part of the daily routine of earning a living. Rituals to mark the beginning of the rainy season, of the hunting season, or of the fishing season were usually accompanied by dancing and singing. Competitive games in activities such as running, throwing, and climbing were common among herdboys, especially during the free time while looking after cattle.

A rare autobiographical account by Olaudah Equiano, published in 1789, shows the enmeshment of sport with daily life. "I was trained up from my earliest years in the art of war; my daily exercise was shooting and throwing javelins." Later, after he became a slave in Africa, he notes, "My young master and I, with other boys, sported with our darts and bows and arrows, as I had been used to do at home" (Spears 43).

As is the case with much of the world, notably North America and Oceania, most of the sports, activities, and games cited in this chapter predate the Renaissance (1350 to 1650) by hundreds, if not thousands, of years. The lack of written records, most of which post-date the period of the Renaissance, add to the difficulty of creating historical context for such sports. Early explorers and slave traders were among the first to record observations of African athletes. The games they saw were developed by entire cultures over time. The aim of this chapter is to present a sampling of traditional sports and games that have developed in Africa over many centuries.

AFRICAN SPORTS

▦ Archery

Archeologists are in general agreement that the use of the bow and arrow began in Africa, perhaps as early as 25,000 B.C. During the Renaissance, the crossbow and firearms began to replace the bow and arrow in

Europe, but traditional weapons predominated in Africa until the 19th century.

The Bambuti people of central Africa (known by the now-derogatory name "pygmies") were accomplished archers, able to bring down huge game, including lions, buffalo, and even elephants with their relatively small (less than two feet) bows.

As with Native American cultures, archery was borne of necessity, for defense during intertribal wars, and for hunting, but also grew in popularity as a sport. Testing one's ability to shoot at specific targets helped develop crucial hand-eye coordination.

▦ Dancing and Gymnastics

Nearly every African culture danced. Usually, the dancing was a group activity for the purpose of giving thanks to spirits and to ask for favors, such as a bountiful harvest, victory in battle, or rain. It was also used as a means of celebrating events such as births and marriages, and also for mourning, such as the loss of a family member. The occasion and accompanying emotions dictated the bodily movements employed.

In a similar vein, gymnastics were also a popular way to celebrate the human form and physical prowess in a competitive venue. Gymnasts might gather under a full moon or after a harvest to see who could perform the most intricate contortions and maneuvers.

The *yakoba* dance typifies a common approach to these activities, combining dance with intricate acrobatic techniques. In this dance, two young men called *simbos* did elaborate movements while balancing small children (called *sangnoulou*) on their shoulders. The movements included the synchronized swinging of the *sangnoulou* by wrists and ankles, and the intricate tossing and catching of them between the *simbos*. The dancers wore masks and costumes.

▦ Rowing

Many tribes in central Africa engaged frequently in rowing races in various types of vessels. The Boloki of the Upper Congo River and the Bachiga of Uganda rowed competitively on lakes and rivers. The Luo people of Kenya used a boat race on Lake Victoria to test that a new boat was better than the old one. European traders witnessed boat races in present-day South Africa.

▦ *Rungu* Throw

This contest originated with the Maasai warrior tribes of Kenya and was popular with the Baganda people of what is now Uganda and is designed to test one's ability to throw a club for distance and accuracy. This contest was used as a training method for young warriors and is associated with battle or cattle raiding missions. Only young males participated in the *rungu* throw, which was often performed in the presence of tribal elders.

The *rungu* is an 18-inch club with a curved neck and rounded head. The *rungu* is thrown from a preset throwing area (as with the throwing circles for the shot put and discus) at target ranges, at stationary or moving targets, or for distance. Matches usually continued until a dominant thrower emerged.

The *rungu* throw is obviously an outdoor contest. A cudgel, nightstick, or any small club can serve as a substitute. A target range can be marked off with lime and specific targets, such as an empty cardboard box, set in an open area.

▦ Running

Racing of all kinds (running, swimming, climbing, canoeing, or rowing) were likely the most popular form of competition among most African tribes. In Northern Africa, conquering Muslim armies spread enthusiasm for horse racing. Among the Sotho tribes of central Africa, oxen racing (jockeys aboard the beasts) became a popular sport. And boat racing has always been a popular team sport.

Running was likely the earliest racing venue as it required no equipment and, as an activity, was more integral to daily life than swimming or climbing. Running was a survival skill necessary for hunting as well as transportation. Hunting parties often covered vast distances in search of game, making the development of stamina essential for any young man wishing to contribute to the work of his family and village.

Apart from its utilitarian purposes, running has been a favorite means of competition for centuries. Races were often run between villages, or as special challenges, including mountain ascents. The superiority of African runners was noted by historians in ancient Rome, and one need only check the results of any major marathon today to see that Africans still produce many of the best runners in the world. The high altitudes, mountain trails, and rich cultural tradition of running in nations such as Kenya and Tanzania produce champions year after year.

It should also be noted that, despite great advances in training techniques and equipment, Africa has produced Olympians in the 20th century that ran in their bare feet, which, until modern times, was the standard.

▦ San Ball Games

There is little evidence to suggest that ball games in Africa attained anything near the popularity they did in Europe and North America. There were some, however, and accounts of two such games of the San people in South Africa, one played by men and one played by women, are well known.

The women played what looked like a communal form of catch, and it is unclear whether the game was competitive or cooperative. The men played a rougher game, vying to catch a ball bounced high off a stone. Ethnographer George Stow described a San ball game as a "dance" in his book *Native Races of South Africa*, published in 1905.

> Some of their dances required considerable skill, such as that which may be called the ball dance. In this a number of women from five to ten would form a line and face an equal number in another row, leaving a space of thirty or forty feet between them. A woman at the end of one of these lines would commence by throwing a round ball, about the size of an orange, and made of a root, under her right leg, and across to the woman opposite to her, who in turn would catch the ball and throw it back in a similar manner to the second in the second, and thus it continued until all had taken their turn. Then the women would shift their positions, crossing over to opposite sides, and again continue in the same manner as before; and so on until the game was over, when they would rest for a short time and begin again.

The men's game also used a special ball made from the thickest portion of a hippopotamus hide, cut from the back of the neck; the fresh piece of hide was hammered until round, and it was quite elastic. A flat stone was placed in the center of a field and players stood around it. The game was similar to the women's game in that it was a form of catch. The first player would bounce the ball off the stone and the next in line would catch it. The catcher would then throw it and the next in line would catch it. The last thrower would bounce the ball very high off the stone and during its ascent, the players would throw themselves wildly into all kinds of positions, make loud noises, and all the while position themselves to catch the ball to become leader for the next game.

▦ Stick Fighting

Traditional stick fighting was once an important skill necessary for warding off both animals and rustlers that might be pursuing one's cattle herd, the source of a family's dietary staple and wealth in many African nations. Mock swordfighting with sticks also figured into warrior training and religious rites and was, after wrestling, the most popular and widespread African sport.

Stick fighting was used to test speed, physical skill, and endurance. It was also an important means of showing one's prowess in courting. The Donga, for example, was an annual stick-fighting tournament among the Surma people of Ethiopia that took place after the harvest. A period of courtship took place, with young people spending peaceful days by the river and perhaps painting their bodies.

The next phase of the rite featured some of the fiercest competition on the continent. The sticks used in this ritualized fighting were hard wooden poles about eight feet long designed to knock down one's opponent. Winning a wife was the chief goal, but this stylized combat was also employed to settle grievances and to test or demonstrate one's masculinity.

The only rule is that one is not allowed to kill one's opponent. At the end of the day's fighting, the victor is carried from the field on an intricate platform of poles, high in the air, toward a group of the most beautiful women in the village. The women do the choosing, however, balancing the ritual.

Stick fighting, like fencing, is not a good contest to try and replicate, given the risk of injury, even when striking the body is not allowed. One form that originated in Kenya many centuries ago shows what is involved in a stick fight.

Warriors would cut forked sticks from the leketwo tree, whose wood marks easily when struck. A modern equivalent might be coating a stick with paint, flour, or chalk so that hits to it are easy to see. No hits to the body are allowed, only to the opponent's stick. A match begins when both players are ready and one says, "Let us begin." The match may last for a preset period of time, such as three minutes, until a player's stick has been hit a given number of times, or until both players are tired.

Stick fighting was immensely popular from Egypt to South Africa, second only to wrestling in terms of cultural importance. In South Africa, the two main Bantu-speaking groups, the Nguni and the Sotho-Tswana, engaged in a form of fighting that used a stick in each hand: one for parrying and one for thrusting or striking, the primary target being the opponent's head. In a chapter on sport in his landmark work, *The Zulu People*, Catholic missionary A.T. Bryant describes young boys' zeal for stick fighting.

> Nothing was more enjoyed than sham-fighting (ukuqakulisana) with the quarter-staves. Every boy, like every man, when away from the home kraal, always carried with him a couple of strong sticks; and, fist or hand-fighting being utterly unknown to the Zulus, their fights were always with these sticks. One stick, held about the middle in his left hand, was used for parrying; the other held near its end in the right, was for striking. This exercise in a way resembled our own fencing, and the boys became great adepts both at parrying and at striking, the aim being practically always for the head.

▦ Swimming

Swimming has always served as a form of competitive play among young African boys and girls. Swimming was both a survival skill and recreational activity. What separates the sport is that it employs no standard swimming strokes—each swimmer tore through the water as best they could. Also, competitions varied: two people might vie to see who could swim under water the farthest, or they might race to an established target.

⊞ Tug of War

Tug of war was one of the few team sports readily practiced in Africa, and was an activity that could accommodate all the people of the village as participants and spectators. The object in tug of war is for one team to pull the center of a thick rope or vine over a line in the sand. It is among the most physically demanding sports, as it puts maximum stress on every muscle group from the fingers to the toes for periods of several minutes or more. Tug of war was both a test of brute strength and team unity, and also gave team members a chance to work out aggressions.

⊞ Watusi High Jump

The Watusi people used jumping for various rituals and competitions. Youths competed in a forerunner of the modern high jump, and leaping and chanting as a group was used to channel energy in preparation for war.

The high jump competition was very similar to the modern high jump event in that the bar (in this case, a long reed balanced atop two poles) was set at incrementally higher levels to winnow competitors who were eliminated if they failed once at any height. They also employed a running start of about 20 yards prior to their takeoff.

The Watusi used a sort of launch pad (a hummock or anthill) to give them a boost. Modern high jumping has no such launching pad. The use of the hummock may account for the Watusi's purported jumps of more than eight feet, which is a modern world record.

The high jump was a right of passage for young men. The ability to clear one's own height was considered a necessary step for becoming an adult.

The Watusi also used jumping as part of a prewar energy-gathering ritual. The tribe gathered together in a circle, spears and shields in hand, and the warriors jumped up and down as high as they could while rhythmically chanting. This traditional method of channeling energy to "get psyched" for battle lives on and can be observed on the football field, with teams chanting or yelling as one while warming up.

⊞ Wrestling

Traditional wrestling is probably the single most significant sport throughout Africa. Often associated with festivals and religious celebrations, wrestling also prepared soldiers for combat, kept the body physically fit and served as a contest of fitness and skill among young boys. In some cultures, including the Igbo, wrestling was part of a young man's initiation into adulthood.

Wrestling matches generally took place after harvest, between November and March. Heralds would go out from host villages and announce upcoming events with horn and drum. The events often featured elaborate masks and costumes and were accompanied by music and ceremonial dance.

In addition to its physical benefits, wrestling also provided a means for a young man to achieve lasting fame beyond his village. Top wrestlers were lauded as heroes and became part of a region's oral tradition, as the opening of Chinua Achebe's classic novel *Things Fall Apart* dramatizes:

> Okonkwo was well known throughout the nine villages and even beyond. His fame rested on solid personal achievements. As a young man of eighteen, he had brought honor to his village by throwing Amalinze the Cat. Amalinze was the great wrestler who for seven years was unbeaten, from Umuofia to Mbaino. He was called the Cat because his back would never touch the earth. It was this man that Okonkwo threw in a fight, which the old men agreed was one of the fiercest since the founder of their town engaged a spirit of the wild for seven days and seven nights. (7)

We see that Okonkwo's personal fame transcended his surroundings, and that the act of wrestling also brought honor to his village. The passage also shows the type of wrestling practiced: the goal is to throw an opponent onto his back. It is also clear that great wrestlers would take on all comers, a daunting, yet no doubt intriguing challenge many young men contemplate.

Wrestling has been an integral part of African culture for centuries and, as a sport, is still largely informal. There are traditional rules, however. E. O. Ojeme notes that rules used in Nigerian wrestling include the matching of participants by age, the outlawing of blows or grabbing below the belt, and the banning of the use of any sort of charm. In general, matches are staged in an open, sandy place. Traditional music plays, and a match is won when an opponent is thrown so that he is lying on the ground in a supine position.

Though wrestling was more popular among young men, women also participated in the sport. Nuba and Ibo women wrestled each year after the harvest. Women wrestlers vied for respect and to attract the attention of young men. In Gambia, the top female wrestler often married the male champion.

AFRICAN PLAY

▦ *Anotoba*

Anotoba is a children's game along the lines of duck-duck-goose, but with a few added subtleties. Players (the game works best with 20 or more) sit in a large circle. One player, chosen to begin the game, stands outside holding a small beanbag or other token, such as a stone, rag, or hat. The holder runs around the circle and quietly drops the object behind one of the seated players, and then races around the outside of the circle to return to the beanbag. If a complete circle is made, the holder gently taps the seated player behind which he dropped the bag on the shoulder. The two then race once around the circle, with the winner getting the coveted seat. If the seated player notices the drop, he or she must run to try and catch the other player before they get around the circle and back to the player's place. If the seated player succeeds in catching the other player, he or she keeps the seat. If the player who dropped the beanbag makes it all the way around, he or she wins the player's seat, and that player must walk the outside and begin the next round. Players sitting in the circle are not allowed to look at the person dropping the beanbag. This game can be played inside or out, and tests not only speed and agility, but also physical subtlety and awareness.

▦ Crows and Cranes

This is a South African game, a form of tag that two teams (crows and cranes) can play, either indoors or out. The two teams stand facing each other along a center line. A teacher or referee calls out either "crows" or "cranes." The specified group then turns and runs back toward an end line, pursued by the others. Any players who are tagged become part of the other team. The teams then face off again and the action is repeated. The caller may flip a coin to see which team is called to keep both teams on their toes. The game continues until one team has captured all the players on the other. One variation on scoring is for players to be put out of the game once tagged.

▦ *Daolikhabo*

This game from Nigeria's Owan tribe is generally played by children and young adults and is a subtle team version of blindman's buff. The game can be played inside or out. Teams sit facing one another so the venue can be opposing rows of desks or tables, or a quiet area outside on the grass. The only necessary equipment is a hood or blindfold of some sort.

A player from the first team approaches the opposing team and puts the blindfold on the first player. Then, a second member of the first team walks silently up to the blindfolded person and touches them on the back or shoulder, and then returns to his or her seat. The blindfold is removed and the person who was touched tries to guess who touched them.

If the guess is correct, the person from the first team comes over and joins the second team. If the guess is incorrect, the one who was touched must join the first team.

In the next round, a person from the second team goes and blindfolds a player on the first team and the touching and guessing is repeated. The game can proceed until one team has captured all the players on the other team or for a preset number of rounds, after which the team with the most players wins.

A key element captured in this game is the silent, subtle ways people both give away and recognize actions.

▦ *Ifi-Uvin*

This group game from Nigeria reinforces the development of hunter-gatherer skills, though its essential element is reminiscent of the "jump ball" that starts basketball games. In *ifu-uvin,* players on two opposing teams vie to retrieve a coconut that is thrown into the air between them.

This works best as an outdoor game, though it could be staged in a full-court (94 feet) gymnasium. Teams line up and face each other many yards apart. A center line is drawn between them, where a referee stands holding a coconut. A bag of rags or a slightly deflated ball can serve as a substitute. The object has to be solid, without bouncing too much, which can cause erratic movement from players, resulting in collisions.

The referee throws the coconut into the air over the centerline as players from each team try to be the first to retrieve it. Each retrieval is worth one point. The game can last for a preset period of time or can be played until one team has scored a specific number of points. No undue physical contact is permitted, such as pushing or holding.

▦ Lions and Goats

This is a chase-and-capture game from the Bini tribe in Nigeria. It is a game that involves a great deal of running and can also incorporate a large number of players. The game is essentially between two teams, the lions and the goats. A contingent of remaining players serves as villagers and creates a ring around and inside of which the action takes place.

The object of this outdoor game is for the lions to catch the goats while the goats avert capture.

The villagers form a large circle by holding hands. The lions and goats each send one player to compete in the first round. The goat goes inside the village; the lion runs around the outside, trying to break in to tag him.

In its traditional setting, a song might be sung as a ceremonial start of the action. A countdown, or shouting, "Go!" can be used in its place. The lion tears around the circle, trying to get in by breaking the human chain or ducking beneath it. The villagers try their best to keep him out. If the lion gets inside, the villagers then allow the goat to slip out of the circle, while they try to hold the lion in.

If the lion catches the goat, the goat goes over to the lion team. If the lion fails, he or she becomes a goat. Since the game is exhausting, the contest might run for a preset period of time, such as 20 minutes. Whichever team has captured the most players is the winner.

▦ *Simbii*

This is a boy's game from the Kalenjns tribe in Kenya that tests both form and accuracy in the throwing of 10 small objects into a hole several feet away.

This game is designed for 10 players. Each player brings one button to the game, taken from an old shirt or pair of pants. A hole is dug in the ground about two inches wide and two inches deep. A bowl or small wastebasket can be used if the game must be played indoors.

After the hole is dug, a line is marked about 10 to 15 feet away to indicate the throwing area. Each player, in turn, is given all 10 buttons and he throws them, one at a time, in an effort to get all 10 into the hole. Each player employs whatever style works best for him. After all the players have thrown, the judge determines who was the best thrower. This style of determination hearkens back to a time when rites were performed before tribal elders, whose wisdom and decision making was respected.

Getting all 10 buttons into the hole, therefore, is only part of the contest. Behavior during the game, adhering to the rules (no going beyond the throwing line), and continued accuracy and composure if the game requires extra rounds (which is common) are all considerations.

AFRICAN GAMES

▦ *Achi*

Achi is a game similar to tic-tac-toe that originated in Ghana. The object, as with tic-tac-toe, is to get three in a row, but instead of X's and O's, each player has three game pieces that are set down one at a time on the intersecting points of the game board, which is a square that is divided into eight triangles as shown in the illustration.

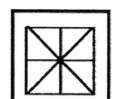

An *achi* board.

The game board is easy to draw. To play *achi*, you need three game pieces, which can be coins, pebbles, bits of paper, etc. Players take turns placing a game piece on any of the dots, or places where lines intersect. Once all the pieces are on the board, players take turns moving one piece at a time to one of the three empty spots. You cannot jump over another piece or an empty spot. The first person to have three pieces in a straight line is the winner.

A similar three-in-a-row game to *achi* is *dara*, which was played by the Dakarkari of Western Africa. The game board was a grid of six spaces by five and was often simply scooped out of the dirt. Each player began with 12 game pieces, which could be any small object, such as stones or seeds. The players took turns placing pieces, one at a time, into the holes—one piece per hole. Once all the pieces were placed, the players took turns moving their pieces one space at a time to create as many rows of three as possible. After creating a row of three, a player could take an opponent's piece from the board. Whoever made the most rows of three was the winner.

▦ *Ipenpen*

This Yoruba guessing game is similar to many played by Native Americans and involves the continued wagering on the guessing, counting, and recounting of small seeds. To play, a quantity of seeds (or small stones) is poured on the ground. One player divides the pile and the other guesses which pile contains more. The seeds are counted and whoever was correct claims the stake for that round. Traditionally, games of this sort are played for hours, but can also end when either player has had enough.

▦ *Kora*

Kora is a Kenyan game similar to jacks, in which six stones are tossed and caught in varying combinations. Generally young girls play the game, and the game works well with several players. The game requires six small stones, one of which is designated the queen or king.

Players can split into small groups depending on the total number of players. For example, if a class of 24 wants to try this game, six sets of four people works well. Basically, this is a toss-and-catch game that tests coordination and depth perception as one works into a rhythm for tossing and catching the stones in various combinations.

A player starts by selecting the queen stone and tossing it into the air high enough to be able to catch one stone at a time before the queen stone drops until all five are picked up. Caught stones are placed in the non-throwing hand. Once all five stones have been caught, they are put back on the ground for the next round.

In the next round, a player tosses the queen and tries to pick up the stones in sets of two, two, and one, or one, two, and two until all five have been picked up again. In the next phase, the players try to pick up two followed by three. Next, the player goes for the one, four combination, and lastly, the five-in-one pickup.

When these steps are completed successfully, the player picks up all six stones, tosses them in the air, and tries to catch them all on the backs of the hands. Both hands are pressed together with palms facing down, index fingers touching. Once these are caught, they are flung back up into the air and caught in both hands in the usual way.

Completing all the steps earns a player one point. Players try to accumulate as many points as possible. Any miss and the stones pass to the next player.

The stones used in *kora* are about the size of dice. Small pebbles can serve as a substitute, as will jacks or actual dice.

▦ Mancala

Mancala is the national board game of Africa. It is actually a family of what are called "count and capture" or "pit and pebble" games that has over 250 variations all played on similar boards. Mancala began in ancient Egypt and was carried by trade down the Nile River valley and was eventually brought to the Middle East, Asia, and the West Indies where it remains popular to this day.

The two most popular versions of mancala are *bao kiswahili* (which we will call *bao*), which is very popular in Zanzibar, Kenya, Tanzania, Malawi, Zambia, and eastern Zaire, and *Oware*, which is common to West Africa and the Caribbean. All mancala games involve the strategic and sequential picking up and dropping ("sowing") of small game pieces around the board, which usually consists of two rows of six pits or hollows. The goal is to distribute the pieces so that the pits in front of a player contain two, three, or four pieces and can be captured and stored in a player's "reservoir" at the end of the board.

This hand-carved wooden mancala board is 20.5 cm wide by 58.2 cm long by 24.1 cm high. Fourteen depressions are carved into the board, two rows of six each, with a reservoir at each long end of the board. A stylized leopard carved into the base is typical of certain traditional Ashanti carvings found in West Africa. This raised base is 2.1 cm high by 38.4 cm long by 17.3 cm wide. (Used with permission of the Elliott Avedon Museum and Archive of Games, University of Waterloo.)

Since each game starts with the same number of pieces in each pit and since both players drop pieces counterclockwise around the board, mancala can develop strategic counting skills while remaining fun enough for players of all ages.

Mancala sets can be purchased at any toy store, and the materials needed for creating a game can range from an empty egg box (a 12-egg carton is a handy way to visualize the board with its facing sets of six hollows) to 12 holes scooped out of the sand on a beach. For the counters (24 per player), you can use small stones, marbles, or seeds. Shape or color does not matter, but they should be small enough so 12–15 can fit easily into one hollow.

▦ Oware (Wari)

Oware, or *wari,* is a mancala variant played on a 12-hollow board that dates back to ancient Egypt and is ideally suited for two players.

Oware is played on a surface consisting of two rows of six hollows. Often, there are two extra hollows normally placed centrally at the end of each pair of rows. Each of the 12 hollows is filled with four counters. There are two large extra hollows at either end of the board that are called "reservoirs." The reservoir on each player's far right belongs to that player and contains his or her captured counters. To decide who goes first, one player hides a counter in a fist. If the opponent correctly guesses which fist, the opponent starts.

The objective is to capture more counters than your opponent. Players take turns to distribute counters. To take a turn, a player chooses a hollow from one of the six directly in front of him or her and picks up all the counters contained in it. The player then drops a single counter into the next hollow in a counterclockwise direction, a single counter into the hollow after that, and so on until they have all been dropped.

When a player reaches the end of a row, sowing continues in a counterclockwise direction in the opponent's row. When a player picks a hollow with so many seeds (12 or more) that sowing them requires a full lap or more around the board, the 12th (and 23rd) counter is not played in the originating hollow: that space is skipped and the counter is played in the next hollow. The originating hollow is always left empty at the end of the turn.

If the last counter is dropped in the opponent's row and the hollow finishes with two or three counters, those are captured and placed in the reservoir. If the hollow that immediately precedes it also contains two or three counters, these are also captured, and so on until a hollow is reached that does not contain two or three counters or the end of the opponent's row is reached.

If a player cannot play because all six hollows in front of him or her are empty, the game ends and all the counters on the other side of the board are captured. However, if the opponent's hollows are all empty, the player must drop at least one counter on their side of the board if possible during their turn.

It is perfectly legal to attempt to capture all the opponent's counters thus leaving the opponent with no move and thereby capturing all the remaining counters in his or her row. Such a play is known as "cutting off the head." A common strategy for cutting off the head is to collect a large number of counters in one hole while forcing the opponent to empty most of the hollows on the other side of the board. A player will then set up a turn where he or she can pick up and distribute a large number of counters so that they are dropped around the board once and into the opponent's territory again, leaving several hollows with two or three counters which are thus captured.

The game ends when one player has captured 25 counters, and that player is the winner. The game ends in a draw if both players accumulate 24 counters or when it becomes clear that the last remaining counters are just being moved around the board with no chance of capturing.

⚏ Bao La Kujifunza

Bao (a word that means "board") is played on a board consisting of four rows of eight hollows. In this variant, a hollow is called a *shimo,* the plural being *mashimo*. The counters are called *kete* and should be hard objects small enough so that 15 of them will comfortably fit in one hollow.

The 48 hollows are filled with two counters each. To decide who goes first, one player holds a counter in a fist. If the opponent correctly guesses which fist holds it, the opponent starts.

The two rows nearest each player belong to that player, as do the counters contained within them. Captured counters are moved from the opponent's hollows into the other player's. The objective is to cause the opponent to have no counters in his or her front row or to make the opponent unable to move.

Players take turns to move counters within their own hollows. On each turn, the player first chooses one of his or her occupied hollows and picks up all the counters contained in it. The player must drop the counters either in a clockwise or counterclockwise direction around the two rows. The player drops a single counter into the next hollow, another into the hollow after that, and so on until all the counters are dropped. When the player reaches the end of a row, he continues in the other row according to the choice of direction.

A *mtaji* is a group of 2 to 15 counters in a hollow that are in a position to capture the counters in an opponent's hollow. If a *mtaji* exists, the player must play a capturing move. Otherwise, the player must make a *kutakata* move.

Capturing Move

A capture is made when the counters of a *mtaji* are distributed one by one in one direction or the other and the last counter falls into a hollow that

- is in the front row
- is occupied
- is in line with an occupied hollow in the opponent's front row.

In this case, the counters in the opponent's occupied hollow are captured and the player takes them and plays them in turn according to the following rules:

The captured counters start in the far left hollow of the front row and are distributed in a clockwise direction in the following cases:

- The captured counters were in one of the two left-most lines.
- The captured counters were in one of the four central lines and the *mtaji* was distributed in a clockwise direction.

The captured counters start in the far right hollow of the front row and are distributed in a counterclockwise direction in the following cases:

- The captured counters were in one of the two right-most lines.
- The captured counters were in one of the four central lines and the *mtaji* was distributed in a counterclockwise direction.

If the last captured counter falls into an occupied counter that is in line with an empty hollow in the opponent's front row, the player takes all the counters in this occupied hollow (including the counters just deposited in it) and begins afresh with the new counters, continuing in the same direction and starting with the following hollow. The player repeats this until either the last counter played falls into an empty hollow or another capture is made.

If the last counter falls into a hollow that matches the three capturing rules above, the counters in the opponent's hollow are captured and play continues with the captured counters as before. When the last counter falls into an empty hollow, the turn is over.

Kutakata Move

The *kutakata* move is performed when a player has no *mtaji* at the beginning of a turn. The player decides upon a direction and proceeds to distribute the counters in that direction. If the last counter falls into an occupied hollow, the player takes all the counters in this occupied hollow (including the counter just deposited in it) and begins afresh with the new counter, continuing in the same direction and starting with the next hollow. The player repeats this until the last counter played falls into an empty hollow, whereupon the turn finishes. *Kutakata* must obey the following rules:

- *Kutakata* cannot be started with only one counter.
- A player can *takata* from a back row hollow only if it is not possible to *takata* from a front row hollow.
- Having started to *takata* in one direction, a player cannot change direction during that turn.
- Having started to *takata,* no captures may be made during that turn.

A player loses when

- All six hollows in the row in front of the player are empty.
- A player has no *mtaji* and cannot *takata* because none of his or her hollows has two or more counters.

▦ Panda

Panda, like *ipenpen*, is another game that involves counting and betting on the sum. In *panda*, one player drops a predetermined number of beans on the ground and then quickly scoops back up a small number of them. The second player, after taking a quick (a few seconds at most) look at the remaining beans, can call for one, two, or three beans to be tossed back onto the pile on the ground. Once these steps are complete, the pile on the ground is counted. The goal is to have the final number of beans on the ground be a multiple of four. If the total is a multiple of four, the guesser wins. If the sum is not a multiple of four, the thrower wins. *Panda* demands a quick eye, nimble arithmetic skills, and luck.

▦　Stone Tossing

Both the Kamba people of Kenya and the Zulu of South Africa had forms of competitive stone tossing that combine elements of sport and play. In this game, stones were piled before each competitor and that person had to throw a stone up in the air, pick up another stone with the same hand as the one used to throw the stone, and then catch the first stone before it hit the ground. The game helped build hand-eye coordination and mental agility.

▦　*Yote*

Yote is a form of African checkers. In this ancient game, players try to capture an opponent's pieces by jumping over them. Unlike draughts or American checkers, *yote* begins with all playing stones off the board. Players place the stones onto the grid one by one. At any time, instead of placing a stone a player can choose to capture an opponent's stone by jumping forward, backward, left, or right—but never diagonally.

A similar game that is still played is *choko*—which is played on a five-by-five grid of squares that, like the game of *dara*, can be scooped in the dirt. Players start with 12 game pieces, such as seeds, stones, or bits of twig, and they take turns placing pieces on the board and then moving them (as in checkers) one space at a time, attempting to jump over and capture the opponent's pieces. Two features make the game different from regular checkers, however. A player can start moving his or her game pieces before all are placed onto the board (one move equals one turn), and the act of capturing enables a player to remove any one piece from the board, not just the one jumped over.

⊞ ASIA

INTRODUCTION

As the world's largest and most populous continent, Asia played a major role in the economic and political life of the Renaissance. Establishing consistent trade with Asia to furnish goods (silk and porcelain from China, pepper from Java, tea and spices from India) for the minions of a new moneyed society led to the age of exploration and set humanity on the path to a global economy. As cash replaced land and service as the main means of exchange (a direct cause of the Renaissance), a new merchant class looked eastward and rushed to create the fastest trade routes to satisfy demand.

Bartholomew Diaz sailed around Africa's Cape of Good Hope in 1487 and Vasco da Gama used that route to reach India in 1498, shifting the center of trade from the Mediterranean Sea to the Atlantic Ocean almost instantly. In between those voyages, Christopher Columbus sailed west across the Atlantic and reached the West Indies, though it took years for people to grasp that this "New World" was far from Asia. By 1521, the globe had been circumnavigated, the Pacific Ocean crossed, and the world set in context.

The period of the Renaissance in Europe corresponded to a time of relative political stability throughout Asia. In China, the Ming Dynasty (1368 to 1644) extended Chinese influence farther than any other native rulers of China. Under the Ming, the capital of China was moved from Nanjing to Beijing, and the Forbidden City—a 9,000-room palace complex—was constructed. Naval expeditions led by Zheng He opened trade with Southeast Asia, India, and Africa.

In Japan, Edo (present-day Tokyo) was chosen by Tokugawa Ieyasu as Japan's new capital in 1603 and became one of the world's largest cities and the site of a thriving urban culture that saw the development of Basho's haiku poetry and kabuki theater. By the end of the 17th century, during the Genroku Period, major urban centers including Kyoto, Osaka, and Tokyo experienced a flourishing of culture among the non-samurai middle class, who enjoyed great wealth, art, and conspicuous consumption very similar to Florence and other European cities during the Renaissance.

Despite associations via trade, Asia was largely closed off from the rest of the world during the Renaissance. It would take centuries for its culture, religions, and ways of life (including sports and games) to be appreciated by the West. Though playing cards and board games such as chess are Asian in origin, the world would not embrace sports such as the martial arts until the 20th century.

Martial arts, including various forms of wrestling, animal sports, races and fights, and water sports (notably boat races), are the foundation of traditional Asian sports, while deceptive simplicity is at the heart of games such as go.

As is the case with most geographic regions during the time period, it is difficult to parse out Renaissance-related developments in Asian sport. It is clear, however, that most countries had rich physical traditions that grew into organized sports with the advent of printing, the growth of leisure time, and a shifting of emphasis from the ways of war to that of nation-building.

ASIAN SPORTS

▦ Animal Sports

As was the case with Europe and North America, many traditional Asian sports were spectacles that pitted animals against each other in various competitions. Such competitions included many that are popular in the west, such as races (horse, camel, water buffalo, etc.) and fights (fighting cocks, bulls, etc.) and others—such as dove-cooing contests—that are unique to the region.

Cockfighting is especially popular in Thailand and the Philippines, with written accounts dating back to the Renaissance. King Naresuan (1590 to 1605) raised and pitted birds while a war hostage in the Burmese court. Cockfighting is still popular today in Thailand, despite its regulation by the government.

In addition to birds, battles between insects (crickets and beetles) are popular in southeast Asia, particularly as venues for gambling. Fish fighting involves placing together in a small bowl two males of the species

Betta spendens; the fish bite at each other until one dies. Bullfights are also common, though in Thailand two bulls face off in the ring rather than a bull and a man.

Among the more eclectic and recent animal sports are the dove-cooing contests, very popular in Thailand, in which specially bred pigeons are matched and judged on quality, technique, and duration of song. Similar singing contests are staged between grasshoppers.

▦ Archery

Archery was a vital military pursuit throughout Asia. As was the case in Europe and North America, the period of the Renaissance saw the role of the bow and arrow shift from essential martial art to one of competitive or ceremonial sport due to the invention of gunpowder.

In Japan, *kisha*—shooting of a bow and arrow from astride a running horse—was a popular sport among the nobility that took several forms. *Kasagake* involved riding a horse at full speed for approximately 100 yards before firing at a fixed target from within 20 yards. A more challenging version was *yabusame,* in which the track was longer (about 250 yards) and riders shot one arrow each at three targets set about 10 yards off the track. Still another type of archery was *koyume,* which featured a small bow and was a popular pastime among all classes. A favorite target was a sparrow tethered by a thread.

In Korea, archery is among the oldest and most lasting of traditional sports (along with wrestling and tae kwon do) and has been practiced as a team sport for centuries, especially during the first 200 years of the Choson Dynasty (1392 to 1910). Teams consisted of 15 archers, each of whom shot five arrows per round for three rounds (225 shots per team), with the winning team being the one who scored the most hits. Korean bows made of birch or jujube wood were regarded as the best throughout Asia.

Nu-shooting was a form of target archery popular in southwestern China in which both the bows and arrows are made of wood and the arrowheads are of bamboo. Archery was also popular in Mongolia and was considered one of the three "manly" sports, along with wrestling and horsemanship.

▦ Ball Possession Games

If one were to boil down football, rugby, and basketball to their common essence, the result would be a game (or, more accurately, a near free-for-all) in which two teams scramble to deposit a ball within a single goal, their efforts unencumbered by such details as yard lines, bounds, and dribbling.

One such game is the *tamaseseri* or "ball struggle" of the Hakosaki Shrine in Fukuoka City in Japan. Founded in A.D. 923, the shrine is the site of an ancient festival celebrated in honor of the Shinto god Hachiman, a kind of patron saint to fishermen and farmers in addition to being the god of war and divine protector of the Japanese people. During the festival, held every January 3rd at 1:00 P.M., a large crowd of men assembles on the grounds of the shrine for the once-a-year appearance of two solid wooden balls, each about 15 inches in diameter. According to legend, these wooden balls, one said to be male and the other female, bestow good luck and happiness on all who touch them. This magic power apparently inspired the *tamaseseri*, because over the years the festival crowds grew and the struggle to touch one became more and more competitive.

After a purifying ritual, the Shinto priests toss the male ball to the crowd, leaving the female ball within the shrine. The crowd, whose members wear only loincloths, is composed of two teams, one representing farmers and the other fishermen. Each team vies for possession of the ball, the smaller men and boys riding atop the shoulders of their teammates to gain a height advantage. As an extra twist, the priests throw buckets of cold water over the crowd making the heavy ball slippery. After much scrambling and general chaos, one team eventually makes it back to the shrine with the ball in its possession. The team thus returning the ball to the priests wins. Tradition holds that if the team representing the farmers wins, a good harvest may be expected for the upcoming year, and if the fishermen team wins, a good catch.

Given the singular nature of the shrine and festival, with all its attendant pomp and ceremony, the *tamaseseri* might be somewhat impractical to reenact, although one can imagine diehard enthusiasts of obscure games satisfying their curiosity with a bowling ball, garden hose, and swimming trunks.

A strikingly similar but somewhat more accessible contest is *yubee-lakpee* or "snatch the coconut," a traditional game played by men in the state of Manipur in India. As in the *tamaseseri*, the object of *yubee-lakpee* is for one team to carry a ball, in this case a greased coconut, into the goal area. Interestingly, *yubee-lakpee* also has mythic overtones, and playing it came to be associated with the Govindaji temple on the royal palace grounds in Imphal, the former capital of the old kingdom of Manipur. Every year at the Govindaji temple, two teams would, by playing the game, reenact a scene from Hindu mythology in which gods and demons struggle for possession of the nectar of immortality. According to the story, Vishnu, the protector of all good, intervened in the contest by assuming the shape of a beautiful enchantress, thereby charming the demons into relinquishing the nectar. She then served the nectar to the gods. Two of the demons, however, were not taken by Vishnu's appearance, and disguising themselves as gods, tricked Vishnu into serving them the nectar. Having thus achieved immortality, the two demons may be seen during eclipses when, it is said, they swallow the moon or the sun.

Unlike the *tamaseseri*, however, *yubee-lakpee* is also played for recreation on ordinary occasions much like a pick-up game of football at the park, its mythic overtones notwithstanding. This form of the game is quite suitable for contemporary reenactment.

The equipment consists simply of a coconut, available at most supermarkets. Where coconuts are not available, an old football inflated until it's quite firm should work. To grease the coconut, use petroleum jelly.

There are no set dimensions to the playing field. The goal is a rectangular area roughly 9 by 15 feet, positioned at the edge of the field much like a soccer goal. The number of players per team is also not set, although the teams typically do not exceed 12 players apiece.

The game begins with the players standing along the sidelines. The coconut is placed in the center of the field, and at the signal the two teams rush forward to gain possession of it. After that, it is a free-for-all. There are few rules other than that the ball may not be kicked. Grabbing, tackling, and wrestling are all part of the game, although for safety, contemporary reenactors may want to ban tripping. To score a goal, a player must carry the coconut into the goal area from the front—that is, the goal line—rather than the sides. The first team to carry the ball into the goal area wins. If neither team has scored a goal at the end of the time allotted by agreement in advance, then both teams line up and run a foot race to determine the winner, the game going to the team whose runner comes in first.

⬛ Boat Races

Boat racing has been extremely popular throughout China and Southeast Asia since the time of the Renaissance and before. Often the boat is carved to resemble a ceremonial dragon, and the sport is as charged with ritual and symbolism as athletic skill. In China, for example, the races are connected to rituals that focus on rains, vital for producing a good rice crop.

The racing of dragon boats (flat boats decorated to resemble dragons) has taken place in China for over 2,000 years and is still done today, with both men and women participating. The boats used today are about 45 feet long and hold 20 oarsmen. Elimination heats pit two boats against each other over a 1,000-yard course. Each boat has a dragonhead and tail. The dragon is the national symbol of China, and the dragon boat was thought to be a sacred vehicle affording one access to the dragon god. The race itself symbolized love of homeland, justice, and peace.

A form of racing called boat tugging (similar to tug-of-war contests) has taken place in China since the 10th century during the summer Lotus Fes-

An ornate ivory carving of a dragon boat from China's National Palace Museum.

tival. Two boats, each with an equal number of oarsmen, are tied together facing in opposite directions. Two lotuses are set on the water the same distance away from the front of each boat. At a signal, the teams begin rowing, trying to pull the other boat toward the lotus directly ahead of them. The first team to pick up a lotus is the winner.

Boat racing also grew as a sport along the many rivers and canals of Thailand. Festival boating took place as early as the 13th century as part of the flowers and candles floating ritual in the Sukhothai Kingdom. Royal processions of barges were vital pageants in Thai society: with sometimes a quarter of a million people watching the progress of over 20,000 boats.

The first recorded boat race in Thailand took place in the 17th century under King Ekatosarus, who made them annual events and provided feasts to the participants. He later inaugurated an annual race between the two royal barges in the 11th lunar month. A victory by the queen's barge assured the country's well-being and fertility for the coming year. The royal barges accommodated as many as 250 paddlers.

Later in the century, King Narai added a race of smaller boats for members of the king's court.

▦ *Buzkashi*

Buzkashi, which translated literally means "goat grabbing," has for centuries been a vital and immensely popular equestrian sport in northern Afghanistan. In *buzkashi*, men on specially trained and very powerful horses compete to get control of and ride cleanly away with the carcass of a decapitated and dehoofed calf or goat set in a hole in the ground.

This sport is believed to have emerged sometime in the late Middle Ages or early Renaissance, carried westward from China by nomadic Turkic peoples (Uzbek, Turkomen, Kazakh, and Kirghiz) and developed fully in northern Afghanistan, most likely as a recreational activity among herdsmen.

Because skilled riders and champion horses are necessary to stage this sport, *buzkashi* requires the sponsorship of powerful local men of political and economic influence, called *khans,* who stage celebratory events called *toois* at which *buzkashi* is played. *Toois* are staged to celebrate major events such as marriages and require amassing sufficient resources to feed and entertain scores or even hundreds of guests and to award prize money. Staging a successful *tooi* can greatly enhance a *khan's* prestige; an unsuccessful event can ruin him. Normally, *toois* at which *buzkashi* is played are held during the winter, when no farming is done and when men and animals can vie for hours without overheating.

There are two main types of *buzkashi: tudabarai* and *qarajai. Qarajai* is slightly more complex than *tudabarai,* although they share similar objectives. In *tudabarai,* the rider must obtain possession of the carcass and then carry it away from the starting circle in any direction in order to score. The rider must stay free and clear of the other riders. In *qarajai,* players must carry the calf around a marker, and then return the carcass to the team's designated scoring circle. In each version, points are awarded for successfully completing the tasks of getting control of the carcass and getting it to the proper scoring area.

Though the term *buzkashi* refers to goats, calves are the animals of choice because their carcasses last longer. In accordance with Muslim law, the calf is bled to death, decapitated, and dehoofed to protect players' hands. Sometimes the calf is gutted, which makes for a faster game, but since durability is an issue and strength is a key component of the contest, the animal may also be eviscerated and filled with sand or soaked in water to toughen the hide.

Buzkashi takes place on a barren plain. The calf is placed in the center in a hole deep enough to make the carcass level with the ground. The object of the game is to get control of the carcass and bring it to the scoring area. Although it seems like a simple task, the weight of the animal and its four legs make it hard to seize without others grabbing on. Because matches may consist of hundreds of riders, only the most masterful players (called *chapandaz*) get close to the carcass. The competition is fierce, often violent. Horsemen batter their way to the center of an expanding melee and try to reach down and grab the carcass. But with four legs available, it is easy for other riders to wrench it away. The calf gets tossed, trampled, dragged, and lifted as players seek to gain control and ride free. Communication between horse, rider, and teammates is essential to success and for minimizing injuries.

Once a single horse and rider emerge from the throng with the carcass, they drop it in the scoring area and play stops for a moment to acknowledge the winner. Over the centuries, prizes have included fine clothing, carpets, and horses. Today, most prizes take the form of cash purses. The next play cycle then begins. By the end of the day, the carcass is in shreds and the last victor carries it off as a trophy.

The evening after a *buzkashi* is a time of feasting and also a time to discuss the day's action and to settle disputes—a vital social component of the sport—whose competitors are often economic and political rivals. *Khans* take great care in adjudicating disputes, because a defection by an aggrieved faction could ruin the *tooi*.

Becoming a *chapandaz* (the best of whom are over age 40) requires years of difficult training. Women do not participate and are forbidden to watch. The horses used in *buzkashi* must be trained for at least five years. For its participants, *buzkashi* is more than a sport; it is a way of life that reflects the attaining of physical, social, and political prowess.

▦ *Chuiwan* ("Whack Ball" or Chinese Golf)

As if inventing fireworks, paper, and pasta were not enough, the Chinese are also credited with creating a game nearly identical to modern golf, centuries before the game appeared in Scotland. Called *chuiwan*, which roughly translates as "ball-whacking," the game consists of driving a small ball with a specialized metal club toward 10 holes positioned on 4 large, open greens. Cloth pennants atop narrow poles marked the location of holes just as in modern golf.

Chuiwan was immensely popular among male and female players during the Song and Yuan Dynasties (960 to 1368). During the Ming Dynasty (1368 to 1644), *chuiwan* became a popular sport of young men living in cities in much the same way that tennis became a popular urban sport during the European Renaissance.

By the early Middle Ages, *chuiwan* was a highly developed sport. The 32-chapter *Book of Chuiwan*, written in 1282 by Ning Zhi, contains specifications on the playing field, equipment, and rules as well as learned commentary on proven approaches to the game.

Chuiwan clubs—at least those used by emperors—were edged with gold and inlaid with jade, and the shafts were elaborately decorated.

When not in use, the clubs—about 10 in number—were stored in brocaded cases.

Just as in modern golf, *chuiwan* courses were laid out on both flat and sloping grassland, with raised and lowered hazards. Play was divided into first, second, and third strokes, with the first stroke having to be played from a "base" area (similar to a modern tee) and each subsequent shot played from where the ball landed.

Hagoita (Shuttlecock)

Hagoita, or shuttlecock, is a Japanese game traditionally associated with the New Year festivities. The object of the game is for two players, typically women, to keep a shuttle aloft by hitting it back and forth with wooden paddles.

While shuttlecock games are common worldwide and originate far back in antiquity, *hagoita* entered Japanese culture by way of China as early as the Hein period (A.D. 1000). The first players of the game were the nobility. To celebrate the New Year, highly skilled artisans and tradesmen would present their noble patrons with gifts of elaborately decorated *hagoita* sets. These early *hagoita* paddles were decorated with traditional good luck charms, a custom that led to their being manufactured and sold as talismans against fire and mosquitoes at temple festivals.

Over time, *hagoita* became popular with the *kamuro*, the beautiful and cultured young women who entertained at the "green houses" or brothels of Edo. Unlike the unflattering stereotype of the contemporary prostitute, the *kamuro* were depicted as gracious courtesans with refined manners and fashionable hairdos. Clients expected the *kamuro* not only to be beautiful, but to be charming, musical, and adept at such genteel pastimes as *hagoita*, typically associated with women of wealthy merchant and noble families.

Keep-Aloft Football Games

Resembling the contemporary pastime of hackey-sack, keep-aloft football games were played widely throughout Asia during the early modern period. Because the objective of these games was so simple—to keep a ball aloft for the greatest number of consecutive kicks—the particular spin any group of people put on the game often offers valuable insights into its culture. Nowhere is this more apparent than in the case of *kemari* of Japan and *sepak raga* of Thailand, Malaysia, the Philippines, and other southeast Asian countries.

Kemari was a wonderfully idiosyncratic pastime. Part tea ceremony, part dance, part juggling exhibition, *kemari* is believed to have descended from a Chinese keep-aloft game introduced into Japan between the 7th and 10th centuries. As often happens, the Japanese added their own inimitable refinements. To begin with, *kemari* players wore dark, expensive silk robes with fine floral embroidery as a kind of uniform during matches. The elaborately costumed players thus were always members of the most sophisticated and elite circles of Japanese society, the wealth associated with the pampered leisure class being a prerequisite not only for the expensive silk robes but for the exquisitely manicured *kemari* court itself. Typically maintained on the grounds of a private estate, the *kemari* court was traditionally a square, roughly six yards to a side, the corners of which were marked by four trees, always the willow, cherry, pine, and maple, pruned to a height of about 12 feet and said to represent universal harmony.

Eight players participated, two at each corner. Play began with one player kicking the ball into the air three times without letting it fall back to the ground. The first player then passed the ball to the next player, who kicked the ball up three times, passed it, and so on.

The object of the game is to keep the ball from falling back to the ground for the greatest number of consecutive kicks. Interestingly, the players are not opponents in the traditional sense of the word. There are no winners or losers. The whole undertaking is a group effort to play in a manner worthy of the game's long tradition and, perhaps, to enter the record books, no small feat considering that outstanding *kemari* scores have been recorded since at least A.D. 1208, when a round lasted for 2,000 consecutive kicks.

At the other end of the spectrum is the humble and egalitarian game of *sepak raga*. The only equipment required was a ball of woven rattan, usually about eight inches in diameter. To soften the rattan, and thus prevent blisters on the bare feet of the players, the ball was often rubbed with coconut oil. Because rattan is readily biodegradable, very few antique *sepak raga* balls survived in the moist climate of southeast Asia, making the earliest origins of the game difficult to trace. It is known, however, that native inhabitants of the Philippines played the game at least as early as the Spanish colonization of the islands in the 16th century, at which time the game lost its status as a pastime associated with the coronation of island kings and other notable events and became a folk game played at weddings and local festivals.

To play, six or seven participants form a circle some 50 feet in diameter and pass the ball around and around by repeatedly kicking and batting it into the air using any body surface—feet, knees, elbows, shoulders, and head—except the hands and forearms. The object of the game is simply to keep the ball aloft for as long as possible, a noncompetitive undertaking that, like *kemari*, is quite alien to Western notions of the sporting spirit. This cultural gap can be so profound, in fact, that in West Sumatra, a region where *sepak raga* has been popular for centuries, it is not unheard of for natives to bar someone who arrives first in a noncompetitive run from further participation, the offense being that he or she violated the cultural taboo on self-aggrandizement.

▦ Martial Arts

Few Asian sports are more highly developed or culturally significant than the martial arts: traditional systems of armed and unarmed combat used for warfare, self-defense, exercise, and spiritual development. Many Asian countries—notably China, Japan, and Korea—are known worldwide for their fighting arts that seek to perfect human character by unifying mind and body through the ritualized learning of forms.

Traditionally, martial arts fell into three categories: techniques used for combat, arts studied for social or spiritual growth, and those arts that were pursued as sports. Judo, developed in the late 19th century, is a prime example: it can be used for self-defense and, since 1964, has been one of two martial arts (tae kwon do is the other) included in the Olympics.

The exact origins of martial arts are impossible to determine due to a lack of written records and a vast number of colorful legends that obscure facts. It is clear that most armed and unarmed fighting techniques began in antiquity, were developed during the Middle Ages, and began to be systematized during the Renaissance.

Here is a brief description of some of the most popular martial arts.

Aikido

Aikido is a Japanese martial art with roots in the Edo Period (1603 to 1867) whose main focus is to control an opponent by using his or her own energy against him or her by employing various striking, joint-twisting, and pinning techniques. Disarming an opponent and knocking him or her off balance to gain control is an essential component of aikido.

The word *aiki* from which the form takes its name has been described over the years, though it defies a one-word translation. One Jujitsu master wrote that *aiki* describes a standstill in a martial arts bout that occurred when both fighters focused on one another's breathing. A more recent definition of the art's goal is "taking a step ahead of the enemy" by anticipating its actions.

Aikido training is comprised mainly of *katas*, the formalized series of movements that simulate moves made during a fight. A typical *kata* may consist of between 20 and 30 specific techniques (striking, thrusting, turning) and can be likened to an intricate dance.

Judo

Judo is one of the more recently systemized martial arts, created in 1882 by Japanese master Kano Jigoro. Judo ("gentle way") emphasizes the use of throwing and grappling techniques intended to turn an opponent's force to one's own advantage rather than to oppose it directly. Initially yielding to an opponent's strength to get him or her off balance is the foundation of many judo techniques.

While jujitsu (from which judo was created) grew out of samurai culture, judo had more of a western influence and was part of a movement to modernize Japan. Judo's philosophical component stressed moral education and spiritual discipline above fighting skills, though it can be used as self-defense.

The opponent must be thrown cleanly, pinned, or mastered through the application of pressure to arm joints or the neck. Judo is now practiced primarily as sport. It became an Olympic sport in 1964; women's judo was added in 1992.

Jujitsu

Jujitsu is a Japanese martial art that employs holds, throws, and crippling blows designed to disable an opponent. The term means "gentle technique" but how "gentle" is interpreted varies: for some schools, "gentle" meant how an unarmed or lightly armed warrior could subdue a larger or better-armed assailant.

Jujitsu evolved among the samurai and later the merchant class in Japan beginning in the early 17th century. A ruthless form of hand-to-hand fighting originally designed for disabling armor-clad warriors, its techniques included the use of the knuckles, fists, elbows, and knees against an enemy's vulnerable points. Chokes and joint-locks were also central to the style. Jujitsu declined in the mid-19th century, but many of its concepts and methods were incorporated into judo, karate, and aikido.

Karate

Karate ("empty hand") is a martial art believed to have originated in China. It was synthesized on the island of Okinawa in the early 1600s and was brought to Japan in the early 20th century. Karate features striking and kicking techniques designed to block an opponent's blows and follow with counterattacks. Emphasis is placed on concentrating as much of the body's power as possible at the point and instant of impact. Thus karate demonstrations often feature the breaking of boards, bricks, and blocks of ice. Blows are struck with the hands (especially the knuckles and the outer edge), the ball of the foot, heel, forearm, knee, and elbow. In practice and in tournaments, blows are stopped short of impact.

Karate has many styles and in the mid-20th century, the fundamental techniques of blocking (*uke*), striking (*tsuki*), punching (*uchi*), and kicking (*keri*) of the various schools were synthesized into a sport. Karate became very popular in the United Sates in the 1960s and 1970s after it was introduced to television and film audiences. Karate remains the most popular

During the relatively peaceful Edo Period (1603 to 1867), samurai warriors pictured here systematized traditional fighting
techniques into martial arts such as jujitsu.

and widespread of the traditional martial arts with millions of worldwide
practitioners.

Kendo

Kendo is a Japanese martial art derived from the sword fighting methods of the ancient samurai and came into its own in the 18th century, following the development of safer equipment, notably the bamboo sword
(*shinai*), which is held with both hands. Fencing, or *kenjutsu*, had existed in
Japan for at least 1,000 years. Traditional kendo training is done through
the perfection of *kata*. During competitive matches, contestants wear traditional protective garments. Points are awarded for blows delivered to
various parts of the upper body, including the head above the temple,

both sides, and the forearms. The fighter who scores two of the first three points is the winner.

Tae Kwon Do

Tae kwon do is a Korean martial art similar to karate. Although tae kwon do was not formalized as a system or named until the 20th century, its striking and kicking techniques were developed over many hundreds of years. The Japanese occupation of Korea beginning in 1909 and a banning of local martial arts practices sparked a hunger to create a system that was distinctly Korean. What distinguishes tae kwon do from karate and other martial arts is an emphasis on kicking, especially flying kicks, and immediate physical response to an opponent's moves.

Tae kwon do incorporates strikes, kicks, stances, and blocks into its fluid movements. *Kata,* sparring, and the breaking of boards and bricks to master the channeling of power constitute the three main training areas. The sport was formalized in 1955, was demonstrated at the 1988 Olympics in Seoul, South Korea, and became an Olympic sport (a proof of its international growth and popularity) in 2000.

▦ Thai Boxing

Thai boxing or *muay thai* is a traditional art of self-defense from Thailand. It is a form of boxing, but differs from international boxing in that the feet, elbows, and knees are used as well as fists. Thus, Thai boxing is both an effective form of self-defense and one of the most physically exacting fighting sports. A Thai boxing match lasts for only five three-minute rounds, with a two-minute rest between rounds.

Muay thai is one of only two professional sports in Thailand and is steeped in legend. In Burma in the 16th century, Thai war hostage Kanom-tom had to fight 10 Burmese boxers to gain his freedom. He won all 10 matches and a place in Thai history.

The best way to explore the martial arts is to enroll in a class. Although many books, videos, and Web sites are devoted to various disciplines, techniques can only be learned effectively from an instructor. There are many places to learn, including schools that specialize in specific forms, and many local YMCAs, health clubs, and community recreation centers offer programs. All disciplines require years of study and practice to master (three to four years is often minimal for a black belt), and the rewards include self-confidence and a high level of physical fitness.

▦ Wrestling

The practice of grappling as a sport was fairly universal among the many disparate cultures of the early modern period. Few wrestling traditions, however, were as refined as those found in Asia, based as they were on eastern notions of physical harmony and balance that so characterized martial arts from India to Japan.

Probably the most well known and distinctive of the Asian wrestling traditions is Japanese sumo wrestling. While the earliest roots of sumo are shrouded in myth (a book entitled the *Kojiki* or "Record of Ancient Matters" from the 8th century A.D., for example, claims that the imperial family of Japan is descended from the god Takemikazuchi, who won possession of the archipelago in a sumo match with another god some 2,500 years ago), reliable records dating back to the early 9th century A.D. indicate that the imperial court held annual sumo tournaments on the palace grounds in the city of Nara, a custom that continued until the end of the 12th century.

Although the basic object of a sumo match in this period was much the same as in modern sumo—that is, to throw an opponent either to the ground or out of bounds—the early contests could be quite a bit more brutal, involving as they did the occasional kick, punch, or choke hold. Little distinction was made at the time between grappling as a sport and grappling as a martial art.

As sumo evolved in the direction of a sport in the modern sense, it began to accumulate many of the stylistic hallmarks for which it is famous. Handed down along family lines generation to generation, the sumo lifestyle, with its special diet and exercise regimen, tended to promote men who were both hugely rotund and nimble, thus the familiar

Sumo wrestlers face off.

profile the sumo wrestler, some of whom weighed as much as 300 pounds. Further, sumo grappling technique became more refined, more a codified system than a no-holds-barred struggle.

In 1578, Oda Nobunaga, a feudal lord and fan of sumo, introduced at his castle the 15-foot circle as an official sumo arena in order to protect spectators and provide a definitive boundary line for determining the outcome of the match. Prior to this innovation, the arena was loosely defined by the spectators standing in a circle around the wrestlers.

Shortly thereafter, in the first years of the 17th century, the practice of sumo began to shift from the exclusive realm of private castles and military academies to public venues, achieving wide popularity as a spectator sport. As professional athletes, the sumo wrestlers themselves became public figures, some of them receiving a substantial cut of the proceeds of paid matches called *kajin-zumo,* held ostensibly for the benefit of shrines and temples. In addition to the income from the *kajin-zumo,* especially promising wrestlers received generous stipends, as well as samurai status, from feudal lords. The growing fame of the sport and its star practitioners resulted in a complex system of ranking whose hierarchy culminated with the designation of *yokozuna* or "grand champion," a title first bestowed upon Akashi Shiganosuke in 1632.

Ssirum is a traditional Korean style of wrestling believed to be a forerunner of Japanese sumo. *Ssirum* dates back nearly 2,000 years, but its first written accounts date from early in the Choson Dynasty, about the time of the Renaissance in Europe.

Ssirum is a man's sport and was, for centuries, a popular contest at village festivals and on feast days such as *Chusok* (Korean Thanksgiving) and *Tano* (the 5th of May). *Ssirum* matches are held in large sandpits. Contestants gird themselves with cloth belts that encircle the waist and tie on the right thigh. The goal is to lift and throw one's opponent to the ground. Matches last three rounds of three minutes each. A wrestler loses a round if any part of his body (other than his feet) touches the ground.

The popularity of *ssirum* declined early in the 20th century but made a comeback in the 1960s with the overall growth of martial sports and a proliferation of Korean culture. Today, *ssirum* is a popular professional sport in Korea.

Like Japan and Korea, early modern India had a rich tradition of wrestling, complete with royal patronage during the Mughal Empire (1526 to 1748) and its own host of star athletes. What set India apart, however, was that instead of refining a single wrestling style as in the case of Japanese sumo, India embraced early on a wide variety of physical activities that incorporated grappling, a reflection, perhaps, of the ethnically diverse subcontinent. A 12th-century Sanskrit text, for example, refers to an unusual form of wrestling involving four participants, two of whom stand waist deep in water while the other two grapple from atop their shoulders. Elsewhere, a 17th-century miniature depicts wrestlers performing a kind of gymnastics on a tall wooden pole (a sport in its own right called *mallakhamb*) as a warm-up exercise for the match. Of the various wrestling traditions that developed in India, two lend themselves especially to contemporary reenactment: *kirip*, a two-man wrestling contest indigenous to Nicobar Island in the Bay of Bengal, and *kabbadi*, an ancient sport popular throughout India, Bangladesh, Nepal, Pakistan, and Sri Lanka that can best be described as a cross between playground tag and tag-team wrestling.

Kirip is a fairly simple sport, requiring only an open, preferably soft, area. The match begins with the wrestlers face to face, each reaching around the middle of the other in bear hug fashion. At the signal, each wrestler tries to throw his opponent to the ground without losing his grip. The player who first touches the ground with any part of his body other than his feet or who loses his grip around his opponent loses.

Kabbadi is somewhat more involved. Here the playing field is a roughly 30-by-40-foot rectangle divided in half the short way like a tennis court. There are two teams, each with 12 players. Before the game, the players decide by coin toss which will be the defending and which will the raiding team. The game begins with seven members of the defending team on one side of the dividing line and one member of the raiding team on the other. The solitary raider must cross the dividing line and tag members of the defending team. Once tagged, a player is out for the duration of the game, the object of the game being to tag out all of the opposing team. Simple enough, but there's one amusing catch: The raider must continuously chant the word "*kabbadi*" on one breath the entire time he is on the enemy side of the court.

If he runs out of breath before crossing back to his side, he is out for the duration and all who were tagged during that particular raid remain in play. Further, his side then fields seven players or, as the game proceeds, however many are left, as defenders, and so on until one team wins by completely tagging out the other. If, on the other hand, he crosses back to his side on one breath, the tags for that raid take effect and he may again venture across for another raid. The game thus becomes a lopsided wrestling event in which the defending team, always mindful of the deadly touch, attempts to grab the raider and physically prevent him from crossing back before he loses his breath.

Mongol-buh is a form of wrestling popular in Mongolia that is similar to Japanese sumo but with key differences: wrestlers are not confined to a small ring, and their palms may touch the ground. *Mongol-buh* matches attract tens of thousands of wrestlers—an amazingly high per-capita participation rate—and is considered, along with archery and horseback riding, one of the "manly sports" of Mongolian culture.

ASIAN PLAY

▦ Firecracker Rings

The sport of vying to catch small metal rings sent high into the air by igniting firecrackers has been popular in China (where fireworks were invented) for more than 500 years, especially among the Dong, Miao, Molao, and Shund peoples.

The contest usually takes place in an open field between two teams of equal number. A "firing zone" is set up in the center of the field with box zones drawn at either end, each of which contains a decorated basket. Baselines connect the box zones to the firing zone and small flags are placed at each line's intersection.

During the time of the Renaissance, only three rings and three firecrackers were used, the catching of each ring symbolizing a hoped-for event. The first ring stood for prosperity, the second stood for a good harvest, and the third for a peaceful life.

Today, the game is popular among young people and is a recognized event in China's National Peasant Games. Each team has 10 players. The rings—which measure two inches in diameter—are launched from the center of the firing zone, and, once caught, the teams try to get the ring into the basket by passing, rolling, and running with it, while the defense tries to gain possession of it. Getting a ring into a basket scores one point. Games usually consist of two 20-minute halves with a 10-minute break between.

The game is easy to reproduce. In places where fireworks are banned, substitutions are made. One possibility is to use glow sticks, which can either be short and straight or long enough to have ends fitted to form rings. The glow sticks are tossed high into the air (about 20 feet) by a teacher or student serving as referee.

▦ *Geune*

The *geune* is a Korean swing made by tying a board with two ropes to a large tree branch or a long log placed across two poles. Swinging on the *geune* was one of the traditional games played on *Dano* Day or *Chuseok.* The contest involved standing on the swing (sometimes two people at the same time) and moving the body to swing as high as possible, the highest swing determining the winner. The competition was usually among girls and women. The *geune* is still popular today.

▦ Japanese Parlor Games

Several refined parlor games were popular among the upper levels of Japanese society during the Muromachi, Azuchi Momoyama, and early

Edo periods of Japanese history, a span of time roughly encompassing the 14th through the 17th centuries of the Western calendar. The common element of these games was that they tended to cultivate an appreciation for the Japanese sense of high culture and aesthetics. Unlike folk games that rely on common, local objects such as pebbles and cowrie shells, the accessories to these parlor games were often exquisitely crafted from precious materials and housed in fine lacquer boxes that only the well-to-do could afford.

One of the more interesting and unusual games in this category was *ko-awase* or the "incense game." A game for two or more players, *ko-awase* was popular with the aristocracy as early as the 11th-century Heian period. The object of this wine-tasting-like game was to identify by smell alone various types of rare incense.

The equipment for the game includes paper and pencil for each player, an incense burner and several types of incense, a luxurious commodity made from fragrant drops of tree resin that had hardened for many years in the ground. (The modern reenactor should be able to find a wide variety of incense at specialty shops, or if the reenactment is intended for children, familiar, fragrant objects such as lemons and cinnamon sticks would be a good substitute, although in this case the guessers would need blindfolds.) Some players also used a game board and carved pieces whimsically depicting such figures as wrestlers and dancers to keep score, each player advancing his or her piece a space toward the goal for each correct guess.

To play, the host heats a bit of the resin in an incense burner, releasing the aroma. On smelling the incense, the players write the name of it on slips of paper and place it in a box. Correct guesses score a point. Of course, guessing correctly presumes prior knowledge of the various aromas, and thus modern reenactors may wish to pass around and preview the incense beforehand or burn a few practice rounds, the primary objective of the game being to enjoy the incense and the ambiance it creates for an evening of elegant conversation.

In addition to appreciating incense, sophisticated courtiers might enjoy refining their literary palates in a card game known as *hyakunin isshu,* or a "hundred poems by a hundred poets." A *hyakunin isshu* deck consists of 100 pairs of cards, one card in each pair containing the opening line and the other the closing line of a poem from a famous poetry anthology compiled in 1235 by Fujiwara no Teika. The opening lines and closing lines are divided, and the closing lines are laid out in rows on the floor. As the host reads each opening line aloud the players attempt to find the card with the corresponding closing line to win the pair. The player with the most pairs wins.

While the knowledge of Japanese language and literature required to play *hyakunin isshu* is probably beyond most reenactors, a determined group of literary-minded participants—members of a book club for example—could certainly undertake a reasonable interpretation of the game by agreeing to familiarize themselves with, say, a number of Shakespeare sonnets or Emily Dickinson poems and making the pairs of cards themselves.

Finally, if memorizing and matching lines of 100 or so classic poems seems overly ambitious, *kai-awase,* a matching game with clamshells, might be a little less daunting. Based on the fact that two sides of a clamshell will only fit one another perfectly, the object of the game is to find the most pairs of matching shells.

Because each pair of shells forms a unique couple, the game became associated with marriage and fidelity. In fact, whenever a highborn lady married, she inevitably brought with her an exquisite set of 180 pairs of *kai-awase* shells as an indispensable component of her dowry. These shells were finely decorated with gold leaf and paint, each matching half bearing an identical miniature depicting a scene from classical Japanese literature, and stored in ornate, hexagonal boxes.

For the modern reenactor, making a *kai-awase* set should provide both an engaging craft project and an excuse to eat a lot of steamers (available at most supermarket fish counters). Keeping the two halves together, thoroughly clean the shells, buffing the rough edges as necessary with fine sandpaper. Place the shell pairs on newspaper concave side up and paint the insides of the shells with gold spray paint. Two coats may be necessary. When the shells are dry, label the faces of each pair with the same number so that after the pairs are separated the mate for each can be found by matching the numbers.

At the beginning of the game, the pairs are divided into two sets, the *jigai* and the *dashigai.* The players arrange the *jigai* face down on the ground while the *dashigai* remain in the container. The players then draw a shell face up from the *dashigai* set and, taking turns, flip over one of the *jigai* shells in effort to find the match. If a player turns over the matching shell, he or she wins the pair. If the turned shell is not the match, that shell is turned back over and the other player takes a turn, and so on until the match is located. When one player wins the pair, another of the *dashigai* set is drawn and the process is repeated until all of the *dashigai* have been paired. The player with the most pairs at that point wins.

::: *Jegichagi*

Jegichagi is a traditional Korean game for boys that was normally played during the winter. A shuttlecock was made from old coins wrapped in paper or cloth with a hole in the center through which feathers were inserted and fanned out into a circle. The shuttlecock was kicked with one foot or both feet into the air. The person who kicked the *jegichagi* the most number of times without it touching the ground was the winner.

Jingluo Balls

In traditional Chinese medicine, the *jingluo* are meridians that mark the flow of energy through the body. The manipulation of specially made metal balls has long been believed to promote good health and long life by improving blood flow, strengthening the hands and forearms, lowering blood pressure, and improving the central nervous system. Health balls became especially popular in the United States during the New Age movement that began in the 1970s as a holistic way to focus energy and relieve stress.

The first health balls were produced during in the Ming Dynasty (1368 to 1644), a time period that roughly coincides with the Renaissance. According to legend, the gods guided a weapons blacksmith to fashion balls of iron that recreated the sound of a roaring dragon and the singing of the mythical phoenix. This was achieved by sealing magnetic balls and soundboards inside the spheres.

Although initially ownership of the health balls was limited to the emperor, the imperial family, and court officials, they were soon manufactured and used throughout China as tools in martial arts and in traditional Chinese medicine.

According to the *jingluo* theory, the 10 fingers are connected with the heart, the cranial nerves, the vital organs, and the bloodstream. The balls stimulate the various acupuncture points of the hands and aid the uninterrupted flow of blood and vital energy to produce harmony throughout the organs and the nervous system.

Men and women of all ages today use health balls. They can be purchased from most health food stores, gift shops, and online. One ball is generally pitched high and the other sounds at a lower pitch. Although their primary use is health, games are easy to create. One version is for two players to place two health balls in the palm of their less-dominant hand and rotate and revolve them as many times as possible. The first one to drop a ball loses. As dexterity increases, one can shift to larger balls, or three or even four balls at a time.

Kite Flying

Scholars debate the earliest origins of the kite, offering such candidates as windblown Chinese farmer hats to early silk battle flags for having inspired them. Whatever their ancient origin, legends involving kites entered Chinese literature as early as the fourth century B.C., and by the Ming

Dynasty (A.D. 1368 to 1644) kite flying was one of the most popular outdoor pastimes not only in China but throughout Asia.

Unlike many pastimes of the era, kite flying was readily accessible to the elite and the common man alike, the toy figuring prominently in epic tales as well as humble folklore. According to Korean legend, for example, the tradition of kite flying began in that country during a battle with Japanese invaders just before the turn of the 17th century. During the battle, the Koreans began to take heavy losses, a reversal of fortune they blamed on the inauspicious appearance of falling stars in the night sky. Realizing this, a Korean general invented a kite to which he attached a small lantern. As the kite and lantern ascended, his troops interpreted the light as the lucky appearance of a new star. Their morale thus bolstered, the troops rallied and repelled the invaders.

While more humble, the kite of the common man was no less meaningful in Korean culture. Constructed of paper over a bamboo cross, the typical Korean kite was roughly square with a round hole in the middle and kite strings of either silk or less expensive hemp. During the New Year festivities, it was traditional for flyers to write wishes on their kites asking that their misfortunes float away with them.

For the sake of completeness, it should be noted here that in addition to casual flying, these kites were also used in the dangerous sport of kite fighting. To play, participants would coat their kite strings with glue and ground glass. Using the rasp-like surface of the string, a flyer would attempt to cut the strings of the other flyers, sending their kites crashing down as free loot for the younger children waiting below. The last flyer with his kite aloft not only won but got to keep his kite. Needless to say, this game was very dangerous and its reenactment should not be attempted.

Buddhist missionaries from China are thought to have introduced the kite to Japan in the early years of the Twang Dynasty (A.D. 618 to 907). As in other countries, a body of lore developed around the popular kite. At the turn of the 17th century, for example, a rival of the Shogun Tokugawa Ieyasu supposedly built an enormous kite on which he ascended to spy on the royal palace. Unlike the lantern-bearing kite of Korean legend, this kite was apparently less effective in its strategic application, and the Shogun handily crushed his adversaries despite their airborne reconnaissance.

One of the most famous of the traditional Japanese kites is the *hata* or "flag" of Nagasaki. The origin of this flag is somewhat unclear, given that its diamond-shaped design is quite different than the rectangular design popular elsewhere in the country. Based on its similarity to kites from India, however, it is thought that the kite was introduced from India by merchants seeking trade with Japan in the late 16th century, a theory bolstered by the fact that foreign merchants of the era, a group including the Dutch, Portuguese, and British, were restricted to the city of Nagasaki, and that the traditional broad red, white, and blue stripes adorning the *hata* resemble those of the Dutch flag.

Like the simple diamond-shaped kite popular in the west, the *hata* lends itself to a fairly easy craft project. To build one, the following components are necessary:

Two 1/4-inch square pine slats, one 70 cm long, and the other 82 cm long

Cotton cord

Wood glue

One 70-by-80-inch sheet of tracing paper

One spool of kite string

One roll of narrow ribbon

Directions for construction:

1. Begin by marking the middle of the 82-cm slat. This slat will be the horizontal beam or "cross-spar" of the kite. Next, measure 16 cm down from the top of the 70-cm slat, and, using the wood glue, secure the middle of the cross-spar to this point, thus forming a cross with the 70-cm slat as the "longeron" or vertical beam. When the glue is dry, add strength to the joint by lashing it with a length of cotton cord. (Traditionally, the cross-spar and longeron were made of strips of bamboo and attached by splicing, then lashing, the bamboo together, but where bamboo is unavailable, the pine slats are a fine, and more convenient, substitute.)

2. Whittle a small groove at the ends of the cross-spar about 1/4 inch from each tip. Placing the cross-spar flat on a table so that the longeron is on top, tie a length of cotton cord around one end of the cross-spar at the groove, then run the string over the longeron and tie it at the other groove, pulling the string taut until the cross-spar bows slightly.

3. Whittle a small groove at the ends of the longeron about 1/4 inch from each tip as in step 2. Tie another string to the right-hand cross-spar at the groove and loop it several times around the bottom of the longeron at the groove, pulling it taut so that the length of cord between the end of the cross-spar and longeron is 56 cm. This will cause the cross-spar to flex downward. Next, continue with the cord from the bottom of the longeron to the end of the left-hand cross-spar and loop it around several times at the groove, likewise pulling it taut so that the length of cord between the end of the left-hand cross-spar and longeron is 56 cm.

4. Continue with the string up toward the top of the kite, looping it several times around the notch at the tip of the longeron, then down to the notch of the right-hand cross-spar where it began, tying it off there to create the diamond outline of the kite. This string will secure the paper sail to the kite.

5. For the sail, cut a piece of tracing paper (in lieu of the traditional, handmade Japanese paper called *washi*) into the shape of the diamond, leaving an extra inch around the perimeter. Place the cross longeron side up over the sail and

fold the extra inch of paper over the string, securing it all the way around with glue. Once attached, the kite may be decorated with traditional wide red, white, and blue stripes.

6. The final components are the two short tassels at each end of the cross-spar. To make them, tie several four-inch pieces of ribbon together at the top. Attach the tassels at the ends of the cross-spars.

7. The last step is to attach the kite string. Cut a 24-inch length of kite string and tie a loop in the center of it. This string, called the "bridle" will connect the kite string to the kite. Tie one end of the bridle to the longeron where it intersects the cross-spar. Tie the other end to the bottom of the longeron. Finally, tie the kite string to the bridle at the loop and the kite is ready to fly.

▦ *Neolttwigi*

Neolttwigi is a form of Korean play that resembles the Western game of seesaw. A long board called a *neol* is centered atop rigid piles of straw or bags of rice. Two persons—usually women dressed in brightly colored traditional costumes—took turns jumping on their end of the board, sending the other person high into the air. Like *geune*, *neal-ttwigi* was enjoyed on traditional holidays such as the lunar New Year, *Chuseok,* and *Dano* Day.

ASIAN GAMES

▦ *Bagh-bandi*

Bagh-bandi is a traditional game from Sri Lanka that is similar to the English game of fox and geese. Bagh-bandi is played on an alquerque board, which is a five-by-five checkerboard on which game pieces are played on the intersecting points rather than the spaces. The lines divide the board into four quadrants with eight triangles in each quadrant.

One player is the tiger; the other is the goats. The tiger has two games pieces (stones), while the goats have 20 game pieces.

The goat game pieces are stacked in four piles of five stones each on the center points of the four quadrants. The tiger stones are placed between them with one on the exact middle intersection and the second on the middle of the end line in front of the person playing as tiger.

The object is for the tiger to capture all the goats and for the goats to immobilize the tigers by moving stones to adjacent intersections.

The tiger player may move one tiger stone to an adjacent cell (adjacency is given by board lines) or may capture a goat by jumping a stack of goats (just capturing the top goat) and landing on the next cell which must be empty. Jumps may be multiple, but a tiger cannot jump into the previous cell (so a tiger cannot jump back and forth to capture one stack of goats).

The goat player may take the top goat of a stack and place it on an adjacent empty cell or move a single goat to an adjacent empty cell. The goats start the game.

The tiger wins if all the goats are caputred, and the goat wins if both tigers are immobilized.

⊞ *Ko-no*

Ko-no is a Korean game of strategy played on the intersecting points of a 16-square grid. Two players or two teams can play the game, which requires 14 counting pieces—seven each of two different colors. The pieces are placed facing each other on the five points of the bottom row, with the last two pieces on the far right and left points of the second row.

Players or teams take turns moving one piece forward, backward, or diagonally to an open intersecting point. Jumping over an opponent's pieces is not allowed. The goal of the game is for each player or team to move all its pieces into the opponent's starting positions. The first to do so is the winner. A *ko-no* board of four squares by four squares can be marked off on a standard chessboard or drawn on a sheet of paper. Checkers, chess pawns, poker chips, or coins can be used as counters.

⊞ *Nim*

Nim is a counting game simple enough for a child to play yet complex enough in its possibilities to be studied by mathematicians. The game involves two players taking turns removing objects (coins, matches, etc.) from small piles, usually three, but the number of piles can vary according to preference. Players take turns removing one or two objects from one of the piles, though it is okay to remove an entire pile. The one who removes the last object is the winner. The game centers on making the best moves amid a sequence of diminishing possibilities.

⊞ *Ninuki-renju*

Ninuki-renju is a classic Japanese game in which two players alternate placing black and white stones on intersecting lines of a standard (19-by-19) go board. Each player attempts to construct a continuous line of five stones of his or her color along a vertical, horizontal, or diagonal line. Players can also win by capturing five pairs (10) of their opponent's stones. Capturing occurs when one player encloses two of the opponent's stones between two of his or her own.

Rules dictate the placing of the first three stones. Black always moves first, and that stone must be placed in the center of the board. White can then place his or her stone on any point on the board. Black's second move must be made outside of the limits of the five-by-five center grid.

From that point on, players place stones anywhere they like. Stones can only be captured in pairs, and all captured pairs are removed from the board.

The first player to construct a line of five continuous stones of his or her color in any direction wins. Either player can pass, but if both players pass in succession, the game automatically ends in a draw.

Ninuki-renju was very popular in the 1920s, spawning a magazine and tournaments. The game was featured in *Master of Go,* a novel by Japanese Noble prizewinner Yasunori Kawabata. This game is known in Korea under the name *Chosen.* In 1978, a simplified version, called Pente, was released in the United States.

▦ *Nyout* (Korean Checkers)

The ancient Korean game of *nyout* is perhaps the oldest ancestor of what game scholars refer to as the "cross and circle race" family of games, a family that includes the likewise ancient Hindu game of *pachisi* as well as the popular contemporary game Trivial Pursuit. Typically, the object of cross and circle games is to be the first player to move all of one's game pieces around the spaces at the periphery of the circular game board (or, if lucky, traverse the central cross as a shortcut) and thereby exit to safety.

The *nyout* board consists of 20 small circles—the spaces on which game pieces land—arranged evenly in a circle. Nine more spaces are arranged in a cross in the center of the circle. The spaces at the center of the cross and at the four compass points of the circle are slightly larger than the rest. The top space is marked with the character *ch'ut* or "exit." The game pieces, called *mal* or "horses," may be any convenient, flat bits of wood, paper, or stone marked to distinguish one player's pieces from his or her opponent's. Finally, the four special dice that govern the movement of the horses around the board are narrow pieces of wood about one inch long, flat on one side and convex on the other. The convex side is blackened by charring, and the flat side is left white. Some players use a bamboo ring two or three inches in diameter supported by a sharpened stick in the ground, like a miniature basketball hoop, through which the players drop the dice in order to ensure that chance rather than skillful throwing determines the outcome of the roll.

The number of players determines the number of horses each player must move around the board. When two play, each may choose to move one to four horses. When three play, each moves three horses. When four play, each player teams with the player opposite him or her, and together they must move four horses around the board.

The game commences with each player casting the four dice. The point value of the roll is based on how many dice land white or black side up as follows:

four black sides up = five points and another roll (a die landing on end is equivalent to a black side up)

four white sides up = four points and another roll

three white sides up = three points

two white sides up = two points

one white side up = one point

Whoever scores highest on the initial roll goes first.

▦ *Pachisi*

Pachisi, or twenty-five, is a board game known to many modern players in a simplified form called parcheesi. The game has been played in India since the late Middle Ages and is considered the subcontinent's national game. The name comes from the Indian word *pacis,* which means "twenty-five," the highest number that could be thrown with the six cowrie shells used to determine moves.

The Indian Emperor Akbar I of the 16th-century Mogul Empire apparently played *chaupar,* a game very similar to *pachisi,* on great courts constructed of inlaid marble. He would sit on a dais four feet high in the center of the court and throw the cowrie shells. On the red and white squares around him, 16 beautiful women from the harem, appropriately colored, served as the game pieces and would move around according to his directions. Remains of these boards can be seen today in Agra and Allahabad.

The object of the game is to move game pieces out from a center area, around the board, and return them safely home. Although modern versions are designed for individuals, traditional *pachisi* pits two-player teams against each other.

Equipment

Pachisi is played on a board that, these days, is usually made from strong cloth, with the gaming pattern embroidered onto it. The board is in the shape of a cross, each arm being divided into three adjacent columns of eight squares. Three of the squares on each arm are highlighted with a cross or some other distinguishing mark—the middle square at the end of each arm plus the fourth square in from the end of the arm on either side. These squares are called "castles." The middle of the cross forms the large square center area called the *charkoni.*

Sixteen beehive-shaped pieces are used: four black, four green, four red, and four yellow. Six small cowrie shells provide the element of chance and have the following values:

- two cowries with mouths up = two
- three cowries with mouths up = three
- four cowries with mouths up = four
- five cowries with mouths up = five
- six cowries with mouths up = six plus grace
- one cowrie with mouth up = 10 plus grace
- zero cowrie with mouth up = 25 plus grace

A grace is a special allowance, which is a critical part of the game.

Modern commercial versions of the game use dice instead of cowries, but this produces a different flavor to the game. Since cowrie shells are hard to come by, a more authentic way to recreate the game would be to use two-sided objects, such coins or pyramids with the tips painted two different colors. Players can also use dice like cowrie shells with the rule that a roll of one, two, or three means mouth up, and a roll of four, five, or six means mouth down.

Preparation

Partners sit opposite each other; yellow and black play against red and green. To begin, the pieces are placed in the *charkoni*. Each player throws the cowries, with the highest role going first and play passing to the right (counterclockwise). It is possible to play the game with two players. In this case, play proceeds exactly as if there were four players, but one player plays yellow and black and the other plays red and green.

Each player's objective is to move all four pieces down the middle of the nearest arm, around the edge of the board in a counterclockwise direction, and then back up the same arm to finish back in the *charkoni*. The pieces are placed on their sides when returning up the middle of the arm toward the *charkoni* in order to distinguish them from pieces just starting.

Pachisi is won when both partners have all eight pieces home. As with all true team games, working together is the key to winning.

Play

Moves are decided by throws of the cowrie shells. To begin a turn, the player throws the cowries. The player moves a piece the number of spaces indicated. If a grace is thrown, the piece moved can be played out of the *charkoni* onto the board, if desired, and the player is allowed another throw and so on until a two, three, four, or five is thrown.

The first piece to leave the *charkoni* for each player can depart using any number. All subsequent pieces are only allowed to start or reenter the game using a grace throw. More than one piece from the same side can occupy the same square. A piece is not allowed to finish on a castle square that is occupied by one or more enemy pieces.

If a piece finishes on a noncastle square inhabited by one or more enemy pieces, the enemy pieces are captured. Captured pieces are returned to the *charkoni,* from where they must start again with a grace. A player making a capture is allowed another throw of the cowries to be taken immediately.

Moving is not compulsory, and a player may decide not to move after having thrown the cowries. This is typically done in order to remain safely within a castle square or to help a partner. A common strategy is for a piece to remain in the castle square at the end of the third arm until a 25 is thrown, thus allowing that piece to finish without risk. It is possible for a piece, upon completing its circuit, to carry on around the board for a second time. This is often done in order to assist a partner who is lagging behind.

Pieces finish the game by reentering the *charkoni,* having completed a circuit of the board. However, a player is only allowed to move a piece into the *charkoni* by throwing the exact number required.

▦ *Shogi*

Shogi, or "the generals game," is Japanese chess and is unique in the chess family in that captured pieces become part of an opponent's army. The *shogi* board is a nine-by-nine grid of noncheckered squares with four small crosses marking the corners of the nine center squares. The three rows nearest each play is the home territory.

Each player has 20 wooden game pieces. The pieces are flat pentagonal tiles pointed in a certain direction. Japanese or modified Chinese characters are written on each piece to signify its value. Most of the pieces can be turned over to become a stronger piece. Some of the pieces, upon entering an opponent's home territory, can be "promoted" to the rank of a stronger piece. Pieces that can be promoted are noted below. The number of each piece each player starts with is in parenthesis.

jeweled king (1): moves like the king in standard chess

gold general (2): moves one orthogonal space or one space diagonally forward

silver general (2): moves one space diagonally or one space forward. Promotion is to a gold general

honorable horse (2): like a knight in standard chess, this piece moves two spaces forward and one space sideways. Promotion is to a gold general

flying chariot (1): moves like a rook in standard chess. Promotion is to a dragon king, which can move like a jeweled king or a flying chariot angle-going (1): moves like a bishop in standard chess. Promotion is to a dragon horse, which can move like a jeweled King or an angle-going

Lance (2): moves forward only any distance. Promotion is to a gold general

Soldiers (9): moves one space forward only. Promotion is to a gold general

The initial setup is similar to that of standard chess, but with key differences. On the back row, the lances are placed on the corners. Next to the lances are the honorable horses. Next to them go the silver generals, followed by the gold generals. The king is placed on the center space, between the two gold generals.

The second row contains just two pieces. In front of the left honorable horse is the angle-going, and in front of the other horse is the flying chariot. The nine soldiers are placed in the third row.

A common opening move in *shogi* is to move the solider in front of the angle-going to free it for diagonal movement.

Re-playing Captured Pieces

Any captured piece can be placed back onto the board. This counts as a move. The chariot, the angle-going, the silver general, and the gold general can be placed on any empty square anywhere on the board. The lance and the horse can never be dropped onto the eighth or the ninth row, and the lance and the solider can never be dropped onto the ninth row because of the rule that a piece can never be set onto a square from which it can never move.

There are several important restrictions on replacing soldiers. A soldier can never be dropped into a column in which there is already a nonpromoted solider. If a player does this, he or she automatically loses. Also, a solider can never be dropped to create checkmate. This again results in an immediate loss. *Shogi* observes strict rules due to the sheer number of pieces involved and the complexity of the game.

▦ Tapatan

Tapatan is a row game from the Philippines similar to tic-tac-toe. The game is usually played on a wooden game board that can be easily reproduced on a sheet of paper. Make a square of nine dots, three each in three rows, and connect them all with lines to form eight right triangles. Each player needs to have three game pieces such as coins. The game begins with the first player setting a piece on one of the nine points. The second player then places a piece. Once all six pieces are placed on the board, players take turns moving pieces, one piece per turn, to a vacant point on the board. Jumping over pieces is not allowed. The first person to line up three pieces in a row in any direction is the winner.

▦ *Wa Tze* (Little Rice Bags)

This is a Chinese variant of the popular toss and catch dexterity game of jacks. *Wa tze* uses five small rice bags that measure about two square inches. The object, as in jacks, is to pick up, toss, and catch the little bags in progressively more difficult combinations. Traditionally, *wa tze* was an indoor game played by young girls (its food connection reinforcing gender stereotypes), though young children of both sexes now play it.

The game begins by tossing a bag into the air and then trying to pick up another from the ground and catch the first as it comes down. This action is repeated until all five bags are collected in one hand at the same time. The first player to succeed in collecting all five bags wins that round.

In the next round, each player holds two rice bags in her hand while tossing up one and grabbing another from the ground. Next, the player has to hold two and pick up two or three at a time. When all the combinations are gone through, players can create their own rules, such as catching the bags on the back of the hand rather than in the palm.

Rice bags are easy to make. All that is needed is pound of raw rice and some small fabric bags sewn shut or small sandwich bags taped closed.

▦ *Wei Qi (Go)*

Go is an ancient war strategy board game for two opponents, one playing black and the other white. The object of the game, much as in modern warfare, is for each player to surround the greatest territory on the board with his or her game pieces.

For a game famous for its sophistication and depth, the equipment and the rules of go are remarkably simple. The game board is a square grid, 19 lines by 19 lines, including the sides. At the beginning of the game, white receives 180 game pieces—small, slightly convex white stones the size of nickels. Black starts with 181 stones for a combined total of 361 stones, a stone for each intersection of the board. Black plays first, and thus is considered to have a slight advantage, a factor that goes into the choice of who will play which color; typically the weaker plays black as a handicap. A turn consists simply of placing a stone on an intersection of the grid. Unlike chess, the piece doesn't move once played. (Because the pieces do not move, an interesting tradition developed in which a player demonstrates his or her conviction regarding the choice of placement by holding the stone between the pointer and middle finger and plunking it down crisply on the board. Finely crafted game boards in fact often had resonating chambers to enhance the *plunk* of a resolutely placed stone.) After black's turn, white places a stone, and so on, the players alternating back and forth in the placement of stones.

As more stones occupy the board, tenuous "skirmish" lines of black and white stones begin to emerge in a connect-the-dots fashion. While capture of pieces may take place at this point, it is not, as in checkers, the primary object of the game. Rather, capture is a tactic designed to acquire or secure territory mapped out by the placement of the stones. Capture takes place when a stone is surrounded on each of the adjacent intersections by enemy stones. When a stone is captured, it is removed from the board.

▓ *Xiang-qi* (Chinese Chess)

The *xiang-qi* game board differs from the modern eight-by-eight square chess board in three notable ways. First, all of the squares are white, as the game pieces move between the intersections or "points" of the gridlines rather than on the spaces. Second, the game board is divided in half horizontally by a strip one square wide called the *hwang-ho* after China's great Yellow River, resulting in two four-by-eight square territories on either side. An X crosses the two-by-two square area centered at the edge of each player's territory, marking the nine-point area known as the "fortresses."

Rather than three-dimensional representations of medieval combatants as in modern chess, the *xiang-qi* game pieces are round, traditionally blue or red disks resembling checkers, each with a Chinese character indicating the piece's rank. The initial complement of pieces for each player is as follows:

one general (G)

two ministers (M)

two elephants (E)

two knights (K)

two rooks (R)

two canons (C)

five pawns (P)

The general is equivalent to the king of modern chess in that a checkmate against it results in a loss. The general's movements, however, are much more limited than those of a king. The general may move one point vertically or horizontally in either direction but not diagonally. Further, the two generals are not allowed to "see" one another. That is, the two generals may not occupy the same vertical line or "file" unless another piece of either color stands between them. This rule on occasion results in a piece becoming pinned between the two generals as they occupy the same file. The greatest limitation on the general's movement is that it must remain within the nine points of the fortress.

The ministers may move only one point diagonally. In addition, the ministers must likewise remain within the nine points of the fortress, effectively limiting their movements to only five points.

The elephants move diagonally exactly two points per turn, and the intervening diagonal point must be unoccupied. The elephants are not allowed to cross the "river," effectively limiting the movements of each to seven points on its own side.

The knight's movement is reminiscent of the dogleg jump of a knight in modern chess, except that it may not jump initially over a piece occupying a point vertically or horizontally adjacent to it. To move, a knight jumps one point vertically or horizontally to a vacant point, then, from there, one point diagonally, the second jump being allowed even if at that point another piece occupies a point vertically or horizontally adjacent to it. The knight may jump across the river as if the vertical lines were continuous.

The movement of the rook is virtually identical to its chess counterpart. It may move any number of points in a straight line vertically or horizontally but may not jump over any intervening pieces. The rook may cross the river as if the vertical lines were continuous.

The cannon is an interesting piece because it owes its existence to a Chinese development in modern warfare, namely, gunpowder. Like the rook, the cannon moves any number of points in a straight line vertically or horizontally, with one caveat: The cannon must jump over a piece on its way. In other words, there must be one piece, friend or foe, between it and its destination, whether the destination is an empty point or one occupied by a piece subject to capture. Thus, of all the games pieces, its movement is perhaps the most evocative of the military equipment on which it is based, the required jump over an intervening piece suggesting the cannon's ability to reach targets beyond obstacles.

⊞ EUROPE

INTRODUCTION

For all intents and purposes, the Renaissance was a European event, though its ramifications were felt around the world. It began with the rise of commerce in Italy from the end of the 12th to the middle of the 14th century and was brought north via trade to Germany and England, where its energy began to dissipate after the first wave of emigration to the New World ended in the early 1640s. Exact chronological parameters, as previously noted, are difficult to specify.

The factors that sent Europe into the dormancy of the Dark Ages that ended with the Renaissance are easier to define. The disintegration of the Roman Empire, which was more or less complete by the end of the 5th century A.D., began an era of great instability in Europe, Asia, and northern Africa. Europe, especially, was invaded from all sides: the Vandals and Goths raced through Italy, the Vikings descended from the north, the Moors attacked Spain from Africa. Strong central governments did not exist; Kings had nominal and mythic power, but no ability to protect citizens from invasion. The absence of hard currency made it impossible for kings to raise money through taxation to maintain armies, provide services, and enlarge their power.

What the kings did have was land, which they could grant to nobles in exchange for loyalty, military service, and the administration of local justice. This economic system, known as feudalism, helped to stabilize Europe. Land was the only currency, and as kings granted it, the lords, in turn, made grants to peasants who worked the land in exchange for protection, and for a meager percentage of the proceeds. As feudalism took hold in the 10th and 11th centuries, Europe was thrust back into an agrarian economy, while town and city life virtually disappeared.

Another force at work in the Middle Ages that added to the social and economic stagnation was the Roman Catholic Church. The church was the chief purveyor of learning in medieval society, with its primary interest being the problems associated with human salvation. Science and literature, though not totally repressed, were given far less importance. In addition, the church was responsible to a large degree for how mankind saw life on earth, fostering the idea that human experience was a veil of tears through which man made a slow, sad journey from this world to the next. The teachings of the church helped to solidify feudalism by adapting St. Paul's metaphor of the body to society, promoting the notion that it is the will of God that society is divided into classes according to each person's role (i.e., peasant, lord, priest), and that it is the duty of each person to labor piously in the field in which God had placed them. Feudalism and the church made any kind of social or economic progress very difficult.

Feudalism never took hold in Italy and had virtually disappeared by the end of the 13th century, as urban life began to flourish in many Italian city-states, notably Florence. The country was perfectly situated between Africa and Asia (the source of luxury goods of the Far East) so that it developed a money economy based largely on foreign trade, and this created a thriving merchant class, able for the first time to accumulate profit, rather than just make a living.

The inland city-state of Florence, especially, became a center of commerce and banking, as well as the home of 12 artist guilds. Banking was a new and vital Renaissance industry through which Italy perfected the commercial administration necessary for capitalism. A Florentine gold coin called the florin was of such reliable purity it became a standard in Europe, as Florence set up banks in London, Geneva, and Bruges. Florence also built a huge international textile industry, turning wool from England and Iberia into fine cloth that was sold throughout the world.

Men of this city and others throughout Italy owed nothing to feudal lords, and, while not impervious to the influence of the church, they became more confident in their own ability to interpret their place on earth. Money led to increased time for self-development, including education that went beyond the teachings of the church. Soon, the great artists began reaching back into antiquity for inspiration, in part as a reaction to what they saw as a stifling ecclesiastical influence of the Middle Ages.

THE POWER OF MONEY

With money the new, reliable means of exchange, kings now had a means of levying taxes and strengthening their governments with the purchase of cannon, gunpowder, and the maintenance of regular armies. Banking enabled them to borrow vast sums for capital improvements. The feudal nobility, whose only wealth lay in their land and who were slow to adapt to economic change, quickly declined and modern Europe began to take shape.

New inventions, notably the astrolabe for navigation and movable type for the creation of printed books, began to open up new worlds inside the mind and around the globe as mankind reached out for wider spheres. The age of exploration, which began with Columbus and de Gama at the end of the 15th century, soon shifted the focal point of world commerce from Italy and the Mediterranean to the Atlantic. The conquest of the New World by England, France, Spain, Portugal, and the Netherlands diffused much of the Renaissance energy, as nationalism replaced humanism in the lust for gold and empire. But a crucial change had taken place, a new atmosphere for achievement, and a consciousness of the world and its history had helped set humanity on a course to build the modern world.

A KEY INVENTION—LEISURE TIME

As economic and social life became more urban, as feudal nobles became courtiers, and as leisure time increased, sports and games took on a greater role in daily life. One major contribution, both technological and conceptual, that the Renaissance yielded was a new way of looking at time, both in its daily and historical senses. The ability to divide leisure time from work, an increase in disposable income in a new moneyed economy, and the sudden rise in popularity of many sports and games enabled pastimes to become entrenched parts of daily life. Clocks, watches, church bells, and calendars gave people the means to measure time and count the days until the next holiday or feast day and the revels associated with them.

THE POWER OF PRINTING

Of the technological innovations that helped people make the best use of their time, printing had the biggest and most immediate impact. Movable type, which was developed in Germany in the middle of the 15th century, meant that the ideal traits of an aspiring courtier or country gentleman could be set down in a book and published widely. The Renaissance was the birthplace of the modern self-help movement.

Two famous books of the era that promoted the harmonious development of human character show how integral the role of sports had become by the 16th century. Baldassare Castiglione's *Book of the Courtier* (1528) said that the ideal courtier would be "well-built and shapely of limb," and partake of "all bodily exercises (swimming, running, leaping) that befit a man of war." Likewise, Sir Thomas Elyot's *Book of the Governor* (1531) expounds on the virtues of such activities as running, swimming, and hunting as exercises that made "the spirit of a man more strong and valiant." Both Baldassare and Elyot cite archery, fencing, and tennis as sports befitting gentlemen of rank, and as a result these sports became immensely popular.

In addition to books, printers produced calendars, playing cards, paper sheets for new games such as goose, and inexpensive substitutes for many board games.

ROYAL SPORTS

The Renaissance was the age of kings. The shift from feudalism to a money economy enabled royal power to increase steadily from the middle of the 13th century onward. The feudal nobility lost their wealth and power and flocked to royal courts, spending their leisure in sporting pursuits, hunting with the king to curry favor, or jousting in outmoded armor to revivify their dying image of prestige.

As with every age, royal patronage played a huge role in spreading the popularity of sports, especially in England, which, along with Italy, brought Renaissance achievements to their apex. One of the most celebrated athletes of Renaissance England was King Henry VIII, as Alison Weir's biography demonstrates:

> He hunted, jousted, played tennis, wrestled, could throw a twelve-foot spear many yards, defeated all comers with his heavy, two-handled sword in mock combats, and could draw a bow with greater strength than any man in England. The benefits of all this activity included a splendid physique, robust good health, and sheer masculine strength. As one observed, "When he moves, the ground shakes under him." (105)

Other monarchs, including Philip of Spain, Queen Elizabeth, King James I of England, and Mary, Queen of Scots, were all either passionate players or patrons of sports that included jousting, hunting, tennis, fencing, and golf.

The promotion of sports by King James I of England was one of many factors that fueled political tensions and hastened the end of Renaissance energy. In 1618, James issued his Declaration on Lawful Sports, in which he endorsed the playing of sports on Sundays. "Our pleasure likewise is, Our good people be not disturbed, letted, or discouraged from any lawful recreation, Such as dancing, either of men or women, Archery for men, leaping, vaulting, or any other such harmlesse Recreation, nor from having of May Games, Whitson Ales, and Morris-dances, and the setting up of Maypoles, and other sports."

James's declaration was an outrage to the growing number of Puritans gaining power in Parliament. The issue of Sunday sports, though far from the gravest issue of the day, became a galvanizing force, exacerbated when Charles I—James's son and heir—reissued an expanded version of the Declaration in 1633. Charles was playing golf in Scotland in 1641 when he heard of the Irish uprising. He was beheaded in 1649 (a moment some his-

England's King Henry VIII was as devoted an athlete as he was a husband.

torians regard as the beginning of the modern era) and England was plunged into civil war. Sports might not have been the cause, but the uses of recreation and opposing attitudes toward sports was an apt barometer.

Although it is hard to say when the Renaissance ended, it is clear that by the early 1640s, its energy had been dissipated to the New World and beyond. The first wave of Puritans had settled in New England and throughout North and South America, the focus of colonization shifted from the plundering of gold to the slow work of empire building. Europe continued to lead the way, though in terms of sports, they would find in and adapt from new cultures as much as they would attempt to impose.

EUROPEAN SPORTS

⊞ Animal Sports

Despite ongoing refinements in art, culture, social attitudes, and the gentility of many games and pastimes, Renaissance sports were, to say the least, steeped in violence and aggression. Humanity was just beginning to develop the compartmentalized sense of time in which sports and games were pursued for their own sake. Most sporting activities of the era, such as archery or hunting, still served either the needs of the military for trained soldiers or the peasant for food. Blood sports were great entertainment, as this passage from Huizinga's *Waning of the Middle Ages* illustrates:

> In 1425, an *"esbatement"* takes place in Paris, of four blind beggars, armed with sticks, with which they hit each other in trying to kill a pig, which is a prize of the combat. On the evening before they are led through the town, all armed, with a great banner in front, on which was pictured a pig, and preceded by a man beating a drum. (26)

Though only spectator sports, cockfighting and bull or bear baiting were immensely popular. Cockfights pitted two fighting cocks against one another in a small ring surrounded by benches. Although the sport was popular throughout the Middle Ages (except during times of plague, when it was suspended), King Henry VIII did not build the first permanent cockpits until early in the 16th century. The activity was so common that young boys even brought cocks to school on Shrove Tuesday (the day before the beginning of Lent) and pitted them against each other. The sport was eventually prohibited by law in 1654 but flourished nonetheless.

In bull baiting, a bull was chained in a large open area while pit bulldogs, usually English Lyme mastiffs, were loosed upon it. The dogs would clamp their powerful jaws on the bull's face, ears, or testicles while the enraged bovine thrashed, stamped, and attempted to gore or crush the attacking dogs. Both cockfighting and bull baiting were occasions for gambling. Puritans frowned upon it, not out of animal rights, but since most matches took place on Sunday. Of the many bull rings throughout England, Paris Gardens in Southwark was the most impressive, at its height housing 3 bulls, 20 bears, and 70 mastiffs. Despite the brutality of the spectacle, the relentless tenacity of bulldogs became emblematic of England's national self-image.

Popular feast-day contests, particularly on Shrove Tuesday, included gander pulling and throwing at the mark. In gander pulling, a greased goose was hung by its feet from a rope line and contestants would ride by and try to kill the bird by grabbing its greased neck and yanking its head off. A contest of throwing rocks to kill a rooster tethered to a spike was also popular and practiced in colonial America. In each case, the dead bird was the prize.

Hunting, usually for rabbits, deer, or birds, was also popular among all classes, though hunting rights were limited to one's own land, giving kings and the nobility the most far-reaching access. In general, hunting was a sport among the aristocracy (an ideal showcase for their thorough-bred horses, hawks, clothing, and weapons) and a source of sustenance among the poor. King Henry VIII of England was a prolific hunter, sometimes wearing out as many as 10 horses in a single day. His daughter, Elizabeth I, was also an avid hunter.

In addition to the killing or pitting of animals, another strain in sports of the era was combat, from wrestling—possibly the most popular sport among the lower classes—to jousts and other ceremonial and mock battles. In Spain, mock battles between those dressed as Christians and Moors were often town-engulfing pageants that combined a sense of history, religion, theater, and physical play.

During the reign of King Philip II, Pope Pius V, appalled at the unconscionable carnage of the bullfights, forbade the practice of the *corridas*. The people, however, ignored the papal decree and continued to relish the *fiesta brava*, forcing Pope Gregory VIII to recant the decree, following the advice of the writer and mystic Fray Luis de León, who said "the bullfights are in the blood of the Spanish people, and they cannot be stopped without facing grave consequences."

▦ Archery

Archery is the skill of shooting with a bow and arrow—in battle, for hunting, or in competition to hit a target. As the bow began being replaced by the gun as both weapon and hunting implement during the Renaissance, archery began a new life as a skill sport, first in tournaments (Charles II of England established the oldest continuous contest in 1673), and later in the modern Olympic Games.

In 1415, the British army under King Henry V won a spectacular victory at the Battle of Agincourt. The British force of approximately 6,000, most of them archers, defeated a flailing French force of 10 times its size. It was a seminal event in English history and one that no doubt fixed archery in the nation's psyche. Prowess with the bow and arrow are a part of European myth, from the 13th-century ballads of the anti-hero Robin Hood to tales of the Swiss national William Tell, who, according to legend, was forced to shoot an apple off his son's head with a crossbow at a distance of 80 paces. William Tell's existence is disputed, but the story dramatizes the mythic level to which bow prowess was raised during the late Middle Ages.

The need for competent bowmen—abating steadily over the next 150 years—resulted in ongoing decrees forcing all commoners to practice archery. Other sports and games were outlawed to prevent them from interfering with archery practice. In 1457, James II of Scotland outlawed golf and football. Twenty years later, Edward the IV banned stool-ball, the forerunner of modern cricket.

The bans never worked and were hard to enforce, but archery still flourished. King Henry VIII was an adept archer and is reported to have hit the bull's-eye on a target 240 yards away at an exhibition in 1520 (the same year the musket was invented). Elizabeth I was an avid archer, and archery was viewed as not only a patriotic pastime, but also a duty.

The military use of the bow remained strong in the 16th century and was a decisive factor in England's victory over Scotland in the Battle of Flodden in 1513. In 1534, King Henry VII ordered that 30,000 longbows be made and stored in the Tower of London. The musket, however, changed the physics of warfare and its clear advantage over bows in defeating the Spanish Armada in 1588 helped hasten the bow's elimination, which was finally decreed in 1595.

During the Elizabethan era, archery competitions took place during festivals and tournaments. Most bows were made from yew wood. Arrow shafts were also made of wood and tipped with heads made of iron that were usually barbed.

Archery and bow hunting are popular in the United States today and it is easy to get involved in the sport, though proper supervision is necessary for beginners. Archery is a popular activity in physical education classes, summer camps, organizations such as the Boy Scouts, and hunting clubs. Most bows today are made of fiberglass and are strung with nylon. Arrows are often metal tipped. Targets are available at any sporting goods store.

▦ Bandy

Bandy would appear to the modern reader as ice hockey played with field hockey equipment. It is an ancient stick and ball game—played widely during the Renaissance—in which teams of players use small bats or sticks to maneuver a ball, usually made of wood or leather, across the ice toward the opponent's goal. It is thought to be a winterized version of the many games, including shinny and hurling, that were played in fields during the summer.

The word "bandy" derived from the Teutonic *bandja* (a curved stick) has come to mean knock something back and forth. The word can apply to objects, insults, or even faces. King Lear chides, "Do you bandy looks with me, you rascal?" (1.4.89).

Early in the Renaissance, when the game was called bandy-ball, its venue and rules were less important than knocking the ball around a frozen marsh on a winter day. The modern game developed in northeast England around 1800 in the marshes of Bury Fen. Marshes (or fens) freeze quickly during the winter and are much safer to play on than ponds because they are shallower.

By the end of the 19th century, bandy evolved into a more rigorous sport along the lines of soccer, pitting 11-player teams for two, 45-minute halves on an ice field the size of a soccer field. A National Bandy Association formed in 1891, and the sport later became popular in Sweden and Russia, where the availability of large ice fields was more predictable.

The sticks were made of willow or ash and were curved or crooked at one end like a modern field hockey stick. Two long branches, often willow, formed the goalposts; the base of the branch was frozen to the ice and its top bent over to define the goal. The original ball was likely a leather-covered ball or small circle of wood. Players would eventually wear metal ice skates to play bandy, but in the game's early days any shoes, boots, or bone skates sufficed.

To play bandy, find a large frozen pond or marsh, mark goals with tree branches, and use field hockey sticks and a rubber ball.

▦ Caber Tossing

Tossing the caber, the hurling end-over-end of a tapered fir pole about 17 feet long and weighing from 90 to 120 pounds, is the best-known throwing event featured in Scotland's Highland Games. The practice is believed to have originated in Scotland by the middle of the 17th century.

Caber tossing requires brute strength and dexterity in measures unequal to any throwing event. Contestants throw toward a target area laid out in a field with points resembling a clock face. The caber is placed on the ground with its small end toward the starting point. The contestant lifts the larger end of the caber above the head and slides his or her hands down its length until the caber is vertical and makes a platform of their hands in which the base of the caber rests. The thrower keeps the caber as low to the ground as possible.

At the starting mark, the contestant stands erect, brings the caber to chest level, takes a run to build momentum, and then heaves it up and away, so that it flies end-over-end away from him toward the circle. The goal is to make the small end of the caber come to rest as closely as possible to the 12 o'clock position. Contestants get three throws each and there is no restriction on the length of the run prior to the toss.

A relatively thin log will work for a substitute if you wish to try this. Even a longish piece of wood, such as a two-by-four would provide a means of practicing the heaving motion necessary for end-over-end propelling. The goal is not distance, but rather style and the ability to have the toss end with the smaller end pointing to 12 o'clock.

▦ Fencing

Fighting with swords in times of war and for military purposes was depicted on the walls of Egyptian tombs as early as 1190 B.C. Every ancient culture had some form of fencing. The sport, or even the art, of fencing, however, is more or less an invention of the Renaissance, with Italy, Spain, and France all claiming its parentage. Modern conventions for equipment and scoring were set in the 18th century.

Although a popular weapon in ancient times, the sword all but disappeared in the Dark Ages as knights donned impenetrable armor. As the Middle Ages waned, swords became lighter as the new tools of war (namely gunpowder and musket) made heavy armor obsolete. Shrinking armor exposed flesh that was now vulnerable to sword and arrow, so for a brief time, skill with such weapons was vital. By the 16th century, the sword had also become a key fashion accessory for any aspiring gentleman.

The birth of fencing can be traced to Germany and the founding of the Fraternity of St. Mark, better known as Marxbruder, in Frankfurt. A systematic approach to fighting was developed by observing human reactions to various moves during combat—moves that could be taught and thus repeated in combat. At first, separate fencing guilds guarded their secret techniques. The sport spread quickly when the first fencing manual, *Treatise on Arms*, by Diego de Valera appeared in 1471. The first official ban on dueling followed nine years later in 1480.

Fencing with heavier bladed broadswords had always been popular in England. The sword was designed for slashing rather than thrusting, and contestants would usually also be armed with a buckler, a small wooden shield. Early in the 16th century, thanks to the influence of King Henry VIII, the Italian school of fencing—using a much lighter rapier and dagger—began to gain popularity in both Spain and England. Italian master Rocco Boncetti opened the first fencing school in London in 1569 and was still going strong as a teacher 30 years later. One outgrowth of fencing's popularity, however, was the invention of the duel of honor, a concept unknown in England until the late Elizabethan period. In 1613, law made death during a dual an act of murder.

While the rapier made its way north from Italy, another sword, the foil, was developed in Paris. The foil was based on the fashionable French court sword, whose size and lightness made it an excellent fencing weapon.

The sport of fencing was added to the summer Olympic Games in 1924. The drama and the glamour of it have been with us since the Renaissance. The climatic moments of two of Shakespeare's greatest plays, *Hamlet* and *King Lear,* are built around swordfights; Sherlock Holmes was a consummate fencer, and swashbuckling pirates became cultural icons in literature and film.

Lessons and discipline are required to participate in fencing. Serious injuries can result from playful dabbling in this sport, even if swords are not used. Classes are available in many high schools and colleges, health clubs, community centers, and studios maintained by instructors.

Vincentio Sauiolo his Practise.

THE THYRDE DAYES
Discourse, of Rapier *and*
Dagger.

Luk..

I Know not certainly, whether it hath been my earnest desire to encounter you, that raisde me earlier this morning than my accustomed houre, or to be assertained of some doubtfull questions, which yester-night were proposed by some gentlemen and my selfe, in dis-
courfe

Fencing was the sport of choice among aspiring courtiers. (Used by permission of the Folger Shakespeare Library.)

▦ Football

Football, called soccer in the United States, began in Europe in the Middle Ages, and, as with the modern game, pitted two teams that try to kick or otherwise maneuver a ball (usually an inflated animal bladder encased in leather) toward a goal. The field might be between two villages or a street. As with many popular sports, football was banned in England on numerous occasions, including 1349, 1541, and 1617, but the game only grew in popularity. Football was played by the lower classes, hence Shakespeare's famous putdown in *King Lear* when a servant is referred to as a "base football player."

The game of football is often perceived as a melee in which inhabitants of two towns clash on a boundless field, using any means necessary, including kicks and punches, to move the ball. This might have been true during the Middle Ages, but by the early 1600s, the game had developed a high degree of sophistication, including the even division of teams (usually with 15, 20, or 30 members to a side), the use of man-to-man defenses, offsides rules, and limitations on physical contact, both with respect to the ball and one's opponents.

Staging a Renaissance-like football game is a great class activity in which everyone can participate. Key elements include picking a special day for the contest, one that has special meaning for the class, such as the day before spring vacation. Shrove Tuesday was a popular day for football games during the Renaissance. Also, making a ball instead of using a regulation soccer ball will add more drama to the contest, because, as with the balls of the time, it will not bounce or roll smoothly. A ball can be made by sewing leather over a wad of cloth. The teams could pit the players in one class, two classes, two grades, or the entire school. The field could be a large parking lot, playground, or any open space that gives a sense of boundary without having specific boundary lines, with the goals set far apart. Be creative, but for the sake of safety, use modern rules of play: no hitting the ball with the hands, no tripping, and no pushing.

▦ Golf

Golf is a game in which a player using special clubs (limited in number to 14 in the modern game) attempts to sink a small, dimpled ball with as few strokes as possible into a series of holes on an outdoor course. A hole usually consists of a teeing area from which the ball is driven in the general direction of the hole, a long, open fairway of short grass, a putting green that contains the hole, and natural and man-made hazards, such as sand bunkers and water.

There are a number of similarities between the development of the games of golf and tennis: both had antecedents that predate the Renaissance, both developed during the Renaissance into a form that modern readers would recognize, and their popularity was enhanced through royal participation, notably of Mary, Queen of Scots and her son, King James I of England. And like tennis, golf has evolved into one of the world's most popular participation and spectator sports.

On the whole, however, golf never rose to the zenith in popularity that tennis enjoyed during the Renaissance. It remained a fringe sport; a rural pastime practiced in Scotland, Belgium, and the Netherlands, and enjoyed a slow, steady growth over time.

Although every world culture boasts stick and ball games, the game that would become the golf we think of today originated from a game played on the eastern coast of Scotland in the Kingdom of Fife during the 15th century. Players would knock a pebble around a predetermined, natural course of sand dunes, rabbit runs, and tracks using a stick or club. Separating golf from other stick and ball games, including the Dutch game *kolven,* was the object of knocking the ball into a hole in the ground, as opposed to hitting it toward a tree, rock, or other target.

During the mid-15th century, as Scotland prepared to defend itself against the British, the popularity at the expense of archery practice prompted the Scottish parliament of King James II to prohibit golf (soccer, too) in 1457, a ban that was reaffirmed in 1470 and 1491, although people largely ignored it. King James IV of Scotland lifted the ban in 1502 after he had taken up the game.

The rise of golf is steeped in Scottish and English royal history, notably that of the House of Stuart. The word "caddie"—the person who assists a golfer, usually by carrying his or her clubs—is derived from the French military "cadets." These young men aided Mary, Queen of Scots, who was raised in France in the court of King Henry II. She later married his son, Francis I, before returning to Scotland. Mary's son James (the future James I of England) was an avid golfer and sportsman. When he became king in 1603, his attendants improvised a course at Blackheath outside London where nobles and dignitaries might ingratiate themselves by playing an occasional round.

Despite being popular with the Stuarts, golf never caught on with the nobility nor the common man. The Renaissance, after all, focused on town and urban life; rural customs and pastimes from outlying areas were far less attractive to aspiring courtiers than what the rich were doing at court. Tennis, fencing, hunting, and horse racing were much more attractive pursuits. Golf, like tennis after its mid-17th-century decline, had to wait until the end of the 19th century to become universally popular.

Golf's popularity today makes it easy to learn. Many high schools have golf teams or clubs, and most country clubs, town recreation departments, and public and private courses offer lessons during which equipment may be rented.

▦ Horse Racing

As the popularity of jousting declined, horse racing emerged as the most popular sport among the aristocracy, offering a venue that was both safe and exclusive. Charles II established the first national races in England, and horse racing also became the first major commercial sport to be developed in the American colonies, with races held on Long Island as early as 1665.

During the Renaissance, most races were match events among two or three horses that included multiple heats. A horse had to win more than one heat to be declared the winner. The modern form of racing, in which many horses are ridden against one another in single-race dashes did not appear until the 18th century.

Only the wealthy could afford to participate, since horse racing required not only the ability to afford horses that could be bred just for racing, but also the facilities (stables and open land) necessary to train them. Like the older tournaments, horse races became ideal venues for flashing all manner of finery and status.

The first race course in England at Langaby, Cumberland, was in use by 1585. King James I built the famous track at Newmarket and introduced Arabian blood into British horse breeding.

▦ Hurling and Related Sports

While sports like tennis, archery, and jousting enjoyed popularity among the upper classes during the Renaissance, many sports that had been played for centuries in rural communities found their popularity enhanced and their social context strengthened as games of the common people. One example of this is the Irish game of hurling—the "national pastime of Ireland"—which is a stick and ball game similar to modern field hockey and lacrosse. Hurling is mentioned in Irish manuscripts dating back to the 13th century B.C., making it perhaps Europe's oldest field sport.

The hurling stick, called a hurley, is a tapered, slightly curved device with a cupped blade at the bottom. The ball is similar in size to a modern field hockey ball, but has raised ridges. The hurling field today is approximately 137 meters long and 82 meters wide. The goal posts are similar to those used in rugby, but with a lower crossbar.

As in lacrosse or field hockey, players (15 to a side in modern hurling) advance the ball downfield toward the opponent's goal. A point is scored by hitting the ball over the crossbar of the opposing team's goalposts, three points by driving it under the crossbar.

Players may strike the ball on the ground or in the air. Unlike hockey, players can pick up the ball on their stick and carry it in the hand for up to four steps, at which point, the ball may be bounced on the hurley and back to the hand. But this move can only be done twice, so one of the skills is running with the ball balanced on the stick.

Variations of hurling were played throughout Europe and the New World. The Irish brought hurling to Scotland, where it evolved into shinty or shinny. The game was also played in England as cambuca or bandy, in France as *jeu de mail* and in the Netherlands as *het kulven*. Early European settlers saw the game played by numerous Indian tribes throughout North America.

Shinty is still considered the national pastime of Scotland. It differs slightly from hurling in the size of the team (12 instead of 15), the type of stick used (those in shinty have a broader face), and rules on carrying the ball (you can use the stick, called the caman, but not the hand). The modern games are close enough in style to have spawned intersport matches.

Any of the games can be played using modern field hockey equipment. A tennis ball, the approximate size of the ball used in shinty, may be a prudent substitute for the hockey ball when playing for the first time, because hockey balls, although rubber coated, can carry bruising momentum.

▦ Jousting

Jousting was a form of ritualized mock combat in which two armor-clad knights on horseback charged at each other with leveled lances in an attempt to unseat each other. Jousts were usually the centerpiece of great festivals at which knights and the nobility could bask in and honor the long-past days of chivalry while currying favor with kings and maidens.

When we think of Renaissance-era tournaments, the first image that might come to mind is of two knights in shining armor jousting, while kings, courtiers, and ladies look on in anticipation of lavishing praise and rewards on the victor. Jousting developed in France during the 11th century, was carried to Germany, and saw the greatest popularity in Italy and England. Jousting most likely grew out of the melee, which pitted large numbers of armed horsemen in mock combat.

The lances used in jousting were blunted, but the sport was still extremely dangerous, often resulting in serious injuries and death.

By the Renaissance, jousting had lost all connection with military training. Knights had not worn heavy armor in over 200 years. As European kings became stronger in the late Middle Ages, they used growing coffers to hire mercenaries and to build and maintain armies that consisted largely of infantry. So Renaissance tournaments were exercises in nostal-

During the Renaissance, jousting was about the only occasion in which knights donned full armor.

gia even then. The knights' chivalric code still captivated peoples' imaginations, so as feudal lords gave up their castles to become courtiers, they took their armor, lances, pomp, and pageantry with them.

Participation was limited to those who owned the necessary equipment and had access to the tiltyard, the venue at which jousts took place. In addition to the arms, one needed many fine horses, time to train them, and time to practice. A popular way to practice was tilting at the quintain, similar to the hanging heavy-bag boxers use, but with a twist: the target hung down from a crossbar balanced with a heavy weight on the other side, such as a sandbag or cannonball. The crossbar tilted when the target was struck, so if the knight were not charging fast or deftly enough, the tilting weight would knock him in the back.

Jousting was especially popular in Italy under the Medicis, who invested considerable resources to promote the sport. The support and participation of Henry VIII made jousting popular in England as well, with its heyday in the early 16th century. Gradually, however, the inherent risks of the tournament, their military irrelevance, and the development of other sports to demonstrate prowess and win courtly love (notably fencing) supplanted jousting, which had all but died out by the end of the Elizabethan era.

▦ An X-Games–Style Tournament

Obviously recreating a joust is next to impossible, and would be as life threatening today as it was during the Renaissance. But training elements of that era might be re-created to give one a flavor of some of the skills necessary to compete in a tournament. Many "X games" of today (including in-line skating and skateboarding) employ a tournament atmosphere, as each competitor tries to outdo his or her predecessor to impress judges and spectators.

A modern quintain might be a one-gallon plastic jug weighted down with a quart or so of water and placed on a four-foot-high stool. The sword could be a dowel rod. The goal of the exercise might be to skate or ride toward the stool, which can be set in a paved, open area, and attempt to skewer the jug with the sword. This activity tests speed, dexterity, concentration, and coordination.

A second stool and jug could be placed on a line with the first stool a safe distance (perhaps 10 yards) away. The two competitors might skate or bike toward their own targets, covering an equal distance from opposite directions (see diagram). This way, spectators can clearly see which competitor wins the race to his or her target, while preventing any chance of a collision. Points can be awarded for reaching a target first or skewering a target. All requisite helmets and padding must be worn at all times, and the event must be staged in an area free of traffic.

Stool 1   ←-----------Competitor 1

^

(10+ yards between stools)

˅

Competitor 2------------→   **Stool 2**

By racing to spear or knock targets off safely separated stools, speed and accuracy replace brute force in a modern-style joust.

▦ Lawn Bowling

As town life began to proliferate during the Renaissance, the village green became a popular gathering place for sports and activities, many associated with popular feast days, including Plow Monday, Shrove Tuesday (the Tuesday before the start of Lent), May Day (May 1), and many others. Lawns and open spaces near taverns also became gathering places for sport. Some lawn games became immensely popular during the Renaissance and are still played today in one form or another. Lawn bowling, also known as bocce, is still popular; the pitching of quoits has given way to horseshoes in the United States, and pall-mall has evolved into croquet. The popularity of lawn games during the Renaissance mark a point in cultural history when sports had become an important enough element of daily life that venues for play were created and maintained.

Lawn bowling, or bowls, is an English game in which a player tries to roll a ball closer to a smaller target ball than his or her opponents. Like billiards and croquet, bowls is one of the many games descended from the universal pastime of throwing rocks or pebbles at targets on the ground.

While articles found in ancient Egyptian tombs suggest a game similar to bowls was played as early as 5,000 B.C., the bowling game that became popular in Renaissance England probably originated with the Romans. Throughout the empire, Roman soldiers passed idle time playing a game whose object was to roll a wooden or leather ball as close as possible to a mark on the ground. Whoever got closest, won. Over time, this Roman bowling game evolved into the games of bocce (in Italy), boules (in France), and bowls in England.

Throughout the Middle Ages, bowls was popular among all classes of English society. Special lawns called bowling greens were set aside for the game. The oldest of these, located in Southampton, has operated continuously from 1299 to the present day. The third Earl of Southampton enjoyed playing at bowls every Tuesday and Thursday accompanied by as many as 40 knights and gentlemen.

Bowls became so popular that in 1511 King Henry VIII, a superb sportsman and athlete and an avid bowler, banned the game for all but the wealthy. Apparently the game distracted "Bowyers, Fletchers, Stringers, and Arrowhead makers" from their military duties. To ensure that only the wealthy would play, the king imposed a fee of 100 pounds on private greens and forbade "play at any bowle or bowles in open space out of his own garden orchard."

The famous explorer and privateer Sir Francis Drake did nothing to improve the game's reputation as a distraction when, according to legend, he insisted on finishing a game before sailing to engage the approaching Spanish Armada in 1588. He lost the match, but, fortunately for him, won the battle. A 1541 statute designed to promote archery practice levied fines for the unlawful playing of bowls and other games. But these were so small (usually four to eight pence) that they were usually seen as more of a tax than a punishment, and play, for the most part, continued unabated.

Playing Field and Equipment

Unlike the 120-foot square of the modern bowling green, Elizabethan greens had no standard dimensions. Bowling greens were, according to one writer at the time, simply "open, wide spaces made smooth and even."

The equipment consisted of four painted wooden balls, each three and a half inches in diameter. The balls were color-coded so that each player had a matching pair—one player red, for example, the other blue. The balls were weighted on one side with a plug of brass or pewter called the "bias." The bias allowed the path of the ball to curve depending on the force with which the ball was cast or rolled. The fifth ball, called the "jack" or "block," was smaller and of a different color. Finally, the "trigg" was a small piece of wood or metal that marked the spot from which the players would cast.

Although lawn bowling balls are available from a variety of sports suppliers, croquet balls or painted softballs are good substitutes (but they will not have bias). A golf ball is a fine jack, and the trigg can be anything from a crushed soda can to a baseball cap.

Rules of Play

Players begin by "footing the trigg," that is, they choose the spot from which to cast and mark it with the trigg. The first player then throws, or "casts out" the jack onto the green ("no further than a reasonable throw," however, as one writer of the period cautions).

Once the jack is cast out, the real play begins. The players take turns casting a ball toward the jack. In addition to aiming for the jack, a player may strike and dislodge an opponent's previously cast ball (thus prompting one Elizabethan writer to observe wryly that bowling is like life in the royal court, everyone strikes to dislodge the person closest to the queen, "the nearest are the most spited, and all Bowls aim at the one the other, to turn out of place").

After the four balls have been cast, the player whose ball is closest to the jack scores a point. If a player's ball is touching the jack, or if both of his or her balls are closer than those of the opponent, the player scores two points. Next, the jack is cast out again and the process is repeated until one player wins by scoring five points (or seven or nine points, if the players agree beforehand).

▦ Pall-mall

Pall-mall (also pail-mail and pell-mell) is a 17th-century game in which a boxwood ball was struck with a mallet to drive it through an iron ring suspended above the ground at the end of an alley. The name was also given to the mallet used, to the place where the game was played, and to the street in London, still called Pall Mall, in front of St. James Palace where the game was often played. Pall-mall was played by men and women and is similar to croquet.

Like many sports and games, the exact origin of pall-mall is difficult to determine. References to the game appear in French texts as early as the 13th century. It was known to be very popular in England in the 16th century and had also reached favor in Italy and Scotland in the late 17th century. Its popularity waxed and waned over the years, but the game never became hugely popular. It reached perhaps its greatest popularity in the mid-19th century after rules were refined and it began to be played on lawns. The game added wickets and eventually became known as croquet.

In addition to spawning croquet, pall-mall is believed by some scholars to have led to the invention of billiards, the earliest forms of which had more obstacles on the table to simulate the stakes in pall-mall, making the game similar to modern bumper pool.

Playing Field and Equipment

Pall-mall can be played with a modern croquet set using six of the nine wickets that generally come with a set. The wickets need to be marked, one in each of the six colors matching the balls. Also required are two stakes, a start/finish stake, and a midway stake.

The standard colors and the order in which they are played are blue, red, black, yellow, green, and orange. The six colors of the wickets and balls are not specified in sources, so while it is convenient to use a modern croquet set to play pall-mall, you could make your own set, using any colors you prefer. Original sets also did not specify a color order for the taking of turns. Using a standard order, however, makes it easier to remember the order in which players take turns.

The object of pall-mall is to traverse the out-and-back course, knocking your ball through the wickets in the correct color order using your mallet, striking the midway stake with your ball, then going back through the course, knocking your ball through the wickets in reverse color order and finally striking the start/finish stake. The first player to complete the course wins.

To start, each player chooses a color. Each player brings his or her ball into play in the order of the colors on the stake: blue first, red second, black third, yellow fourth, green fifth, and orange sixth. Once all players have selected a color, they are given the corresponding ball and a wicket marked with their color.

Next, the course is established. The start/finish and midway stakes are placed at the ends of the playing field. There is no set distance for a pall-mall field, though a recommended range is between 50 and 100 feet for length and between 30 and 50 feet for width. Boundaries may be marked out via string or some other method, but usually natural boundaries are sufficient to give people a sense of the playing field.

After the stakes are placed, the players set their wickets on the course. Unlike croquet, pall-mall does not have a set layout for the wickets. Players may place their wickets anywhere on the course, at any angle. Hence, players may have to go toward the far end of the course to go through one wicket then come back to the other end for the next. Each game of pall-mall becomes unique, to say the least.

Rules of Play

To begin, the player who chose blue sets his or her ball to either side of the start/finish stake, then strikes the ball toward the first wicket. Each player follows in the order of his or her color. Players then take turns in respective color order. A turn consists of one stroke or hit upon a player's own ball, plus any additional bonus strokes earned. Players must knock their balls through each wicket in the correct color order, from either side of the wicket.

Knocking one's ball through a correct wicket earns one bonus stroke. No penalty stroke ensues if a player knocks his or her ball through the wrong wicket (i.e., one not in the proper order), but the player cannot count that wicket as having been played through and gets no bonus stroke.

If an opponent knocks someone's ball through the wicket that the player has to go through next, that player is credited with having made it through the wicket, and may continue toward the next wicket (or stake), but is not awarded a bonus stroke.

Should a ball rest for some reason in an unplayable position (i.e., a place where the ball cannot be struck with the mallet), the ball may be moved the length of one mallet head to a position where it can be struck. If a ball goes out of bounds (whether by a player's own stroke or a ricochet off an opponent's), the ball is brought back to the boundary nearest the place it went out and is played from that spot.

⽥ Pelota

Pelota is a name for a number of court sports that involve propelling a small ball using one's hand, a racket, a wooden bat (*pala*), or a basket *propulsor*, either directly to players on one side of a net or line, or indirectly off a stone wall. The games were derived from the French *jeu de paume* (a forerunner of real tennis) in the Basque provinces of Spain and France. The most widely known form of pelota played today is jai alai.

Like tennis, pelota games evolved throughout the Middle Ages and the Renaissance. Basques first batted the ball back and forth with their bare hands. By the 15th century, they used leather gloves, wooden paddles, and primitive rackets. The cesta, the woven basket that is the throwing and catching tool used in jai alai, came into use in the mid-18th century.

The game had many variations, including rebot and pasaka, which were the most popular versions played during the 16th and 17th centuries. Rebot is played in an open courtyard with five players per side, each wearing a leather glove or basket on one hand. Pasaka is an indoor game similar to real tennis that features two players per side with the ball struck with the bare hand or a glove.

As with nearly every type of game in which a racquet is used to propel a ball, the introduction of rubber discovered by Spanish explorers in Latin American added new levels of speed, complexity, danger, and fan appeal to pelota games, especially jai alai, where the ball can be whipped from the chistera at great speeds.

⽥ Quoits

Quoits is a game in which flat iron rings, small hoops of rope, or flat stones are pitched at a stake driven into the ground, with points awarded for encircling it. Quoits is very similar to horseshoes in terms of the object of the game, the main difference being that horseshoes are open at one end.

Like many sports that became popular during the late Middle Ages and the Renaissance, the origins of quoits can be traced back to ancient Rome, but no formal rules were set down until 1881. Some believe that quoits developed as a more formal version of horseshoes, while others, including Peter Brown, President of the National Quoits Society in Great Britain, believe that since the word *quoit* in ancient Greece meant discus, the words were interchangeable and thus quoits might have developed from the Olympic sport of throwing the discus.

Quoits-like objects were tossed as early as the Minoan empire of 2000 B.C. Ancient Romans brought the game to Britain, and it was common by the year 1000, especially among agricultural and working-class people, in particular among those in the mining industry. Quoits of this era were often made from lower-grade mine forge leftover, which may explain why the game seemed to flourish most fully in mining communities.

By the Renaissance, quoits had become a popular and well-organized game, evidenced by numerous attempts to ban it. Quoits was considered to be somewhat dangerous and to have seedy ties to public houses and gambling.

Playing Field and Equipment

To play quoits, you need only an open area, two stakes driven into the ground (but protruding only a few inches above it) 11 yards apart, and either actual quoits (which can be purchased from specialty retailers, including online at www.mastersgames.com), or a reasonable substitute, such as a flying ring (a Frisbee with no middle) or a heavy metal ring. A flat stone will also work.

Rules of Play

Quoits is designed as a game for two people. A flip of a quoit decides who throws first. The rules of play are very simple. A single game is played by two people and each person throws two quoits alternately each turn. The players then walk to the other "hob" or stake and, standing alongside it, throw the quoits at the opposite hob. The player with the quoit nearest to the stake wins the end and scores two points if both quoits are nearest to the stake or otherwise just one point. The game is won by the first player to reach 21 points.

▦ Real Tennis

Of all the sports that gained prominence during the Renaissance, tennis has no doubt maintained the greatest popularity, developing into one of the most universal sports played today. The object of the game is to hit a light, elastic ball over a net dividing the playing surface and into the opponent's half of the court in such a way as to defeat the opponent's attempt to reach and return it. Today, tennis is played indoors, outdoors, and on courts made of clay, asphalt, and grass.

Quando pilà et Sphæræ flectuntur corporis artus, *So oft ich thue den Ballen schlagn /*
Corpus erit levius, pectus erit levius. *Erfrisch ich mir hertz.tragen vnd magn.*

Real tennis, as seen in this image, was a real hit during the Renaissance. (Used by permission of the Folger Shakespeare Library.)

The hitting of the ball is done with a racket, an innovation first introduced during the Renaissance. The modern rules and scoring were first set down in 1555 by an Italian monk, Antonio Scaino da Salo, and have changed little since his treatise was expanded and published in English in 1592.

Tennis was played in France by the 11th century, though some scholars argue the game has roots in handball-type games that served as solemn fertility rights in ancient Egypt. The Egyptian town situated on the Nile, known in Arabic as Tinnis is offered as evidence. It is more likely that tennis takes its name from the French word *tenez*, which means "hold" or "take head," an exclamation that was probably uttered prior to a player's serve.

The game we associate with and which most closely resembles modern tennis was first played in courtyards and quadrangles next to monasteries in France and Italy. Monks would run a string between two walls to serve as a net, over which they would hit a ball back and forth with their bare hands, hence its early name, *jeu de paume* (game of the hand). The ball, usually a leather covering stuffed with feathers or hair, could be struck off the walls (just as in modern squash or racquetball) as well as stone underfoot. Early rules varied depending on the surroundings.

Gradually, as monks traveled to other monasteries, the more enjoyable rules were generally adopted, the more bizarre rules abandoned, and people started to add features to their courtyards that improved the pastime and demolish or modify others that detracted from it. The monks enjoyed the game so much that in 1245, the Archbishop of Rouen issued an edict forbidding the clergy from playing because it consumed time felt necessary for prayer. By the 14th century, the game had spread from cloister to castle and had become a game of the nobility.

As play improved and the game developed, players began wearing gloves, which protected the hand and enabled the ball to be struck harder. Later, players began stitching a webbing of cord between the fingers of gloves, adding more power. And by the 15th century, the racket had arrived, a taut striking surface made of sheep-gut at the end of a handle, and the modern game was born. Tennis is the oldest of all racket sports.

High Culture

Tennis appeared in England in the 15th century and was soon entrenched in popular culture, both by the patronage of King Henry VIII, reported to be an avid and highly skilled player, and by the writings of Shakespeare, who mentions tennis six times in his plays. Shakespeare's most famous reference to tennis is found in *Henry V*, based on Henry's response to an insulting gift of tennis balls sent to him by the French Dauphin Lewis. To the notion that leisure might be a better pursuit for him than war, Henry says:

> His present, and your pains, we thank you for:
> When we have match'd our rackets to these balls,
> We will, in France, by God's grace play a set,
> Shall strike his father's crown into the hazard.
> Tell him, he hath made a match with such a wrangler,
> That all the courts of France will be disturb'd
> With chases. (1.2.272–78)

Professional players hired by his father might have taught King Henry VIII the game. It is known that he maintained a tennis coach. He had his tennis balls (leather stuffed with dog's hair) made especially for him by the Ironworkers Company of London. Two such balls were found in the 20th century embedded in the roof timbers at Henry's "tennis plays" (courts) at Westminster and Whitehall.

The enclosed courts had hard floors, nets of fringed cord, painted black walls, and window frames painted red. Protective wire covered the windows. The Keeper of the Tennis Plays was responsible for many aspects of the game, including building maintenance, racket stringing, keeping score, and coaching.

While playing, the king would strip down to his "slops" (drawers) and wear soft shoes. After the game, he'd don a "tennis coat" of black or blue velvet to prevent catching a chill. Henry's favorite tennis play was the one he had installed at Hampton Court (the world's oldest still in use), the palace he received as a gift from Cardinal Thomas Wolsey.

Scoring

The mysterious scoring system unique to tennis dates back to medieval France. The word "love," which means a score of zero, likely comes from the English pronunciation of the French word *l'oeuf* (egg), which resembles a zero. Even today, the term "goose egg" is synonymous with zero. The word "deuce" is shortened from the French *à deux du jeu*—two points away from game.

Points in tennis were scored in units of 15, going 15, 30, 45, and game (60). Over time, 45 got shortened to 40. The number 60 had special significance in medieval France, representing the whole; much the same way 100 does today in the United States. The dividing of games into four points likely had to do with gambling: laws in medieval Germany forbade stakes greater than 60 *deniers*. At the same time, there was a coin in circulation called a *gros denier tournois* worth 15 *deniers*. So it is possible that French tennis players vied for one *gros denier tournois* per point up to the maximum stake of 60 *deniers* for a game.

Its popularity among the nobility made tennis immensely popular during the Renaissance among all levels of 16th-century European society. French kings of the 16th century were fond of the game. Francis I had an indoor court built on his royal yacht. In granting a charter to racket makers in 1571, King Charles IX called tennis, "one of the most honorable, worthy and healthy exercises which princes, peers, gentlemen and other distinguished persons can undertake." At one point, France had nearly 1,600 public tennis courts. The popularity could not last, however. Once commoners can partake of royal sports, much of their allure is lost. Courts also took up space while seating comparatively few spectators. The many public courts soon became rentals for other sporting and cultural events. The expense of building and maintaining courts is the main reason tennis never caught on in the United States until late in the 19th century.

☷ Stoolball

Stoolball is a primitive bat and ball game, a forerunner of cricket, in which the object is for a batter (striker) to prevent a pitcher from knocking over a stool with a ball by hitting it away with a bat. The stool is thus similar to the wicket used in cricket. Indeed, stoolball developed into a team sport that is much like modern cricket.

Stoolball is documented as early as the 13th century and is cited in the *Doomsday Book,* as well as Fitzstephen's *Sports and Pastimes of Old Time Used in This City,* which depicts London life in the early 1200s: "The scholars of every school have their ball, or baton, in their hands; the ancient and wealthy men of the city come forth on horseback to see the sport of the young men." By then it appears the rules for stoolball as a budding sport were well developed. In his translation of *The Odyssey,* George Chapman in 1592 stumps for stoolball as the game Nausicaa and several girls are playing that wakes Odysseus in Book VI when he washes up on the shores of Phaeacia.

The sport is believed to have developed from a game, which now seems like a sort of organized flirting, in which young women seated on milking stools tried to prevent a ball tossed by another person from hitting the stool by swatting it away. The ball was about the size of a modern baseball, usually leather covered and stuffed with animal hair or feathers.

If successful in knocking the ball away, the striker would run to another stool positioned several yards away and try to defend it while the pitcher fielded the ball for a clean shot at the second stool. Points were scored by either hitting the ball away and moving to the next stool or by hitting the stool. As Sally Wilkins notes in *Sports and Games of Medieval Cultures,* the traditional prize for winning was either a kiss or a cake for each point.

The game has special significance in early American history. On Christmas Day 1621 at Plymouth Plantation, Governor William Bradford came upon a group of newly arrived young men "at play, openly, some pitching the bar and some at stool-ball, and such-like sports." These men had refused the morning call for all able-bodied men to work, telling Bradford it was against their conscience to do so on Christmas. But on seeing them playing at noon, Bradford told them it was against his conscience for them to play games on Christmas, and he confiscated their equipment. A telling anecdote in many respects, among them what a popular and portable pastime stoolball was.

The game later developed into a sport with two 11-person teams and is still played today with many thriving associations in England.

Equipment Needed

Here is an easy approach to recreating the more fun, colloquial version. You will need two lightweight three-legged stools, a ball such as a tennis ball, and a bat or paddle. A Ping-Pong paddle is a fine substitute.

Place the stool in the middle of an open space, such as a yard or playground. The striker sits on and defends the stool. The pitcher stands behind a line about 10 to 15 feet away.

The pitcher tries to knock over the stool while the striker tries to knock the ball away. For every hit successfully deflected, the striker receives one point. When the pitcher is successful at knocking over (or hitting) the stool, or catching the ball in midair, he or she takes the striker's place. You can treat turns like innings in modern baseball and set whatever limit is appropriate.

There are many variations to this game, and you can make up your own. For example, you could use two stools and have the striker only score points when the far stool is reached. Another variation is to not use a bat, but instead use the hands or any part of the body except the hands.

EUROPEAN PLAY

Children's Games and Activities

One of the best depictions of Renaissance games was created by Flemish artist Pieter Brueghel, in his painting *Young Folk at Play*, painted in 1560 and which hangs in the Kunsthistorisches Museum in Vienna. The painting is a veritable action poster portraying over 200 children participating in some 80 games and pastimes, most of which are ancient in origin and still played today. Brueghel was famous for his paintings and drawings of

Pieter Brueghel's *Young Folk at Play* (1560). Kunsthistorisches Museum, Vienna, Austria. © Erich Lessing/Art Resource, New York. (Used by permission.)

landscapes and peasant life. Some of the games he depicted include king of the hill, follow the leader, odds and evens, and leapfrog.

▦ Get the Hat

Get the hat is like American football without goals or rules. The object is for players on two teams to try to recover a hat that is dropped between them and hang onto it while players on the other team try to pull it away. The item fought over can be a hat, cap, ball, Frisbee, or almost any small object. This was a children's game in Elizabethan England and it can get a little rough.

▦ Dwyle Flunking

Adult games were common occurrences in and around pubs. These games could be quite puerile, despite the age of the competitors. In dwyle flunking, a string from a stick suspends a bag containing a foul liquid, such as beer or muddy water. One player is chosen to be it, and attempts to hit others with the bag, thereby soaking them as with a water balloon. Whoever got hit became the next it.

▦ Bilboquet

The origins of bilboquet are somewhat obscure, though the game is known all over the world. It is sometimes called cup and ball or ring and pin. The game was played in France as early as the 16th century. The game features either a ball or ring tethered with a string to a handle. The handle has a cup or small hoop at the end of it. The object is to catch the ball in the cup or hook the ring on the end of the stick as many times as possible. Whichever player successfully catches the ring or ball the most number of times in a row is the winner.

▦ Cherry Pit

Cherry pit is a marble game in which a one-foot wide hole is dug in the center of a 10-foot circle. Players surround the hole by placing about a dozen marbles near its edge and then take turns trying to knock marbles into the hole. As long as marbles are knocked into the hole and the taw (shooting marble) remains in the ring, players may continue to shoot. If a taw goes into the hole, the owner must forfeit a number of marbles and place them around the hole to "buy back" his shooter. Cherry pit is mentioned in Shakespeare's play *Twelfth Night*: "Tis not gravity to play at cherry-pit with Satan" (3.4.129).

▦ Running Games

Many favorite forms of play required no equipment. Running and walking have always been popular, and both children and adults in many countries, especially England, took part in many sorts of structured activities. These ranged from simple strolls in the country (very popular among the aristocracy), to footraces of various distances, to the games such as leapfrog and tag and vaulting. The skipping game of hopscotch, invented by Roman soldiers stationed along Hadrian's Wall—the defensive barrier built by Roman emperor Hadrian in A.D. 122 to protect Britain from northern invasions—remained a popular game.

▦ Barley Break

Barley break was a chasing game played by three couples stationed in three bases or plots next to each other. The object was for the two couples standing at either end of the playing field to run toward each other to form new couples, while the third couple occupying the middle base—called hell or prison—tried to catch them.

The couples would start their run toward each other holding hands, but would break apart to avoid being caught. If the middle couple caught and tagged any two players, they would be sent into the middle and receive the distinction "last couple in hell," a phrase used widely in popular literature throughout the late Renaissance and Restoration, as in these lines from Robert Herrick's poem "Barley-Break; or, Last in Hell":

> We two are last in hell; what may we fear
> To be tormented or kept pris'ners here?
> Alas! if kissing be of plagues the worst,
> We'll wish in hell we had been last and first.

To play, three couples stand in a straight line at opposite ends of a field. A good way to visualize the layout is to think of a baseball diamond, with one couple standing on home plate, another at second base, and the third couple, the "last couple in hell" occupying the pitcher's mound.

The couples standing at home and on second hold hands. Those at home shout out "barley" and those at second shout out "break" and they race toward each other. Their goal is to get around the couple in the middle and form a new couple by tagging a member of the other couple. The third couple is trying to get out of the middle. They can do this by tagging two people, either both of the members of one couple, or one from each couple.

As they run, couples drop hands at strategic moments to avoid capture. If the two couples can meet before the middle couple catches them, then the middle couple stays in the middle. If two players are caught, they become the new couple in the middle.

The flirtatious elements of barley break, with an endless forming of new couples, provide a courting aspect to many such chase and capture games common in the Elizabethan era.

▦ Prisoner's Base

Prisoner's base is a game in which two teams try to capture opposing players by tagging them and bringing them to a prison, or base. During the Renaissance, the game was simply called "base" or "prison bars."

The origins of this game are unclear. Like many forms of chase and capture play, base may be rooted in ancient bridal raids, in which men of one tribe or village attacked another and carried off its nubile women. The game's structure and language, however, owes much to warfare, as the two teams line up facing each other and there is a well-defined field of battle. The game seems never to have caught on as an adult game; the exertion seeming to nullify any possible flirtatiousness.

The game can be played almost anywhere from a playground to a gym to a street. Two teams select sides and decide on the location of a home base and a prison. These might be trees, garbage cans, or a section of grass between a street and a sidewalk.

The game begins by the members of each team linking hands and forming a chain, with one player touching their home base. The last player on each team's chain then drops from the chain, and runs into the field of play, chased by a counterpart breaking off from the other team. One by one, team members break from the chain and pursue members of the other team.

The goal is for players to capture members of the other team by tagging them and bringing them to their prison. In some versions of the game, a player can only tag the player on the opposing team who breaks from the team chain at the same time he or she does. More commonly, any player on one team can tag and capture any player on the other team. As prisoners pile up, they form a chain and await rescue, which happens if one of their team members makes it through the fray and tags the last person on the chain. Once freed, neither can be tagged again until they re-enter the field of play.

The game ends when one team captures all the players on the other team.

▦ Kitty in the Corner

Kitty in the corner is another chase game that is similar to musical chairs. The game is designed for five people, four of whom stand on predetermined "corners" or bases. These can be trees, playground equipment, the bases on a baseball diamond, or articles of clothing. The fifth player stands amidst the other four guarding their bases and calls out "kitty in the corner" three times. After the third utterance, all five players race for a new corner. Whoever reaches a new corner first gets to keep it. The player who is left without a corner becomes "kitty" for the next game.

▦ Blindman's Buff

Another chasing game, this one played indoors as well as outdoors and among adults as well as children, was blindman's buff. The game is also called hoodman blind, because an easy method of blindfolding someone was to simply turn a hood around to cover his or her face. The game is simple: a person is blindfolded, spun around three times (sometimes a rhyme is chanted), and then tries to catch the other players around him. The others can dart in and out and gently strike ("buff") the blindfolded person. If the blindfolded person catches someone, that person is it and wears the blindfold for the next turn. Variations of the game include having to identify the person caught before taking off the blindfold.

Another game popular to the era among children and young adults that also involved identifying those striking you was hot cockles, in which a person places his or her head in someone's lap while others slap that person's hands, which are held palm up on their back.

EUROPEAN GAMES

Board games were immensely popular in Europe during the Renaissance, and it was during this period that many ancient games were carried by war or trade from one region to another and standardized into many of the games we enjoy today, especially chess, draughts (what we commonly think of as checkers), and backgammon, which was one form of several games grouped under the name "tables." Boards and game pieces were commercially available, but more often they were made by hand or improvised, and one component, such as a chessboard, would accommodate many different games.

▦ Billiards

Billiards, or pool, is one of the most popular bar games in the world. This game of knocking balls into holes positioned at the edges of a specially designed table came of age during the Renaissance, though, like most games, antecedents stretch back thousands of years. The first written documentation of the existence of a billiard table was found in a 1470 inventory of the possessions of King Louis XI of France, where the modern game was thought to have been invented.

The notation is significant: billiards, like most popular games of the Middle Ages, was banned by both kings and the church for several hundred years. As the modern era began, however, the participation of kings guaranteed that billiard tables would soon be status symbols throughout the courts of Europe.

Early tables had no standard dimensions, and the game more closely resembled the ground games on which billiards is based, with an assortment of posts, pegs, and arches. The maces were smaller, recontoured to accommodate the raised surface. Rails were affixed to keep the balls in play. Tables were designed to meet the specifications of kings and others wealthy enough to own one, and as a result, game rules varied depending on the table layout and the whims of its owner. It is not clear when the standard layout of six pockets at the four corners and midway up each side was adopted or invented. King Louis XI's table had a hole in the center.

By the end of the 16th century, tables could be found in taverns, inns, and other public places in France and England. As the need for tables increased, monarchs throughout Europe hired the finest artisans in an unspoken quest to create the most magnificent tables and gaming rooms on the continent.

One of the most famous billiards enthusiasts was Mary, Queen of Scots, executed in 1588 for her part in an assassination attempt on Queen Elizabeth I. Initially, upon her imprisonment, she had the use of her billiard table inside her prison cell. When this privilege was revoked, she wrote a letter of complaint to the Archbishop of Glasgow. Although she never played again, her body, following her beheading, was draped in the cloth allegedly taken from her beloved billiard table.

It is clear from that account and from a reference in Shakespeare's *Antony and Cleopatra* that when the Egyptian queen suggests to her handmaiden, Charmian, "Let's to Billiards" (2.5.5), that the game appealed to and was played by women as well as men.

▦ Cards (Three Elizabethan Games)

The royal images we see on playing cards today come straight out of the Renaissance, even though cards were invented hundreds of years earlier. The earliest references to playing cards in Europe date to around 1370, and the playing of various games exploded in popularity in 1500. The cards and suits we know were invented in France, though similar sets sprang up in other countries. The earliest known deck comes from 13th-century Egypt, though there is speculation that playing cards were first made in ancient China, where paper was invented.

One thing is clear: cards became popular fast. By 1420, German and Swiss manufacturers printed decks by the thousands via stencil and woodblock printing and later, after printing was invented, with engraved plates.

By the early 15th century, playing cards were included among items commonly burned in bonfires of the vanities that religious leaders inspired in the hopes of stamping out the evils of gambling in a society where the power of the church had begun to wane. In less than a hundred years, cards would be one of the most popular pastimes in Europe, common to all layers of society.

During the Elizabethan era in England, cards were block printed, had blank backs, were unwaxed, and bore a single image in the center of the card. The innovations of mirror image printing, having the suits and numbers appear in the corners for easy reference, and the joker all came later. English cards used the suits of the French system (clubs, diamonds, hearts, spades), while German and Swiss cards favored shields, acorns, flowers, and bells. The range of numbers from ace to king was the same. The deck itself might be referred to as a bunch, pack, or pair of cards. The first technical description of cards games in England appears in 1564, the year Shakespeare was born.

The printing and selling of cards has always been controlled. In Spain under Felipe III, the printing and sale of cards was controlled and sold under license. Heavy fines were imposed for using any other cards. In England, in 1628, the Worshipful Company of Makers of Playing Cards was chartered, after which the importation and use of foreign cards was outlawed. Even today in the United States, cards, unlike all other readily available games, are subject to tax, the seal of which you can see when you crack open a new pack.

Some of the most popular games of the era are played in similar forms today but with different names. Elizabethan favorites included maw, primero, and piquet.

▦ Maw

Maw is a trump and trick-taking game that is fun, easy to learn, and can pave the way for learning more complicated bidding games such as pitch and bridge. Maw developed in 16th-century Ireland and was also popular throughout the British Isles. It is alleged that maw was a favorite game of King James VI of Scotland.

The object of maw, which can be played with anywhere from 2 to 10 players, is to win either three tricks or to prevent other players from doing so. The winner of three tricks wins the pot. If there is no winner, a second hand is played, with each player anteing up. A player who wins the first three tricks automatically wins the pot. If the player plays to the fourth

Playing cards, standardized in the 14th century, became immensely popular. (Used by permission of the Folger Shakespeare Library.)

trick, he or she must win the rest of the tricks to win the pot, sweetened by additional wagers. If the player does not take the final two tricks, he or she loses half the pot, which stays in for the next hand.

Each player is dealt five cards from a standard 52-card deck. The top card of the remaining cards is flipped up to determine trump. The trump cards rank: five, jack, ace of hearts (regardless of the trump suit), ace of trump, king, and queen. If the trump suit is red, the remaining cards rank from 10 down to 2, and vice-versa if the trump suit is black. Non-trump cards of the same color rank the same as trump cards.

The person to the dealer's left leads, playing one card. The other players must follow suit, or play a trump. If a player can do neither, he or she can play any card. Players may hold the five and jack of trump or the ace of hearts if they want to, but lesser trumps must be played if the player cannot follow suit.

▦ One & Thirty

One & thirty was invented sometime around 1450 in Spain (it was also popular in Ireland) and is a forerunner to modern blackjack. Instead of trying to get as close to 21 as possible without going over, 31 is the goal here.

Any number of people can play. Beginning at the dealer's left, each player is dealt three cards, face down. Starting with the player to the left of the dealer, each player can discard one card by turning it face up. The top card on the deck replaces the discard.

The object is to get as close to 31 as possible with three cards of the same suit. The discards continue, one at a time, until a player knocks twice on the table. After the knock, the players get one last discard. The hands are revealed and the hand closest to 31 wins. A player who hits 31 exactly wins automatically.

Card values are the same as modern blackjack: aces count 11, face cards count 10, and the rest are their face value. A three of a kind (different suits) is worth 30 ½ points.

A game similar to one & thirty is bone ace, first mentioned in 1611. Like one & thirty, the dealer deals three cards (three at a time) to each player, only this time, the third card is face up. The player with the highest face up card wins the "bone," which is one coin or the previously agreed-upon wager from each player. Aces are high, and the ace of diamonds (the bone ace) is the highest of all. The eldest hand wins in the case of a tie.

After the bone is won, the player with the hand closest to 31 without going over wins the game. Card values are the same as in one & thirty.

▦ Primero

Invented in Italy early in the 16th century (the earliest reference dates to 1526), primero, a form of poker, was the most popular card game during the Renaissance, and unlike many games of the period, is still played today, notably in Spain.

Primero is played with a 40-card deck: the 8s, 9s, and 10s removed from a standard deck, though there are special decks made just for this game. Primero works best with four to six players.

There are no existing written rules for 16th-century primero, only descriptions.

The object of the game, as in poker, is to attain the highest possible hand, or at least bluff your competitors out of betting against you.

The card point values are as follows:

Face cards = 10

2 = 12

3 = 13

4 = 14

5 = 15

Ace = 16

6 = 18

7 = 21

Following are the primero hands, high to low:

chorus—four of a kind

fluxus—a flush, all cards in the same suit

punto—ace, 6, 7, and jack cards in any suit

supremus—ace, 6, 7, and ace card from any other suit

primero—one card from each suit

numerus—two or three cards in the same suit, value of the hand is the sum of the cards

Because this is a gambling game, the first step is for all players to ante into the pot.

The deal is counterclockwise, starting with the dealer. Two cards go to each player, which is followed by the next phase of betting. Two more cards are dealt to each player, then eight cards are dealt face down on the table or the remaining cards are left out as a draw pile. There are two ways of playing the draw. The first is to draw from the deck and discard into a separate discard pile. The other way is to lay out eight cards and draw and discard from only those cards.

The play moves counterclockwise from the dealer. Each player in turn may draw and discard one card from the eight cards on the table. When a player is satisfied with his or her hand, he or she may knock on the table, calling out "vada." A player may either knock or draw in a turn, but not both. Once a player knocks, he or she may no longer draw. When two players have knocked, the play stops, and hands are shown.

Betting starts after the first two cards are dealt and can continue after the next two cards are dealt, and then at every round just before the dealer's turn. The dealer always bets first. Players may match, raise, or fold any time during wagering. If all players refuse a bet, it must be withdrawn.

▦ Chess

Chess began to emerge in Europe at the end of the 15th century. The game was invented in India in the 6th century, was spread by trade, and developed in many countries in the Middle and Far East with slight variations among the types of pieces and how they can move on the board. The game is a symbolic battle in which the object is to capture the opponent's king.

Chess became the most prestigious of all board games played in Elizabethan England, because chess sets were costlier to create than games such as draughts. Chess was also unique in being one of the only contests that did not involve gambling. The game evolved during the Renaissance; pieces changed and new moves were added. The elephants of the original

Indian game became bishops, which could move diagonally any number of spaces, and the fer became the all-powerful queen, which could move any number of spaces in any direction. Pawns were also allowed to move two spaces on their opening move, and castling, the king-rook interposition, was added.

The basic design of chess pieces (the king wearing a crown, the bishop a miter, and the knight on a horse) did not become standardized until the mid-19th century. During the Renaissance, pieces varied widely in quality from the intricate and ornate, to barely distinguishable wooden carvings.

▦ Coin Games

Coin games were quite popular in Elizabethan England because the chance of pocketing a single coin was a more compelling prospect during the Renaissance than it is today.

In penny prick, a coin, usually a penny, was placed atop a stake driven into the ground. Players threw knives at the stake to try to knock the penny off, or, as in quoits, players stick their knife in the ground so as to block the target from competitors. Whoever dislodged the coin or came closest to the target won the prize.

Cross and pile was even simpler, tossing a coin and guessing if it would come up heads or tails. The cross was the marking on the backs of English coins. The coin toss is still a major part of our culture, usually used to set parameters at the beginning of a game. Winning the toss in modern American football gives a team the right to receive or decline the opening kickoff.

▦ Darts

The game of darts is believed to have begun in the Middle Ages. Bored soldiers passed the time throwing arrows in a spear-like fashion at barrel covers and the rounded upturned stumps of trees. The word "dart" is derived from *dhart,* which means spear. The trees' annual rings provided a useful way to determine whose shot was closest to the center. The hurling of full-length arrows was not practical for indoor play during the winter. Shorter arrows were developed and a popular pub game was born. At the end of the 20th century, darts was the most popular pastime in England, with over 6 million participants.

Dart-type games flourished during the Renaissance. Anne Boleyn gifted her husband, King Henry VIII with a set, and a popular children's game called blow-point involved firing a dart through a pipe at a numbered target. The Pilgrims played darts on the Mayflower.

What we think of as darts today, with its standardized boards divided into 20 triangular sections with double- and triple-scoring zones, did not appear until 1896 when Lancashire carpenter Brian Gamlin created the erratic clockwise numbering sequence (1, 18, 4, 13, 6, 10, 15, 2, 17, 3, 19, 7, 16, 8, 11, 14, 9, 12, 5, and 20). In 1908, in a celebrated sports law case, William Annakin proved through a courtroom exhibition that darts was a game of skill and not chance, and by so doing made the sport legal in British pubs. Dart boards are available through sports retailers and discount stores.

▦ Draughts

Draughts is the very popular game known in North America as checkers. The game is played on the white spaces of a standard 64-square chessboard. The object is to capture all 12 of an opponent's game pieces (small, round disks) by making diagonal jumps over them.

The game is a descendant of the ancient Egyptian game of alquerque, which was played on a five-by-five-point board. As with draughts, each player had 12 pieces, but these were arranged in a sort of interlocking "L" shape, with only one open square, with jumps made along the line intersections. It is believed that a form of alquerque was brought to Europe when the Moors invaded Spain in the 8th century.

Draughts is the result of the northern European recasting of alquerque using a chessboard and game pieces from tables to create a more simplified, though no less popular, game. A book on how to play draughts appeared as early as 1547 in Valencia, Spain, and it now resides in the Royal Library in Madrid. London mathematician William Payne wrote the first English book on draughts in 1756.

The game was played at court and in the taverns of England by all classes. The Earl of Leicester had a set made whose game pieces were made of crystal with inlaid silver and bore his family's heraldic crest. Any small, flat disk or stone will work, however.

Draughts evolved in varying forms throughout Europe, including the French game *jeu force*, invented in the mid-16th century. *Jeu force* forces a player to take an opponent's piece whenever possible (as does the ancient game alquerque), while draughts does not. Draughts is widely popular today, and the Polish version, played on a 100-square board with more complicated capturing rules, is now the internationally recognized standard.

▦ Fox and Geese

In most games, all players start with the same number of game pieces or at the same spot on the board. But some games pit unequal forces against each other whose pieces have compensating powers. One of the popular Renaissance games of this type was called fox and geese.

Fox and geese descended from a group of northern European games known collectively as tafl. Tafl is cited in the Icelandic sagas, but like most

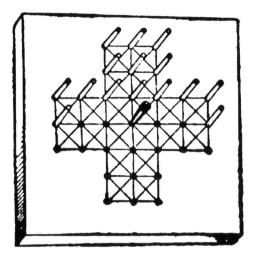

The cross-shaped board for fox and geese.

games, likely has antecedents that are thousands of years old. The game is played on a cross-shaped board covered with squares bisected by diagonal lines that create 33 intersecting points.

One player is the fox and has one game piece. The other player is the geese and has 13 pieces (sometimes pegs) that are arranged to fill the points at the top of the board. The fox starts in the center of the board. The object of the game is for the geese to pen the fox so it cannot escape and for the fox to capture all the geese by jumping over them. The fox also wins if the geese are left with too small a gaggle to surround it, usually five.

The fox moves first. Each side moves one counter per turn. Moves are made from one intersecting point to the next. The geese can move sideways, downward, or diagonally downward. They cannot backtrack. The fox can move in any direction. The fox can also jump over a goose to an empty point, capturing the goose and removing it from the board. Multiple jumps are allowed (as in checkers) as long as the fox is able to jump to an empty point after jumping each goose.

The geese try to immobilize the fox by penning it in, either into a corner or by surrounding it. The geese win if the fox cannot move.

▦ Goose

If it seems that popular board games such as The Game of Life and Monopoly are 20th-century inventions, one need only look at the Spanish game of goose to see that race and journey board games have been with us for hundreds of years.

Goose is a race-around-the-board game played with dice in which fates befall players landing on certain squares. The spiral board varies; some boards have 63 spaces, some 49. The object is the same: finish first.

Goose was a very popular traveling game because it was very portable; all that was needed were the game board, which, if on paper could be easily folded, and dice. Adults and children could also compete on an equal footing. The game is thought to have been invented for Francesco de Medici, who gave it to Phillip II of Spain.

Players roll to see who goes first and advance by rolling dice and moving their game piece along. The winning roll, the one to land on the final square, must be exact. If the final roll is too high, the player doubles back from the last square until the full count is reached.

Only one player can occupy a space on the board. If a turn ends with one player landing on an occupied space, the player on the space is bumped back to the spot the roller just left.

Squares 5, 9, 14, 18, 23, 27, 32, 36, 41, 45, 50, 54, and 59 have a goose on them that, in essence, doubles your roll. If you land on a goose, you again move the number of spaces on your roll. The sole exception to this rule is rolling a nine on the opening move. A player who rolls six and three on the first throw goes directly to square 26. A four and five on the opening roll is even better, shooting the player to square 53. Rolling a nine only has such significance on the opening roll.

Several other squares have additional features. Square 6 is the bridge, which sends a player landing on it to square 12. Conversely a sop on square 42 (the maze) sends the player back to square 30. Square 19 (the tavern) costs a player two turns. A player who lands on the well, square 31, must remain until another player joins him or her, at which time the first player goes back to the space where the second player's last turn began. Square 52 (the prison) is played exactly the same as the well. Square 58 is death and sends the player back to square 1.

Goose game boards are easy to draw on a large piece of paper. Goose also lends itself to live action: a life-sized game board can be constructed either in a classroom or gymnasium by fastening several pieces of paper (one for each square) together and numbering them as described above. Large dice can be drawn on paper folded over two photo cubes. Props can be set down to mark and decorate the specialty squares.

▦ Hazard

Dice games were especially popular in Renaissance Europe, though the tossing of cubes and betting on which side comes up is thousands of years old. Dice games fueled the Elizabethan penchant for gambling, particularly among the lower classes, as the objects are cheap and easy to make. Shakespeare's Richard III, after offering his kingdom for a horse, rejects help; "Slave, I have set my life upon a cast, and I will stand the hazard of the die" (5.4.9–10).

Hazard was the most popular dice game of the age, although by the end of the Renaissance, a simplified version called craps began to emerge. In both games, players bet on a shooter's chances of rolling specific numbers. Dice games were tremendously popular throughout Europe, even in countries such as Spain where their manufacture was illegal.

Hazard is played with two dice, which, during the Renaissance could be made of anything from gold to ivory to bone (hence the dice term "bones"). Anyone could play by laying down a bet. The shooter, or caster, set the wager by paying the first stake and could accept or refuse any bet. In situations with a set number of players, contestants rolled one die to see who cast first.

The caster first rolls to establish the "main," a number between five and nine inclusively. Any other number and the caster either rolls again, or, if playing with a group, the dice pass to the left.

Once the main is established, the caster rolls again to set the "chance," a number between 4 and 10 inclusively that is not the main. It is possible, however, for the caster to win or lose the opening bet without establishing the chance. If the caster rolls the main, he or she wins. If the caster rolls a two or three, he or she loses the bet but retains control of the dice and may roll again. If the caster rolls a 12 when the main is even (6 or 8), he or she wins. If the caster rolls a 12 and the main is odd (5, 7, or 9), he or she loses. Rolling an 11 wins only when the main is 7 (see illustration).

Main Point	Wins On	Loses On
5	5	11, 12
6	6, 12	11
7	7, 11	12
8	8, 12	11
9	9	11, 12
Any	main point	2, 3

Winning and losing roll combinations for the dice game hazard.

Thus, on the chance roll, the caster either wins or loses immediately, or the game proceeds to a third roll, in which the caster wins only by rolling the chance, or loses by rolling the main. The caster rolls until he or she wins or loses. If the caster wins, he or she rolls to establish a new main. If the caster loses, dice pass to the left.

The immense popularity of dice games, especially among the nobility, led to the development of special facilities and accommodations at taverns and gaming houses—such as food, toilets, and entertainment for the convenience of the gambler—and helped lead to the creation of casinos.

▦ Shove Groat

Shove groat developed as a tavern game during the 15th century, a sort of tabletop version of shovelboard (a forerunner of shuffleboard), in which players try to shove or knock a coin between a series of horizontal lines with ascending values drawn on a table.

The game took its name from the groat, a popular coin of the day that bore King Edward IV's image. The coins, in fact became widely known for the game in which they were used. "Quoit him down, Bardolph, like a shove-groat shilling," says Falstaff in Shakespeare's *Henry the IV, Part II* (2.4.180–81).

For such a harmless game, which seems to be a slightly more complex version of nudging a triangular paper football across a cafeteria table, shove groat was subject to many laws. A 1522 proclamation from Henry VIII is supposed to have said, "None of the society shall play at the game called Shoffe boorde or Slypgrote." Such laws were rarely enforced. Another law prevented defaming the likeness of the king by sliding the coin face down. Adherence to this law varied widely depending on time and location.

A similar coin-sliding game might have been played by the Vikings to pass the time on long sea voyages. Shove groat later developed into the game of shove ha'penny, virtually the same game played on a specialized board made of polished wood or slate.

Equipment Needed

To play shove groat, you will need a table with a smooth surface, and ten coins, five for each player. Quarters or 50-cent pieces are ideal, though in the absence of coins, metal washers will also work.

Partition the game board by drawing ten horizontal lines, each between three-quarters of an inch and an inch apart. Mark the spaces between the lines from one to nine.

If you are playing on a conference or cafeteria table, a convenient way to create a game board is to use a ruler to draw bold lines on two sheets of paper that can be taped side by side while leaving a 10-inch wide gap, the game surface on which to slide the coins. Photocopy the sheets and tape them on both sides of the table so two people can sit across from each other and play.

Object and Scoring

The object of the game is to knock coins into each of the sections of the game surface. Only coins that land between the lines count. Each player "shoves" five coins per turn. A coin is placed half off the table edge in front of the player and pushed forward with either the heel of the hand or the backs of the fingers.

Scoring varies. Traditionally, a player is supposed to land three coins in each of the nine sections, and the first player to do this wins. But you can also decide to play up to a predetermined score and award or deduct points for coins shoved off the end of the table or those that hang over the edge.

▦ Tables

Tables is a generic name given to a number of games played on a backgammon board. All the games involve rolling two dice to move 15 "table men" (flat disks), around and/or off the game board, which consists of four quadrants, each with six points. Tables, which was very popular in the taverns of England, most likely made its way north by soldiers returning from the Crusades. Table games, derived from the Middle Eastern game called *nardshir*, were played throughout Europe during the Middle Ages, and were the most popular games in England until the 15th century, when chess grew in stature. Playing at tables often included gambling, which led to its being outlawed for nearly a century, ending during the reign of Elizabeth I.

Modern backgammon did not appear until late in the 17th century. The name is said to derive from either the Saxon words *baec* (back) and *gamen* (game) or the Welsh *bac* or *bach* (little) and *gammon* or *cammaun* (battle). No matter what the origin of the name, the modern game is virtually the same as the table game Irish played during the Renaissance.

Irish is midway in complexity among the popular table games of the era. The object of the game is to move one's 15 pieces—positioned on the various points—around the board according to the roll of the two dice. Rolling doubles (i.e., two fours) entitles a player to four moves of that number instead of two. One can play Irish by following the rules of modern backgammon with the exception of the doubling cube, which was not introduced until 1920.

Another popular table game was doublets, a precursor to the modern game of acey-deucy, which involves the stacking and removal of pieces from one side of the board only. The most complex table game was the

French version called trictrac, in which all 15 pieces are stacked on one point and moved around the board to the opposite point, with points scored for various plays and piece positions. Unlike most table games, trictrac is not a race to remove all of one's game pieces.

▦ Tablero de Jesus

Tablero is a 15th-century Spanish gambling game in which players use their own money for game pieces and play until they run out or quit.

The board is seven rows by seven columns and can be created using a chessboard, with one row and column blocked off. Pennies make good game pieces. Two standard dice are used.

Players roll the dice to determine who goes first. The high roller places one coin in each of the two right-most columns in his or her home row. The low roller places one coin in each of the remaining columns in his or her home row and goes first. The object of the game is to remove an opponent's coins by forming rows of coins in the center of the board.

Each player throws the dice and moves any two coins either forward or backward in his or her own columns by the number of spaces indicated by the dice. The number on each die must correspond to a separate coin.

When a player succeeds in getting two or more coins in adjacent columns on the same row, other than either home row, he or she may either remove them from the board and end the turn or continue to throw the dice hoping to make the row longer and capture more coins.

If a player throws 7, 11, or 12, the dice must be surrendered immediately to the opponent without removing any coins from the board. Dice are also surrendered when a player throws a roll that cannot be played—for example, a six with no coins on either home row.

When a player removes coins from the board, his or her turn ends and the dice are handed to the opponent, who must fill any empty columns by placing new coins in those columns in the home row. If a player is forced to surrender the dice when there is a row of coins on the board, the opponent may take the coins and return the dice without ever making a throw. When a player no longer has enough coins or desire to fill empty columns, he or she has lost the game.

OTHER SPORTS AND ACTIVITIES

As in our own time, people of all ages enjoyed many outdoor activities, including swimming in rivers (the idea of going to the beach had not yet arrived), fishing, and sliding (a precursor to ice skating in which the shinbones of animals were strapped to the bottoms of shoes with leather thongs; the iron skate and even the term "skating" would not reach England until after the Renaissance). A wide variety of dancing was also popular, from country or Morris dancing on festival days to courtly dances designed for two people. Dancing was an essential skill for any courtier and, as now, an important point of interaction between men and women. Another important activity relevant to recreational pursuits was gardening, especially in countries with less open space such as Italy. The cultivation of gardens was both a vigorous physical activity in itself and created places where people could meet, relax, gossip, tell stories, hear music, read love poems, and pass the time in a variety of playful and intellectual pursuits.

Although the Renaissance was an exciting time, and one that saw the standardization of many modern sports, including tennis, it was still a very sedate time intellectually and emotionally when compared to our over-stimulated age. There was little mass culture and, despite the invention of printing, news traveled excruciatingly slowly compared to today. It was an age where a game of naughts and crosses (tic-tac-toe) or flipping a coin was an engrossing leisure activity. It is hard to overestimate how a raucous, draining football game on a muddy spring day, or seeing a rare display of fencing prowess by a visiting master, or catching a glimpse of a king, his men, and his horses plunging through the woods on the chase could erupt in the imagination of a young person who might have grown up exposed to little else besides his or her seasonal chores.

The Renaissance helped to etch sports and games into the psyche more deeply. They became more than diversions and things to pass the time; they became activities worthy of pursuit for their own sake, for the physical, emotional, and social good they gave people.

▦ LATIN AMERICA

INTRODUCTION

For nearly two decades following its discovery, what we think of today as Latin America was the "New World." Columbus landed in the West Indies in 1492 and on later expeditions, "discovered" South America. The exploration of North America, which began in Florida, took nearly 20 years to commence. As time went on and other European powers began carving up the New World, the Spanish, beginning with Columbus, maintained an ever-growing social and religious influence over Mexico (included here as part of Latin America), Central and South America, and the island nations of the Caribbean.

One major consequence of Spanish conquest was the attempt to ban the sports and games they observed, which were seen as pagan and at times barbarous practices. Even as whole civilizations were destroyed by war and disease, attempts to outlaw traditional sports never totally succeeded. Latin America would exert a significant influence on the development of world sports, especially in the use of rubber balls and another phenomenon unknown in Europe: a heightened emphasis on team competition.

Though a discovery for European explorers, indigenous peoples were long established in the New World. Tribes that crossed the Bering land bridge (in present-day Alaska) near the close of the last ice age had pushed to Tierra del Fuego at the southern tip of South America as early as 12,000 B.C., and Latin America had already witnessed the rise and fall of several influential civilizations and cultures.

The Olmecs thrived in the lowlands of southern Mexico as early as 1200 B.C. They developed far-reaching trade and elaborate art, architecture, and religious iconography. Olmec society was supplanted by the Toltec empire, which flourished in central Mexico from the 10th to the 12th century A.D. The Toltecs introduced the cult of the feathered serpent deity Quetzalcóatl (a major religious development) and were known for their fine metalwork and gigantic statues, which featured carved human and animal standard-bearers.

The Maya developed one of the most advanced pre-Columbian civilizations from about A.D. 250 to A.D. 900. The Maya built immense stone cities (over 40 with more than 5,000 inhabitants) containing palaces, temples, plazas, and ball courts. The Maya had sophisticated hieroglyphic writing, mathematics that featured positional notation, and the use of zero; astronomy that featured an accurately determined solar year, and elaborate rituals to propitiate a pantheon of gods. The civilization declined rapidly for unknown reasons after A.D. 900.

The Aztecs built the last great empire prior to the Renaissance. At its peak in the 15th century, the Aztec civilization numbered between five and six million and was destroyed by the Spanish conquistadors beginning in 1521. The Aztecs took irrigation and farming to new levels of efficiency. Their society was despotic and sharply stratified, with human sacrifice—a practice borrowed from the Mayans—an integral part of their rituals, especially connected with the "ball game." The empire crumbled after Hernando Cortez took the emperor Montezuma II prisoner and conquered the great city Tenochtitlán (present-day Mexico City).

Throughout their conquest, the Spanish observed many Aztec sports and games, among them the ball game, patolli, and totoloque, and immediately tried to abolish them. To the Spanish, who sought to spread Catholicism, the elements of such games, including human sacrifice and divination through the casting of dice, were abhorrent pagan practices, and the culture was seen as one that placed an unholy emphasis on play. Even the curious bouncing of a ball made of rubber (a substance unknown in Europe) seemed charged with suspiciously magical energy.

Though the pre-Columbian cultures died out, their influence on world sports is still felt today each time a ball bounces or teams take the field. The advantages of rubber, a strange, new substance to the Spanish, were seen almost immediately back in Europe, where balls for most sports tended to be painfully heavy and dead. Rubber afforded the creation of lively balls, which demanded enhanced physical skills, and in turn made games faster and more enjoyable to watch.

Most sporting contests in Europe, including fencing, tennis, and archery, pitted one competitor against another, and prowess was often regarded as a vital aspect of one's individual development. In Latin America, however, the team concept dominated, from sports that necessitated team interaction such as the ball game, to relay races that placed a team's cooperative movement of an object above raw speed, to mock battles that involved entire villages. This team orientation is at the heart of most international competitions today.

Nearly all Latin American sports were variations on what is simply called the "ball game," an immensely popular sport that involved the violent volleying of a rubber ball between two teams on a specially constructed stone court. There were many versions of this contest, each with its own rules and equipment, and it is clear the sport was a focal point of social, economic, and religious life throughout this part of the world.

As was the case in North America, Latin American culture was one of play: sports and games served many purposes, from passing the time (dolls, string figures, tops, and stilts were popular), to developing life skills (target games that taught and enhanced hunting and fishing reflexes) to grasping the nature of existence (gambling and divination made casting dice a powerful act).

The Mexican god of sport was Macuilxochitl, the "god of five flowers." As they played, gamblers would pray by rubbing the five patolli beans between their hands, and as they threw them on the mat, they shouted his name and clapped their hands together, craning forward to see their score.

Latin American culture put sports and games at the center of existence and from this legacy the world plays on.

LATIN AMERICAN SPORTS

▦ The Mesoamerican Ball Game

The Mesoamerican ball game (referred to as simply the "ball game") is truly a sport out of time and may represent the Americas' greatest contribution to world sport. The ball game is one of the oldest sports on record, dating back to the Olmec empire c. 1500 B.C., and yet many of its aspects, including its team orientation, its staging on specialized venues, and the sublime levels of fanaticism, ritual, gambling, and social conditioning it generated give the game a distinctly modern feel.

The ball game contains elements that are similar to sports such as tennis and volleyball. The object was to propel a heavy rubber ball across the midline of a specialized I-shaped stone court using only the knees, elbows, feet, and buttocks. Points were scored when one team could not return the ball on one bounce within the court boundaries. At least one version of the game contains an element that looks ahead to the invention of basketball—a vertical stone hoop suspended 15 to 20 feet off the ground with which teams could achieve instant victory by driving the ball through.

The ball game began deep in the jungles of Mexico and was played by all of the major Mesoamerican civilizations: the Olmecs, Toltecs, Zapotecs, Mayans, and Aztecs participated in versions of the ball game and developed its many rituals. At its height, the game even reached as far north as the American Southwest, with the remains of rubber balls and the stone ovals on which versions of the game were played unearthed in present-day Arizona. The game also spread east to the Caribbean islands and north (possibly) up the Mississippi River valley.

One element that has cemented the ball game in the world's sporting psyche its sometime use of ritualized human sacrifice, which may be seen as the ultimate form of dedication. The exact nature of such sacrifices is difficult to trace since the only written records of the game come from the Spanish conquistadors who quickly banned the pagan game. How often sacrifices occurred, and whether only losers were sacrificed, or if winners, as some believe, earned the right to enter eternity in the full flush of victory cannot be known.

Even if human sacrifice was never employed, the ball game has many aspects that enabled it to shape the course of world sport. As previously noted, the game's team aspect made it unique to Europeans, a continent on which, as was the case with most of the world, individual sports testing skill or strength were the norm. Another unique aspect was the use of rubber for game balls, a substance unknown in Europe and Asia. The game's pervasiveness throughout Mesoamerican culture also underscores the crucial nature of play in the emotional and spiritual life of these Native Americans—aspects modern sports fans will readily understand.

The Venue

The most well-known version of the ball game was called *ullamalitzli* and was played on a special white stone court called a *tlatchli.* The basic form of the ball courts remained the same over 3,000 years, despite regional variations. Each *tlatchli* had parallel masonry walls that enclosed a long narrow alley, some of which widened into end zones that gave the courts their familiar I shape.

The average size of these courts was 120 feet by 30 feet, though some were small enough to accommodate just two players while others were as large as a modern football field. Often, the walls were decorated with stone sculptures of birds, jaguars, and skulls, as well as carved stone friezes depicting human sacrifice. The high stone rings were added above the center line next to both walls c. A.D. 800, which ushered in a new period of the game with, one assumes, new rules. Most of the courts were torn down following the Spanish conquest that began in 1519, although the sites of more than 600 courts have been discovered throughout Mexico.

Equipment

The ball was made of solid rubber and weighed approximately six pounds. The bouncing rubber ball amazed the conquistadors who thought the substance magical. Cortez took ball teams and many rubber balls back to Spain in 1521, and teams exhibited their skills at the court of Charles V. The superior elastic qualities of the new ball were immediately apparent, and rubber began to replace the wood and stuffed leather balls common in Europe.

Ball players wore protective equipment to prevent injury (the heft and speed of the ball often caused serious injuries and even death) and to enable them to hit the ball harder. Helmets protected the head; quilted cotton pads covered the elbows and knees. Leather or woven belts secured the waist. Some belts had special attachments known as *palmas* that were made of heavy stone, though it is not known whether they were used during play, or as a ceremonial part of the uniform. The yoke-like apparatus weighed as much as 50 pounds, though it fit comfortably, and does appear to offer an efficient means of hitting the ball. Players protected their hands during falls with *manoplas,* or hand stones, though striking the ball with the hand was not allowed.

A number of ways of playing the game are known; one used a bat, another used a paddle to hit the ball, and still another allowed the ball to be kicked with the feet. However, in the dominant and best-known form of the game, the ball could only be struck with the hips, buttocks, knees, or elbows. Points were scored when opposing ball players missed a shot at the vertical hoops or were unable to return the ball to the opposing team before it had bounced a second time or allowed the ball to bounce outside the boundaries of the court.

The ball game can be seen as a metaphor for, if not the epitome of, risking one's life for a sport. Besides the serious injuries that often occurred, the captain of the losing team routinely lost his head, cut off with an obsidian knife by either the captain of the winning team or by a priest. Most of this evidence comes from decorative depictions on court walls. The use of human sacrifice is connected to the game's religious symbolism, especially its association with fertility cults. Decapitation is a means to offer sustenance to the sun god, and the blood is seen as fertilizing the earth so that crops and communities grow.

Rite and ritual pervaded every aspect of the game, from its core symbolism as representing a never-ending battle between the sun and moon (light and darkness, good and evil), to the ritualized habits of the players, who often fasted, abstained from sex, prayed, and chanted. The atmosphere of each contest, accompanied by music, dance, drama, and pageantry, also helped articulate and reinforce the sacred nature of the game.

Balancing the ball game's extreme danger was the opportunity for glory that the greatest players enjoyed, including close connections with kings and special privileges. Most honored of all was the player who was able to send the ball through one of the stone rings. As Fray Diego Duran points out in his *Book of the Gods and Rites and the Ancient Calendar:*

> The man who sent the ball through the stone ring was surrounded by all. They honored him, sang songs of praise to him, and joined him in dancing.

Artist's rendition of Mesoamerican ball game with its high stone hoop.

He was given a very special award of feathers or mantles and breechcloths, something very highly prized. But what he most prized was the honor involved: that was his great wealth. For he was honored as a man who had vanquished many and had won a battle. (315)

Ball Game Variations

Many of the most popular sports played throughout Latin America during the Renaissance were variations on the ball game—team sports whose focal point was mastery over an opponent through the skillful propelling of a rubber ball. In these variations, we find innovations in rules that will find their place in later sports.

Batey

Popular among the Arawakan people of the Caribbean, *batey* featured a long, narrow ball court (roughly 20 by 60 feet) and a kneaded rubber ball that was heavy, but spongier than ones used in Mesoamerica. Teams ranged in size from 10 to 30 players, and women and children participated, though competition was not coed. Women could drive the ball with their fists; men used their heads, shoulders, hips, and elbows. Points were scored by driving the ball over the opponent's goal line, or if the ball died (began to roll) in the other team's end of the court.

Chaah

This Mayan game was the most popular ball game version until the Aztec took the sport to its zenith with *ulamaliztli. Chaah* courts were especially long and narrow and had broad end-courts that yielded the famous I shape. Playing the caroms and keeping the ball from dying in the end-courts was a crucial skill and likely gave rise to the game's first professionals (another innovation), who often owned their own equipment, especially safety gear and the hip belt used to strike the ball, which in this game, was about a third larger than a softball. One Mayan innovation used in many sports is the "side out," a rule by which scoring a point gives one's team the serve.

Matana-ariti

This version, played by the Paressi people in what is now Bolivia and western Brazil, used an inflated rubber ball about nine inches in diameter. Any open area could serve as the venue. The object was to knock the ball over the opponent's goal line using only the head. The game began with the ball on the ground. Diving players wearing no protective clothing headed the ball into the air.

Nucaepoto

This version, also from Bolivia, used an extremely heavy ball said to have weighed 25 pounds. Adding to this game's uniqueness was its use of stages: teams first kicked the ball back and forth using their feet and legs; later they opened up the field and used only their heads to propel the ball, which was allowed to hit the ground once before being returned. The object, as in most versions, was to score points by making it hard for the opposing team to return the volley. A similar game from that region called *toki* used larger teams (as many as 20 to a side), a smaller ball (about the size of a tennis ball), and also volleyed using just the forehead.

Otomac Ball Game

This is one of the few truly coed versions of the ball game: men and women played together on the same team, though rules allowed them to strike the ball in different ways. The Otomac people of Venezuela played this game on an almost daily basis, starting with 12 players on each side. The rubber ball weighed about two pounds and had great bounce. Men hit the ball with their right shoulders or their heads while women used a short wooden racket. Players covered a specific area of the court and rotated after each point as in modern volleyball.

Modern Versions

At least two forms of the ball game are still played in Mexico today. In the states of Sinoloa and Oaxaca the solid rubber balls are still made and teams compete in village streets and city plazas. In northwestern Mexico, Sinoloa teams play a game called *ulama* that closely resembles the game the Aztecs played. In the southern highland valley of Oaxaca, another game also related to the pre-Columbian sport uses a solid rubber ball hit with a leather glove heavily studded with nail heads.

Recreating the essential action of the Mesoamerican ball game is difficult given how the courts were constructed. A racquetball court or even a long brick or cement corridor can yield a slight sense of the type of venue once used. Specify a center line, use a basketball or kickball for the ball, and volley it back and forth. The ball can bounce off the walls and must be returned before it hits the ground twice. Knees, hips, elbows, and buttocks are the only parts of the body that can be used to propel the ball. Another option is to play on a basketball court. There are no walls here to bounce the ball off of, but the baskets conveniently offer a difficult target for an instant victory: make a basket and your team wins.

▦ *Palitun*

Palitun was a shinny-type game played by the Mapuche people of Chile and Argentina, lands that had not cultivated rubber at the time of the Spanish conquest. The game involved advancing a small leather ball with sticks on a long, narrow field approximately 300 by 30 yards. Sticks had hooked ends like those used in modern field hockey. The leather ball was stuffed with grass.

As in modern sports such as soccer or lacrosse, *palitun* began with the ball in the center of the field. The object was to drive the ball across the opponent's goal line.

▦ Running Races

Many of the indigenous peoples of the New World enjoyed running and used footraces as competition, warrior training, and entertainment. Some tribes, such as the Zunis of what is now the American southwest, possessed an almost mythic endurance, able to run races lasting for days.

In keeping with the team orientation of Latin American sports, relay races, such as the *buriti* races of Brazil, were popular among the Xavante, Ge, and other tribes. The *buriti* is a type of tree, and this relay race featured two teams, each of which had to lift and carry a heavy section of log around a circular route through the rain forest.

The log measured about two feet in length and weighed over 200 pounds. One runner on each team hoisted a log onto his shoulder and carried it until fatigue forced him to pass it off to a teammate. The first team to return the log to the starting point won the race.

A similar relay can be run on a track, field, or cross-country course—any circular route. The weight could be a piece of cut wood or a tightly packed sandbag—something too heavy for any person to be able to carry for any length of time, but easy to carry on one's shoulder. Each team must have an equal number or runners.

Another type of relay was the ball race of the Tamahumara peoples of what is now northern Mexico, as well as the Pueblo, Pima, and Papago peoples. This race, run to one village and back and covering distances of 25 miles or more, involved teams of runners who would kick a small leather ball among them as they ran. The ball was about the size of a modern tennis ball and would be kicked high into the air, the runners not breaking stride.

A team usually consisted of six runners and the race began with the leader at the starting line kicking the ball down the trail with the teammates sprinting after it. The one closest to the ball launched it again. Accuracy was everything, given the narrow trail and the rule that runners could not touch the ball with their hands.

This type of relay can be recreated on a cross-country racecourse. Make a small ball out of leather stuffed with sand or sawdust.

▦ Wrestling

Wrestling was a vital social custom throughout much of Latin America, performed on feast and festival days, and on a regular basis among men visiting other villages. For the most part, only men and boys engaged in wrestling.

Styles varied among rain forest tribes, but normally matches began with the two wrestlers facing each other and bent at the waist. On the signal, they would grapple each other around the chest. As in Africa, the object was to throw one's opponent so that his back, shoulders, or nape of the neck touched the ground. In other regions, wrestling matches began from a seated position.

Wrestling matches can be staged in any open area. Gym mats offer protection. Contestants should be matched according to age and weight. A referee should supervise matches.

LATIN AMERICAN PLAY

Children's games ranged from hide and seek and follow the leader to elaborate "bag attacks," a play-fight courting ritual wherein young boys pelted girls with bags stuffed with grass. Much play was in imitation of adult behavior, whether in playing with dolls, shooting at targets, or mastering functions of the ball game.

▦ Children's Circle Ball Games

Kalaka is a type of ball game played by the Yahgan people of Tierra del Fuego at the southern tip of South America. The game resembles the modern game of hacky-sack, in which a circle of people attempts to keep a ball aloft and in the circle by hitting it into the air and to each other. A key difference is that in this game, unlike most Latin American ball games, players can hit the ball with the open hand. The Yahgan people did not have rubber so game balls were made of different animal parts, such as an albatross web stuffed with feathers or an inflated seal bladder.

A net bag stuffed with pieces of foam rubber or even a water balloon would make a fine substitute for simulating the game.

The *mojo* circle game, which seemed to be a children's training exercise for the ball game, is reminiscent of dribbling drills in modern soccer. Eight to ten boys stood in a circle and passed the heavy rubber ball around using only their knees, feet, and ankles. The sole object was keeping the ball from touching the ground.

Yet another circle ball game was *uike*, played by the Witoto people. A rubber ball about six inches in diameter was tossed into the air, and the first player it came near had to strike it with his right knee. The next player had to bounce the ball off his left knee. As always, the aim was to keep the ball from striking the ground.

▦ *Xocotl* Climb

The *xocotl* climb was an annual contest for young men and boys whose object was to climb one of many ropes hanging from a specially erected pole and be the first to seize a dough figure placed at the top. The victor would crumble the figure in his hands, and strew the crowd below with the pieces.

For nearly a month surrounding the Aztec great feast day of the dead, many fire sacrifices were held in central Mexico in which the deities Yacatecuhtli, Xiuhtecutli, and Xocotl were worshiped. On the day itself, boys competed in a ceremonial pole climb. A great tree was selected and felled in the forest and brought to Tenochtitlan (Mexico City) with great pomp and ritual. The tree was publicly groomed and adorned. Great sacrifices that involved the roasting and cutting out of victims' hearts took place as special tribute to Xiutecuhtli, the fire god.

The *xocotl* climb was steeped in ritual: men and boys formed a line and danced a serpent dance through the streets to the tree, which was guarded by eleven "warriors" wielding pine swords. The dance dissolved as the men and boys lunged toward the tree, warding off blows. Many men might have clung to one rope as they all fought to be the first to the top.

The dough figure that was wrapped in festive paper represented bounty from the sky, an image reinforced by the beneficent sprinkling of its bits by the one first reaching it.

The *xocotl* climb is hard to reproduce because no conventional climbing apparatus offers multiple ropes leading to the same height and to recreate one would entail danger. The closest substitute might be a cargo net hanging from the wall of a gym on which several people can climb at once. Gym ropes could also serve as a substitute: a dough figure (or plastic flag) could be attached to two ropes, with warriors guarding each. The race would be won by whoever attained and climbed his or her rope first.

LATIN AMERICAN GAMES

▦ *Patolli*

Patolli is a traditional Aztec game similar to pachisi that is played on a diagonal cross-shaped board around which players race red and blue markers. *Patolli* takes its name from the Aztec word for fava or kidney bean, as beans are used as dice during play.

Patolli was played throughout Mesoamerica, beginning with the Teotihuacanos, who built Teotihuacan (c. 200 B.C.–A.D. 650), and was passed on to every culture (Toltec, Mayan, Zaptotecs) until the Spanish conquests that began in the late 15th and early 16th centuries. Every strata of society, from peasants to kings, played *patolli* for enjoyment or gambled on its outcome. During the Renaissance, Spanish conquistadors noted that Montezuma loved the game as both a player and spectator, and, during his captivity, taught the game to the Spanish.

Like the Mesoamerican ball game, *patolli* received messianic scrutiny and was banned by the Spanish missionaries, who brought ardent

Catholicism along with their lust for gold. What outraged the Spanish was the apparent use of the game for divination and religious rituals: using the outcome of throws and contests to foretell the future. The game still flourished and has survived to this day in various versions. Gambling is still a part of the thrill of this game.

Equipment

To play *patolli,* you will need six red and six blue "jewels" (markers such as painted stones, shells, etc.) and a game board in the form of a diagonal cross or what modern players would call X-shaped.

During the time of the Renaissance, *patolli* "boards" were woven mats with the cross painted on using liquid rubber. Many explorers saw game enthusiasts walking around, rolled-up mat tucked under their arm, a small basket containing game pieces, and the mighty dice tied up in a cloth.

As in the ball game, players and spectators, especially the nobility, bet heavily on the outcome, wagering everything from precious stones, gold beads, fine turquoises, elaborate clothing, land, homes, and slaves.

Each player enters his or her game pieces onto the nearest central square of the cross (where the footprints turn) and moves clockwise around the cross. Each piece must circle the board and is borne off on a roll that is one space past the last square.

Since *patolli* is a gambling game, the real object is to bankrupt one's opponent, by winning stakes in the betting pool while trying not to lose one's own assets via penalties. Each player begins the contest with 10 "assets" (these can be money or tokens) that he or she can bet. After the first game, one contestant will be richer depending on rolls of the dice and gambling skill. Players compete until one is bankrupt, and that might take one or several games. A player is bankrupt when he or she bets all of his or her assets and loses or when a player lacks sufficient assets to pay a penalty.

The *patolli* board has eight special spaces—the rounded cells at the end of each arm of the X—that when landed on give a player an extra turn. There are also eight spaces—black, triangular-shaped cells—that when landed on, require a player to pay a penalty to the opponent. The four central squares and the four squares immediately in front of them are danger zones where "bumping" can occur.

Rules of Play

No authentic rules of *patolli* survived the Spanish conquest, in which priests destroyed all records and manuscripts of the game. The earliest written record, therefore, dates back to 1552. Since the game appears to be very similar to pachisi, rules are not hard to surmise, though the intricacies of how the Aztecs played has been lost.

Play begins with each player lining up his or her game pieces on the edge of the board. Each piece is entered according to the throw of the dice, or the five *patolli* beans, each of which has one dot painted on or drilled into one of its sides. Throws score as follows:

zero dots showing = 0

one dot showing = 1

two dots showing = 2

three dots showing = 3

four dots showing = 4

five dots showing = 10

Before the first game of a contest, players put an agreed-upon amount into the pool. Red rolls first, then blue. Pieces are brought onto the board only by rolling one. Once a piece is on the board, it can be moved any number of spaces on subsequent rolls. Rolls of zero (no dots showing) are re-rolled until a player rolls a positive number. All pieces move clockwise.

Only one piece at a time is allowed on any space. If a space is occupied, it is blocked to one's opponent. Exceptions are the four central squares and the square just before each of them. These eight squares form a "bumping zone." If a player lands on one of these occupied spaces, the opponent's piece is bumped back to the start—that is, off the board.

A player always has a choice of which pieces to move, but if only one piece can be moved, it must be moved, even if it is to the player's disadvantage. If a player cannot move any piece and has at least two pieces on the board, the player forfeits one asset into the pool and loses a turn. A player landing on one of the black triangle-shaped spaces forfeits two assets directly to the opponent. Moving into one of the semicircles at the end of the crosses gives the player an additional roll.

A player's piece must land exactly on the last square of its journey around the board in order to be taken off. As each piece is borne off, the opposing player pays that player one asset. The player removing all of his or her pieces first wins the pool. Games then continue until one player is bankrupt.

⊞ *Pulac*

Pulac is a journey game on the order of *pachisi* that has been played for centuries and is still played today by the Ketchi peoples of Guatemala.

In this game, ears of corn (perhaps 10 to 15) are laid in a row on the ground with their tips pointing in opposite directions. The "trail" along which the game proceeds is made up of the spaces between the ears. Five game pieces, made of flat bits of colored wood, are marched along from their own "village" to that of their opponent.

Four split sticks or corncobs colored on one side serve as dice. The sticks are tossed, and a player moves one space for each colored side that lands face up. Pieces enter the game from the near end of the row and exit from the far end. As pieces are being brought into the game, a player has the option of using a roll to introduce a new piece or move one further along the trail.

Two pieces of the same color cannot occupy the same space on the trail. If a piece lands on a space occupied by an enemy, that piece is captured but not removed from the board. The capturing piece is placed atop the captive piece and is taken along on the journey around the board. If a third piece lands on this double piece, it tops the stack and takes the two pieces captive. The stacks can thus grow and the pieces change directions several times during the game.

When a warrior and any captive pieces reach the far end of the trail, the captured pieces are taken out of the game, and the warrior and any of its own pieces reenter the game from its own end. Play continues until one player has lost all of his or her pieces.

Making a game set is easy: use Indian corn to create the game board, small bits of wood painted or marked to distinguish one player's pieces from another, and a corncob cut in half or small sticks painted on one side for the dice.

▦ *Totoloque*

Totoloque was a popular Aztec gambling game whose object was to toss small, golden pellets as close to a target (usually a slab of gold) as possible. Each player had five tries, and the player with the most scoring hits would win the stake. The great Aztec emperor Montezuma II was fond of this game and often wagered items of great value, such as precious stones or gold ingots, on its outcome. He is alleged to have lost with good humor and often bestowed winnings on his attendants.

Totoloque was one of the games Montezuma played while being held captive by the Spanish, and the conquistadors were averse to the game, as was the case with most Aztec sports and games, as it seemed to have a strong religious basis. In truth, *totoloque* was played almost exclusively as an opportunity to gamble.

To play *totoloque*, create pellets from aluminum foil and take turns tossing them to a large silver dollar set on the ground. After each participant has had a turn, award points for pieces that land on the coin and for pieces that land closest to it.

▦ *Tuknanavuhpi*

This board game, played throughout Mexico, is similar to modern checkers. The object is to capture all of an opponent's 20 game pieces by jumping over them. Unlike checkers however, pieces can move in any direction and no "kings" can be created.

The board is similar to the ancient *alquerque* board in that pieces are placed on the intersecting points of squares rather than on the squares themselves. The *tuknanavuhpi* board is made up of 16 squares (four by four), each crisscrossed by diagonal lines that create 41 total points. Thus the center point is the only empty point when play begins.

The player who goes first moves a piece into the empty space and the opponent jumps over and captures it. Pieces can move in any direction and can jump over any piece, provided there is an empty space on the other side. Multiple jumps are allowed. Once a row has been emptied, however, it is closed off and no piece can land there.

A board is easy to draw in sand or on paper. Game pieces can be corn kernels, beads, coins, or any small object.

▦ *Wak Pel Pul* and Other Target Games

Wak pel pul is a Mayan target game played by throwing cocoa beans at a circle of specially cut sticks. Sticks were cut so they could stand upright on smaller protruding branches. Each stick was assigned a point value from one to six, with the one worth six points inside the circle of the other five. Players took turns tossing their beans in an effort to knock the sticks down. Any number of players could participate. The one who reached a preset number of points was the winner.

To recreate *wak pel pul,* cut reeds or branches similar to those described above or make targets from cardboard, dowel rods, pieces of cut wood, or hollow tubes such as curtain rods—any shaft that will stand by itself and fall easily when hit squarely with a bean.

Other forms of target shooting contests no doubt used the *atlatl,* an ancient hand-held device used to propel spears that was still in use in Latin America long after most cultures had switched to the bow and arrow and the gun. Despite its antiquity compared to the firepower European explorers wielded, the *atlatl* was a feared weapon, capable of whipping a spear at great speeds over 200 yards right through a breastplate of Spanish armor.

Though primarily a weapon of war, competitions that enhanced skills and channeled aggression of villagers were common, especially among the Kalapalo people of present-day Brazil. The Kalapalo staged elaborate intervillage *atlatl* competitions that involved throwing at straw effigies and mock battles that included individual duels using blunted darts.

▦ MIDDLE EAST

INTRODUCTION

The Middle East was the cradle of Western civilization and for centuries was the crucible of culture and crossroads of trade routes connecting Europe to the East. This large section of the world, which includes northeast Africa, the nations southeast of the Mediterranean Sea, and parts of southwest Asia, saw empires rise, fall, and then slowly scatter as explorers took to the oceans during the Renaissance.

Apart from distance running, the Middle East is rarely viewed as a hotbed of sports activity today. But nearly every known sporting pursuit has roots in Egypt, from fencing and ball games, to tantalizingly simple board games for which no rules survive. During the centuries leading to and following the birth of Christ, sporting events—which included the Olympic games and the Circus Maximus—were an integral part of life, providing spectacles that entertained and distracted the public.

Like every region of the world, the Middle East had its traditional sports, including animal sports, archery, hunting, and wrestling. Hunting innovations such as the use of dogs and falcons to kill game and horse racing were born in this region.

But the fall of the Roman Empire and the rise of Christianity and later Islam took their toll on the development of sports in the region. Christianity frowned on both gambling and male nudity, the state in which many athletic competitions (e.g., the Olympics) took place. By the late Middle Ages and on into the Renaissance, much of what is now the Middle East practiced Islam. The Koran prohibited gambling, which eliminated a major impetus for the proliferation of certain sports and games. Islamic law also forbade animal fighting, another popular spectator sport and gambling venue, and looked upon any sporting activity other than archery and other war training as a waste of time. Islam is not a culture of play, but many prohibitions were ignored and games and gambling thrived in secret. Overall, though, the harshness of the region, both in terms of climate and fundamental beliefs, hindered the growth of sports until the beginning of the modern era.

MIDDLE EASTERN SPORTS

▦ *Ad-dahw* (Arab Golf)

Ad-dahw is a traditional stick and ball game from Saudi Arabia played since the Middle Ages that is similar to modern golf. The object is to drive a wooden ball toward a hole dug atop a small sand hill using a wooden bat.

The hill should be somewhat higher than the area surrounding it and the hole should be slightly larger than the ball. A wooden croquet ball and stickball bats can be used.

The ball is set on the ground near the mound. A coin toss determines who goes first. The first player hits the ball up the hill toward the hole. If it goes in, the player scores a point. If not, the player tries again. After the player has put the ball in the hole, the next player takes a turn.

The match can be won by the player with the most balls holed per set number of turns or (as in golf) the fewest strokes taken to hole the ball.

▦ *Al-qall* (Arab Hockey)

Al-qall is a form of field hockey from Saudi Arabia played mainly by young adult men. Traditionally, the game was played between villages over an entire day, with players entering and leaving the game based on their fatigue. Some games were played on into the night.

Today, the sport's parameters are more in line with modern venues: any large, open field such as a high school soccer field can be used for a game. Two medium-sized stones are used to mark the goals at both ends of the field.

The ball is made of cloth stuffed with wool or plant fibers; the sticks are made of hooked palm tree branches (*qalls*).

A coin toss determines which team starts the ball downfield from the center. Teams decide in advance whether to play for a set period of time or up to a certain number of goals to determine the winner.

This traditional sport is based on the ancient Egyptian field hockey game of *al-hoksha*. In modern times, beginning in 1975, *qall* has been integrated into Saudi physical education programs.

▦ Falconry

Falconry is the sport of training falcons or other hawks to hunt and re-trieve game, usually wild fowls. Falconry has been practiced in the Mid-dle East for thousands of years and is still popular today, especially in Saudi Arabia, although the endangered status of much of the falcon's tra-ditional prey has led to tight regulations on the sport.

During the late Middle Ages, falconry flourished among Europe's upper classes and began to decline as firearms introduced during the Renaissance replaced traditional hunting techniques.

The bird most commonly used is the peregrine falcon. Birds are caught wild or raised from birth. Training involves selective use of a leather hood called a rufter and leg thongs (jesses) to keep the animal under control while familiarizing it with its new environment.

Training the bird to be comfortable around people is the first major step and is accomplished by keeping the bird isolated in a covered cage and then getting it used to one-on-one interaction (especially feeding) with its trainer. Deprivation of light, food, and sleep are also employed to make the bird compliant. Once trained to return to the hunter's arm, the rufter was used to eliminate distractions and focus the bird's energy. Tethered game (including rabbits and small birds) was employed for kill training. Eventually, the falcon is released to bring down prey and return it to its hawker.

Falcon wearing its rufter.

▦ Horse and Camel Racing

Horse and camel racing are two very popular sports that have roots in Middle Eastern antiquity. Chariot races—popular into the early Middle Ages—were eventually replaced by horse racing and acrobatic riding by the Renaissance. Popular forms of racing included speed races over fixed distances and relays. Horse racing was one sport where women and children participated. Their lighter weights gave them an advantage over men as jockeys—although their involvement was more like servitude than athletic career.

The famous Arabian horse has a bloodline that dates back thousands of years and has produced some of the most beautiful, intelligent, and loyal breeds in the world. This reputation gave poignancy to Caroline Norton's beloved poem "The Arab's Farewell to His Steed."

My beautiful! My beautiful that standest so meekly by,
With thy proudly arch'd and glossy neck, and dark and fiery eye,
Fret not to roam the desert now, with all thy winged speed;
I may not mount on thee again,—thou'rt sold, my Arab steed!

An Arab on his horse.

Modern race tracks in Saudi Arabia and throughout the Middle East resemble similar facilities throughout the world, though Muslim law prohibits gambling.

Camel racing was a traditional desert sport of Bedouin tribes. Great in scale and spectacle, races once involved thousands of animals speeding across the open desert. Modern races take place on a 13.6-mile track.

The annual King's Camel Race in Saudi Arabia, instituted in 1974, has quickly become one of the world's most prestigious events, drawing nearly 30,000 spectators. Over 2,000 camels and jockeys compete in the annual races during the National Heritage and Culture Festival at Jenadriyah.

Although honored as a traditional sport in the region, camel racing has come under fire for its use of child slaves (many of whom are kidnapped and sold in India) as jockeys.

⠿ Hunting

Domesticating dogs and training them to hunt game was one cultural adaptation that helped the Middle East become a cradle of civilization almost 9,000 years ago. The swift saluki hound, named for an ancient city in southern Arabia, is widely considered to be the world's oldest domesti-

A saluki hound.

cated dog. Over the centuries, the saluki, known in ancient times as the "royal dog of Egypt," came to symbolize hunting prowess and its image was often depicted in the ancient region's arts and crafts.

The saluki breed is keen-sighted and hardy, resembling a greyhound with long ears and a silky coat, and weighing from 45 to 60 pounds. It was primarily used to hunt gazelles. Salukis hunt by sight, which differentiates them from other hounds such as bloodhounds which track by scent. Salukis also run alone, as opposed to foxhounds, which run in packs.

In addition to gazelles, lions have long been a quarry of hunters in North Africa and the Middle East. The caliphs and other nobility of the Islamic empire loved to hunt and prized the lion above all. Lions were hunted on horseback, and this required considerable training to break the horse of its instinct to flee from the lion. Lion decoys and live lions in cages were introduced to the horse slowly to get the horse accustomed to the animal's scent and presence.

Horses were used to draw the lion into runs that would exhaust it, while the hunters mounted on them would fire arrows at the beast.

▦ Wrestling (*Al-mussara'a*)

As in most world cultures, wrestling in the Arab world was a vital part of teaching youths how to build strength and demonstrating the levels of strength and tenacity they will need as men in order to defeat a foe.

Traditional wrestling in Saudi Arabia was very similar to matches held throughout Africa: the goal was to force an opponent's shoulders to touch the ground. Matches had no time limit: they ended when someone won.

Wrestling has long held a symbolic vitality in the Muslim world, representing the ability to struggle for life against one's enemies as well as the harsh bitter heat of the desert. Famed in Islamic lore is the wrestling duel waged by the great wrestler Rukanah against the prophet Mohammed at al-Battha. Rukanah wagered three of his prized goats, but after dropping the first two matches, he not only bowed out but also converted to Islam. Mohammed gave him back his goats.

Modern wrestling in Saudi Arabia has the following rules: matches start and finish from a standing position; matches are made up of three, three-minute rounds with a minute rest before and after the second round; and wrestlers can compete against anyone whose weight falls within three categories of their weight class. Putting an opponent's shoulders to the floor determines the winner.

MIDDLE EASTERN PLAY

▦ *Ad-da* (Search for a Missing Object)

This is a conceal and guess game played by teams of young people in Saudi Arabia that is very similar to games played by Native Americans.

Players pass a small object (a marble or small stone works well) back and forth to one another while their hands are concealed under a blanket or cloth. After the passing stops, the fists are displayed and players on the other team try and guess who is holding the stone.

Also required for this game is a twisted piece of turban cloth called a *mi'kara*. The *mi'kara* represents a stick used for the playful punishment of teams that fail to guess the stone's location.

This game is best played with two teams of four sitting across from one another at a table, but it can also be played outside kneeling on the ground. A coin toss determines which team hides the stone first. Hands fly under the cloth as the stone is secretly passed from player to player. Sometimes teams keep a steady chant to distract the other team. Suddenly all hands stop and the eight clenched hands are displayed, backs of the hands facing up.

The team other gets one guess. If they succeed, they win the blanket, stone, and *mi'kara* and start the next round. If they fail, each player gets whacked with the *mi'kara* in a playful manner. A foam swimming "noodle" makes a good *mi'kara*.

Normally, play continues until both sides want to stop; alternatively, point values can be assigned to guesses and teams play up to an agreed-upon number.

⊞ Buqari and La'b al-dabb

Buqari was one of many simple guessing games common to the region; this one from Abbasid, in what is now Iraq. One player makes a pile of sand and, holding an object in one hand (a trinket, marble, etc.) buries both hands in the sand while the other player tries to guess which hand is holding the object. In a similar game called *fiyal,* the player hid the object in one of two piles of sand, and the other player tried to guess which one.

Yet another guessing game, this one from the Bedouins, was called *la'b al-dabb*, or the lizard game. *La'b al-dabb* had two variations: in one, a player drew a lizard in the sand and covered a portion of it with his hand while the other player, blindfolded or with back turned, tried to guess which part of the lizard was covered. In the other version, the blindfolded person was told to touch a specific part of the lizard drawing. If successful, the player got the next turn to name a spot to be touched.

⊞ Fanzaj

Fanzaj was one of many circle games played by women and young girls in what is now Palestine. Eight to 10 girls joined hands and faced one another in a circle. The circle first turned in one direction, and then the other. Then the players ran into the center, raising their clasped hands in the air. Then they ran back out until their arms were once again outstretched.

Next, the leader let go with one hand and moved back along the line, weaving through one pair of outstretched arms and then back through the next, with the whole line following. When she reached the end of the line, the circle closed and then danced in and out again. The next girl in line repeated the sequence by letting go with one hand and dancing through the line.

MIDDLE EASTERN GAMES

▦ Alquerque

Alquerque is one of the oldest and most ubiquitous board games in history. It is believed to have been played in Egypt and carried throughout the Middle East long before the birth of Christ, and its adaptations and variations are known the world over as draughts in Europe, checkers in America, and *tuknanavuhpi* in Latin America. The latter version is closest to the original because both of those games begin with just one empty space on the board.

Equipment

The alquerque game board is a grid of five by five points (called *oyoons*) with lines between them to indicate allowed moves. To draw a board is easy: first draw a five-by-five orthogonal grid; then draw two diagonal lines to connect opposing corners; finally draw four diagonal lines in the form of a square that connects the midpoints of each side.

Each player begins a game with 12 disk-shaped game pieces called kelbs, usually black or white as in draughts.

Play

The objective of the game is to take all of the opponent's pieces or to produce a position such that the opponent is unable to move.

A coin toss decides who goes first, which is generally thought to be a disadvantage due to the lack of options in moving pieces. The player of the black kelbs places them on the 10 points of the two rows nearest him or her and the two rightmost points on the middle row. The other player sets up the white pieces in exactly the same manner, leaving the middle point as the only one without a kelb on it.

Players take turns moving one of their kelbs. A kelb may only move along the lines inscribed on the board. For each turn a kelb makes either a capturing or noncapturing move. Whenever a kelb is adjacent to an opponent's piece and the point immediately beyond the opponent's kelb is vacant, the opponent's piece can be captured. Capturing is done by simply hopping over the opponent's kelb into the vacant point beyond and removing it from the board.

Multiple jumps are permitted. The move ends when the position of the capturing kelb no longer allows it to take any more pieces or when the player could make another capture but decides not to.

A noncapturing move is made by moving a piece along a line to an adjacent point.

The first player to capture all the opponent's pieces, or who has captured more pieces when it becomes apparent that no more pieces can be taken, is the winner. A player can also win by rendering the other player unable to move.

Draws are very common and can occur by agreement at any point during the game. If it becomes apparent that no more pieces will be taken and both players have the same number of pieces left, then players will agree to a draw.

▦ As Nas

As nas is a Persian card game designed for five players, which, along with *primero*, is considered a forerunner to modern poker. The game is played with a special deck comprised of 25 cards, five each of five suits.

The deck can be simulated using a standard 52-card deck. Use the aces through fives of each regular suit, and then make the fifth suit (which you can call the "face suit") using the four kings and a joker.

king of hearts = five of face suit
king of spades = four of face suit
king of diamonds = three of face suit
king of clubs = two of face suit
joker = ace of face suit

If you make a deck specifically for this game, it will be easier to mark the face cards permanently with their numeric value.

Play

The cards are shuffled, and two cards are dealt to each of the five players. Each player, starting at the dealer's left, either places a bet or drops out. Each player remaining in the game is dealt two more cards. The remaining players, in turn, starting at the dealer's left, make an additional bet or drop out. Each remaining player gets a fifth and final card. The remaining players then bet a final time or drop out. Those who are still in the game show their hands and the highest-ranking hand wins the pot. The rank of hands from highest to lowest are

Five of the same suit (five hearts, spades, faces, diamonds, or clubs)
Five of the same rank (five fives, fours, threes, twos, or aces)

Four of the same rank (four fives, fours, threes, twos, or aces)

Three of one rank and two of another rank (full house)

Three of the same rank (three fives, fours, threes, twos, or aces)

Two of the same rank (two fives, fours, threes, twos, or aces)

▦ Basra

Basra is a Middle Eastern card game that is somewhat similar to the game casino; it is a poplar coffeehouse game throughout the Middle East. Basra works best with four players, but two can also play. The game uses a standard 52-card deck.

The Deal

The dealer shuffles and the player to the left cuts the deck. Starting on the dealer's right, the dealer gives four cards to each player. The next four cards are dealt face up in the middle of the table in a space called the "floor." If the cards on the floor include any jacks or the seven of diamonds, the dealer buries them back in the deck and replaces them with new cards dealt from the top of the deck.

The player to the dealer's right plays first and play continues counterclockwise. Each turn consists of playing one card face up on the floor, attempting to capture one of the exposed cards. Captured cards are placed face down in front of the player. With four players, partners keep captured cards in one pile.

When all players have played their four cards, the dealer gives them each four more. No more cards are dealt to the floor. When the entire deck has been played, the hand is scored and the deal passes to the right.

Capturing and the Basra

A player who plays a card whose rank matches one of the cards on the floor captures that card and places both cards face down in front of him or her. For example, a king captures a king, a two captures a two, and so on.

Numeral cards equal to the sum of one or more cards on the floor capture that entire group. For example, if the floor contains a two, four, seven, and ace and you play a six, you capture both the two and the four.

In addition, cards of equal rank and sums of other cards can be taken in the same play. For example, if the floor contains a 2, 5, 7, and 10, playing a 7 captures the 7, 5, and 2.

Played cards that do not match any on the floor remain face up on the floor and can be captured in future turns. Players are not forced to capture a card just because they can. However, played cards that result in captures must be taken.

Kings and queens have no numeric value. Kings capture kings, and queens capture queens. The only other way to capture a king or queen is to play one of two special cards: a jack or the seven of diamonds.

A "basra" occurs when a player captures all the cards from the floor, leaving it empty. The player scores a 10-point bonus for this, and the capturing card is placed face up in the player's capture pile, as a bonus reminder when scoring the hand.

Jacks have a special power: when played, they capture all the cards from the floor. This, however, does not score as a basra and no bonus points are awarded. A jack played when the floor is empty merely remains on the floor.

The seven of diamonds behaves in a similar way to a jack: it captures everything on the floor. If the cards on the floor are all numerals, and their values add up to 10 or fewer, this counts as a basra and scores the 10 point bonus. If the floor adds up to more than 10, or includes picture cards, the seven still takes all the cards but it does not count as a basra. As with the jack, a seven of diamonds played to an empty floor remains there and can be captured in a future hand.

After the last card has been played, the player who last made a capture takes any remaining floor cards, but this does not count as a basra.

Scoring

When all cards have been played, the cards in each player's or each team's stack are counted. The team with the most cards (27 or more) scores 30 points. In the event of a tie, the 30 points are held over until the next hand and the team with the most cards wins 60 points.

In addition, one point is scored for each jack and each ace in one's pile, two points for the two of clubs and three points for the 10 of diamonds, plus 10 points for each basra, as already mentioned. Thus, the total points to be scored in each hand are 43 plus 10 for each basra.

The team or player that reaches a score of 101 points first wins.

If both teams reach 101 in the same hand, the team with the higher score wins. If the score is tied, additional hands are played until the tie is broken. It is customary to play basra as a best-of-five series, with the first team to win three games winning the match. A deciding game five is usually played to 150 rather than 101.

In the Middle East, the losing team or player pays for the food and drink consumed throughout the match.

▦   *Ganjifa* (Playing Cards)

The *ganjifa* were playing cards that likely originated in India in the Middle Ages and were brought to Persia by the 14th century via trade. The cards were made from either ivory, wood, or more often layers of paper glued together with gum. The cards were cut into small circles, elaborately painted, and then lacquered to protect them.

A deck consisted of 96 cards—12 cards each of eight different suits. Each suit had numeral cards one through ten and two court or trump cards, usually the king and his minister. The suits included slaves, crowns, swords, coins, haps, and scrolls.

Ganjifa cards were small works of art, and the images painted on the cards included dancing, hunting, worshipping, playing chaupar (the royal game of India), and holy processions.

The Persian version of *ganjifa* was known as *ganjifeh* and became known throughout Arabia as *kanjifah* (a word that appeared in an inscription on one of the circa 1400 mameluke cards), and was expanded by the addition of a third court card.

Most of the games played with the *ganjifa* deck are lost; the two best documented are *hamrang* and *ekrang,* both of which are trick-taking games that do not use trumps. The rules for each are extremely complex and each game has strong restrictions on which cards can be led or played to a trick. Because of the large number of cards in the *ganjifa* deck, an excellent memory is essential. To play by the strict rules, it is necessary to know at all times what are the highest outstanding cards in each suit.

In all *ganjifa* games, the suits are divided into two groups, strong and weak. The king and minister are always the highest-ranking cards, but strong suits rank the numerical cards from 10 down to 1, while the weak suits rank them up, from 1 to 10. This is similar to early European trick-taking games such as hombre and maw, and also in the Chinese money-card game ma diao, hinting at common ancestry for card games that came of age during the Renaissance.

▦ *Nardshir*

Nardshir is an ancestor to the modern game of the Irish "tables" game that has come down to us as backgammon. The game is believed to have originated in Mesopotamia and is one of the oldest recorded games in history, being over 4,000 years old. *Nardshir,* or *nard* was typically played on wooden surfaces using stones as markers, with dice made from bones, wood, or pottery. Early versions of the game used three dice and nard reduced it to two.

The word *nardshir* is taken from the Arabic word *nard,* which means battle, and *shir,* which means wooden table. The etymology suggests why Europeans called all such games "tables."

In *nard,* two players sat across from each other and moved 15 game pieces in opposite directions around a board made of 24 long, triangular points.

According to Islamic tradition, the board represents a year; each side contains 12 points for the months of the year; the 24 total points represent the hours in a day; the 30 playing pieces represent days of the month; the sum of opposing sides of the die (seven) represent the days of the week; the contrasting colors of each player's game pieces represent day and night.

The object of the game was to roll dice in order to move one's pieces around the board and into a home quadrant where they can be removed (borne off) with exact rolls. The first player to remove his or her pieces from the board was the winner.

To begin, two pieces were placed on the board in the near right corner and five in the near left corner. On the opposite side of the board, three pieces were placed on the fifth point from the left and five on the sixth point from the right. Players moved counterclockwise and thus began with five pieces already in their home quadrant, two as far away as possible, and eight more in between.

Dice rolls dictated the moves. Players rolled a single die to see who went first. Each number on each die was played separately, so a player could move one piece according to one die and another according to the other. A player could also add the dice and move one piece the total number of spaces (e.g., a roll of four and five could enable a player to move one piece nine spaces), as long as the point four or five spaces away could be landed on.

A piece could land on any vacant point or any point occupied by one of an opponent's piece or by up to four pieces of its own color. If a piece landed on a point occupied by a single opponent's piece, that piece was bumped from the board and had to reenter at the far end with an exact roll to an uncovered point. Thus, covering all the points in one's home quadrant and then bumping an opponent's piece was incapacitating, since players must reenter all bumped pieces before making any more moves.

By the time of the Renaissance, backgammon, or tables, was popular as a gambling game throughout Europe, and even in Islamic nations, although gambling was strictly prohibited.

▦ Senet

Still played during the Renaissance, *senet* was an ancient Egyptian race game that in some respects is a forerunner to modern backgammon. As with many ancient games, especially the royal game of ur, game boards exist but the exact rules are a matter of conjecture. The rules that were handed down are likely a simplification of the original version.

Equipment

The senet game board, which can be drawn on a large sheet of paper, is a large rectangle of three rows and 10 squares to a row. The "final square" in one corner is marked with a single stroke. The next space in that row is marked with two strokes, the next one with three strokes, the fourth has a diagonal cross, and the fifth has a symbol with a circle and a cross.

The squares specified above are spaces 26 to 30 of the 30-square board that starts in the opposite corner, travels along one row, back down the middle row, and finishes along the row ending in these special squares. As in the European game of goose, some squares have special names and properties. Square 15 is called the house of rebirth—a game piece that lands here is bounced back to square one. Square 26 is known as the house of happiness, which must be landed on with an exact throw. Square 27, marked with a cross, is the house of water, which sends a person back to the house of rebirth.

Each player has five game pieces of contrasting color or pattern (checkers work well). The pieces are placed on the first row with their colors alternating and leaving a space after each pair. Movement of the pieces is determined by the throw of four split twigs, dark on one side and light on the other.

Play

Players take turns moving a single piece per turn based on the value of the roll:

zero light faces up = five spaces and one bonus roll

one light face up = one space and one bonus roll

two light faces up = two spaces

three light faces up = three spaces

four light faces up = four spaces and one bonus roll

A square can be occupied by only one piece at a time. If a player cannot move any of his or her pieces, the turn is passed. If a piece lands on an opposing piece, the opposing piece is moved back to the square from which the attacking piece started its current roll.

Pieces can only bear off the final three squares by throwing the number indicated on the square. The first player to bear all pieces off the board wins.

⃞ NORTH AMERICA

INTRODUCTION

During the Renaissance, European explorers "discovered" the "New World," the continents of North and South America—landmasses over which societies and cultures had moved and developed for nearly 15,000 years.

It was an amazing accomplishment to finally conceptualize the layout of the globe, to realize that an immense, uncharted universe separated the Atlantic Ocean and the Far East, which was the destination of the early explorers. Christopher Columbus landed in the West Indies in 1492 and believed he was off the coast of China. For the next 100 years, European explorers kept returning on various missions of conquest, conversion, and reconnaissance to get through the land (the elusive search for a passage to the east persisted for 200 years), or, failing that, to get from it whatever they could: gold, beaver pelts, timber, etc.

The first permanent European colony in what would become the United States was established in 1565 in St. Augustine, Florida. The English landed in Jamestown, Virginia, in 1607 and the Pilgrims settled in Plymouth, Massachusetts, in 1620. The French landed in Quebec. By 1640, Renaissance energy had dissipated in Europe, and the first substantial migration to North America, including the founding of half of the original 13 colonies, was complete.

When Europeans first encountered Native Americans, they saw them as backward, undeveloped, and savage. That indigenous tribes from Alaska to Florida had developed their own religions, rituals, and cultures went largely unnoticed, except, perhaps, for many of the sports and games they played. During this period, as Betty Spears points out, Europeans got their first glimpses of such things as lacrosse sticks, kayaks, and rubber balls.

They also saw native peoples playing a stick and ball game that bore a remarkable resemblance to Irish hurling.

In 1619, the first Africans were brought to Jamestown in chains to labor on tobacco plantations. Slavery was not unknown in Africa during the Renaissance. Prisoners of war often became slaves of victorious tribes, though they were never bought and sold as property or subjected to the levels of cruelty they would encounter when they were dragged into the New World. Like the Native Americans, the Africans who were brought to North America had highly developed cultures that included many competitive sports and games that served as preparation for war, hunting, or friendly competition among individuals and tribes.

The sports and games that would develop in North America sprang from three main influences: sports and activities brought to the New World from Europe, those played by indigenous peoples, and those brought from Africa. As the nations of North America developed, new sports (such as baseball and American football) would be invented and would exemplify the character of life on this continent.

This chapter, however, is concerned with what was being played during the first 30 years of colonization, mainly in the region that would become the United States: what sports and games the Europeans brought with them, and what sports they found Native Americans playing when they arrived. Despite the unquestionable contribution of Africans on American sport, the time period covered in this chapter precludes an examination of their influence, which would emerge later in the nation's history.

As with most sports and games, almost none were introduced during the Renaissance, though this period of history helped shape their overall development as well as the role sports and games play in daily life.

NATIVE AMERICAN SPORTS

Sports and games were an integral part of daily life for Native Americans. Survival depended upon the development of physical endurance (running, rowing, swimming), dexterity, and technical skills (archery, horsemanship, hunting)—feats of athleticism that are either at the core of or have evolved into many modern sports. Sporting contests were vital components of religious rituals, and many tribes used various games of chance as a means of divination. Sports and games had significance for most Native American tribes that far exceeded that of the industrialized European nations that began to explore and colonize the continent during the Renaissance. This culture and mindset of play was often mistaken for laziness by the Europeans, but it can be argued that play is an equally viable approach to life as a Puritan work ethic or economic development. Also, in many areas of human development, especially sports, Native Americans were far more advanced than their European conquerors. French explorer Samuel de Champlain was amazed at the strength and lightness of Iroquois birch-bark canoes. The shipwrecked Cabeza de Vaca noted that the bows of the Apalachee Indians (Florida) were so strong that no Spaniard could bend them (see Archery). And Europeans were unable to match the hunting prowess of the Native Americans until they began to adopt aspects of their clothing and technique. Native Americans contributed a great deal not only to the sports and games played today and how they are played, but also to the manner in which Americans tend to view the world through sport.

▦ Archery

Long before the Renaissance and the coming of Europeans, Native Americans developed archery technology to a very high level and used the bow and arrow as a weapon, as a tool for hunting, and for sport. Competitions included shooting at stationary or moving targets for accuracy and speed shooting. An example of the latter is the Mandan contest in which an archer tried to shoot as many arrows as possible into the air before the first shot hits the ground.

Contests for accuracy might consist of aiming at small, stationary targets, such as an arrow sticking upright in the ground or a suspended bundle of grass or husks. The Inuit made archery an indoor sport, hanging small wooden bird targets from the roof of a communal center and shooting at them with miniature bows and arrows.

Although early Spanish explorers brought the crossbow and harquebus and wore chain mail armor, they were often no match for the Apalachee bowmen, who not only fired bows of Ulysses-like tension, but also knew how to use the natural cover of swamp and forest to better track their prey. As Cabeza de Vaca writes in his *Relacion*, "There were those who swore they had seen two red oaks as thick as the upper part of the leg, pierced through from side to side by arrows."

Prowess with the bow and arrow improved even more when Native Americans added the ability to shoot while on horseback, an adaptation they learned from the Spanish conquistadors, who reintroduced the horse to North America early in the 16th century.

As was the case in Europe, the development and increasing availability of more accurate and powerful firearms supplanted the bow and arrow as the weapon of choice. The bow remained the primary weapon and means of hunting for Native American tribes untouched by European trade and lives on today as a popular outdoor, field, and Olympic sport. (See also Target Games.)

▦ Distance Running

Foot races were extremely popular contests throughout the Western Hemisphere, and most legendary among Native American tribes were the long-distance runs. The Tamahumara Indians of northern Mexico were known to run the equivalent of six modern marathons (over 150 miles) in a single stretch and competed in sports that involved running and kicking a ball or carrying a log over stretches of 75 miles or more. The Zuni and Pueblo Indians of the southwestern United States held races that lasted for days.

▦ Double Ball

Double ball, once a fairly widespread team sport in the area now encompassed by the United States, belongs to the family of sports including lacrosse and field hockey, in which each player uses only a stick to drive the game ball across the playing field and into the goal of the opposing team. The term "double ball" refers to the fact that the game ball was actually a pair of balls tied together with a short leather cord. During the game, the player in possession of the double ball carried it draped across his or her stick while moving down the field.

Unlike lacrosse, double ball was never adapted for play by European colonists, nor did any version of it survive by way of a European counterpart, as did field hockey and football. Perhaps the apparent lack of interest in double ball on the part of the Europeans, and its subsequent failure to enter the repertory of modern sports, was due to the fact that, with few exceptions, double ball was a young woman's sport and thus subject to the prejudices that women's sports have long sought to overcome.

Considering the physical fitness required to play double ball, the game certainly did not fit European stereotypes of acceptable female pastimes. Goals positioned up to a mile apart, for example, were not uncommon. Further, the women who played the game, typically the unmarried women of the tribe, did not shy away from the rough and tumble physical contact that often accompanied the movement of the double ball, occasionally resulting in minor injuries.

Interestingly, the double ball itself was sometimes considered a magic travel device when associated with female participation in the game, much like the flying broomstick of European witch legends. The Wichita of Oklahoma, for example, said that the moon, a female, gave women double ball, teaching them not only how to play the game, but also how to use the double ball for flying. Thus several Wichita legends speak of young women eluding their pursuers by flinging the double ball into the air and joining it in flight.

Conversely, in the somewhat rare instances in which men played double ball, the game was not without metaphysical peril. The Hupa of California, for example, told a story in which a boy defeated the immortal Wildcat, Fox, Earthquake, and Thunder with a set of magic double ball equipment his grandmother made, only to discover upon returning home that, much like Rip Van Winkle, he had been gone for as many years as days he believed he had been playing the game.

The equipment for the game was quite simple, consisting only of the stick and the double ball. The sticks were between two and five feet long and some had a curve or were tapered at the end. A broomstick or a modern field hockey stick would provide a good approximation of the original. There were several styles of double balls. Some were stuffed leather pouches or pieces of wood the size of small hand weights fastened together with several inches of leather thong. Others were made from a leather tube with weighted ends resembling a pair of joined sausage links. A good double ball can be made by filling the toes of two socks with several ounces of dried beans, enough to form a ball three or so inches in diameter when the beans are cinched into the toe area with string, then stitching or tying the open ends of the two socks together.

There were no official dimensions to the double ball playing field. In fact, depending on the tribe, the field might be anywhere from 50 yards to a mile long. The Sauk and Foxes tribe of Iowa played between two trees up to a quarter of a mile apart. The trees marked the length of the field and also served as the goal posts. In this version of the game, players would cast the double ball into the lower branches of the opposing team's tree, scoring points by draping the double ball over an outstretched limb.

Where two such trees are unavailable, contemporary reenactors may try playing on a modern football field, scoring goals by pitching the double ball through the uprights of the goalpost.

The game begins with all of the players forming a circle in the middle of the field. Any number of people may play as long as the teams are even. A nonplayer tosses the double ball high into the air in the center of the circle and play begins, each player attempting to gain possession of the double ball and drive it to the opposing team's goal. A player in possession of the double ball may either run with it draped over the stick or pass it forward to a teammate. Players may not use hands to catch or move the double ball. The team to achieve the winning number of goals to which all have agreed in advance wins.

▦ Field Hockey

Played in antiquity by both the Egyptians and the Greeks, field hockey is a good example of a sport that appears to have been invented independently by many cultures around the world, including those of the native inhabitants of North America. The object of the game is for members of one team to drive a ball across the ground and into an opposing team's goal, using only specially made wooden sticks to propel the ball forward.

Field hockey was quite widespread throughout North America. Depending on the tribe, both men and, more frequently, women of various ages would take part in games sometimes having hundreds of players. While wagering on the game was common, participants did not generally attach to it the ceremonial significance characteristic of a game like hide the ball. Some tribes did, however, play field hockey as part of the festivities associated with particular times of the year. For example, the Wichita of Oklahoma played the game during the spring to commemorate the field hockey victory of "After-birth-Boy," a hero of several legends, over the evil "Headless Man." During the match, After-birth-Boy used a hockey stick carved from a green sapling, and thus his victory was associated with the young foliage of spring. The Makah of Washington State played the game to celebrate a successful whale hunt, associating the game so closely with the hunt that they carved the ball from one of the soft bones of the slaughtered whale and played right on the beach.

The equipment for field hockey consisted of two elements. First, each player has a stick typically between three and four feet long and curved at the end. A modern field hockey stick is ideal. Second, a hard ball about three inches in diameter was used. The native players often carved balls from knots in wood or made them by stuffing leather pouches tightly with animal fur. For contemporary play, an ordinary baseball is fine.

The playing field was typically a flat area from 100 to 400 yards long, although very long fields, up to a mile, were not uncommon. The area of a modern football field is probably a fair approximation for contemporary play. The wooden goalposts were usually set up between three and six feet apart on opposite ends of the field. Several tribes added an extra degree of difficulty by using only one goal post. To score, a player had to hit the post with the ball.

Unless the game involved teams from competing villages, play began with the selection of team members. The Omahas of Nebraska had an interesting tradition to accomplish this. Each player would mark his or her stick distinctly, then place it along with everyone else's in a pile. One of the players would put on a blindfold and pull from the pile two sticks at a time and make two piles, thereby creating two teams, as the owners came forward to claim their respective sticks. There were no set limits on how many players were allowed. A team could have as few as three to as many as 100 players. Once the teams are chosen, the players agree to the number of goals required to win, typically basing this decision on the length of the field. Thus for a field three quarters of a mile long, the winning team may need to score only three goals.

After these preliminaries, the game begins. There were two basic methods of starting the game, either of which modern players might use in reenacting the game. For the first method, the players line up on opposite sides of the field, and the referee tosses the ball between them at the midway point. Once the ball hits the ground, both teams charge forward to take possession of it, and the game is off and running as each team attempts to drive the ball into the other team's goal.

For the second method, the teams again line up on opposite sides of the field, but this time one team is in possession of the ball. The game begins with the team in possession driving the ball forward toward the opposing team's goal much like returning the kickoff in modern football. Rather than flipping a coin, however, to determine which team will take possession first, one member of each team takes a turn dropping the ball and attempting to keep it from hitting the ground by kicking it back up as it falls. The team of the player who kicks the ball up the most times without it hitting the ground gets first possession. Possession then switches after each goal. The team to score the number of goals to which all have agreed in advance wins.

▦ Football

Shortly after arriving to settle Jamestown, Virginia, in 1607, the first English colonists observed the local Native Americans playing a familiar game. The colonists called it "football" after the popular English pastime to which it bore such a remarkable resemblance. The object of the game, as with its Old World counterpart, was for members of one team to kick a leather ball through the goalposts of the other.

Unlike English football, however, most versions of Native American football did not rely on aggressive physical contact such as tackling and blocking. Consequently, men and women of all ages took part, often in coed games that included children and the elderly. The game was so open in terms of who could play that girls and women were allowed to pass, catch, and carry the ball with their hands or even with a special basket in order to compete more successfully against men and boys, who were only allowed to use their feet. This handicap occasionally resulted in the amusing tactic of a female player passing the ball to an elderly woman, who would then carry it across the goal line knowing that no male player would attempt to strip the ball from her hands, as was sometimes the case when a younger female carried it.

The Algonquin of Massachusetts had another interesting tradition designed to keep the game friendly when played between teams composed of men from different villages. Here the players would disguise themselves with paint to discourage thoughts of future revenge in the event of a player accidentally injuring or angering another during the game. Considering that this version of the game might have goals a mile apart and a team might score only once during two continuous days of play, it is not difficult to imagine tempers occasionally flaring.

In addition to the east coast of what would become the United States, the game was quite widespread throughout the rest of North America, with versions played as far west as California and as north as the Bering Strait, where the Eskimo described the Northern Lights as ghosts playing football with walrus skulls. The version played by the Eskimo of Labrador, Canada, was noteworthy because players drove the ball with leather flails in addition to kicking it. Further, the ball was irregular in shape, thereby increasing the excitement as the ball rolled and jumped erratically down the playing field.

Elsewhere the game ball was typically round, between four and seven inches in diameter and made of leather stuffed with fur or feathers. Because the ball was not inflated like a modern soccer ball, it had much less bounce. Thus, when re-creating the game with a modern ball, some of the air should be let out to simulate the dead bounce of the original. Alternatively, a foam rubber softball is probably fairly close to an authentic ball in size and density.

The playing field had no official size, and even during play there was no concept of the ball passing out of bounds. Tribes living on the coast, for example, often played on the soft sand of the beach and considered the ball in play even when it went into the surf. The distance between the goals, as opposed to marked boundaries lines, determined the general area of the playing field. As mentioned above, the goals might be as far as a mile apart. For contemporary play, however, goals set between 150 and 300 feet apart would be sufficient. The goals themselves were typically two wooden poles set three to six feet apart.

The game begins with the teams facing each other on opposite sides of the field. An umpire rolls the ball between them and the players rush forward to take possession of the ball. Females may pass and carry the ball with their hands in addition to kicking it, although if they carry the ball, the men may attempt to strip it from their hands as they pass. No other physical contact is permitted.

Men may catch the ball with their hands but may not pass or carry the ball with their hands; they can only move the ball by kicking it. To score, a team must drive the ball through the goalposts of the opponent. Possession of the ball switches after each goal. The score is tallied with 12 sticks. A team receives a stick every time it scores until all the sticks are gone. The team that has the most sticks at that point wins. If the sticks are split six to six, then the team that scores the next goal wins.

▦ Hoop and Pole

A popular boys' game with many variations throughout North America, hoop and pole involved throwing a stick or reed through a rolling hoop in order to knock it over as it moved past the players. In addition to the dexterity required to hit the hoop, chance often played a role in winning the game because the number of points scored with a successful throw was based in part on where the pole landed on the hoop when it came to rest.

As with many Native American games, hoop and pole had symbolic significance for the players beyond mere entertainment. In one version of the game, for example, the hoop was laced with strips of leather in a pattern resembling a spider web. These webbed hoops represented the magical cloud shields carried by the twin war gods. The playing of the game, therefore, could be viewed as a kind of re-enactment of celestial warfare or as the means by which a player called upon the power of the war gods themselves.

In another version of the game, this one requiring a plain hoop and four poles, the hoop symbolized the circle of day and night, and the poles symbolized the four directions of the winds, north, south, east, and west. When played in this context, the game equipment took on a secondary function as magic implements for use in healing rituals.

As the name of the pastime suggests, there were two basic pieces of equipment, the hoop—typically made from a green, flexible branch and ranging from a few inches to two feet in diameter—and the pole—a stick or reed ranging from two to six feet long, depending on the diameter of the hoop. Some versions of the game required elaborate webbing in the center of the hoop, the opening through which the pole passed determining the point value of the throw, much like the pie wedges on a modern dart board.

For contemporary play, a plain hoop such as a toy flying ring should suffice. Before the game, four marks are spaced evenly around the hoop and are labeled with four point values of 5, 10, 15, and 20 points, respectively. A short paint roller extension pole available at any hardware store is a suitable pole for a hoop of this diameter.

The playing area is any flat, hard surface, such as a blacktop, on which the hoop will roll. For added difficulty, some versions of the game require the hoop to roll past piles of loose straw through which the pole must travel before entering the hoop as it rolls by. A rock is placed in the center of the playing area to mark the position from which the players will throw the poles.

In its simplest form, the game requires three participants, one to roll the hoop and two to throw the poles. The game begins with the two throwers by the rock and the roller some distance away with the hoop. Some experimentation will be required to determine how far away the roller may stand and still manage to roll the hoop past the throwers, this distance depending on the size and weight of the hoop.

The game begins with the roller rolling the hoop past the throwers. As the hoop passes, each thrower attempts to stop the hoop by throwing his or her pole through it. When a player stops the hoop, the point value of the successful throw is determined by the mark closest to the place on the hoop on which the pole has landed. This process is repeated until one of the throwers reaches a winning number of points to which the players have agreed in advance. The loser of the game then becomes the hoop roller for the next game.

☷ Lacrosse

Probably the most famous Native American sport, lacrosse was an almost exclusively male game played among tribes inhabiting the eastern half of North America from Florida to Ontario, Canada. The object of this team sport was to convey a ball down a playing field by means of a round, webbed pocket at the end of a stick, ultimately depositing the ball within the goal of the opposing team in order to score a point.

French Jesuits first described the game in the Huron area of Canada in the 1630s, referring to it generically as *crosse,* based on the stick's resemblance to the curved stick used in a French version of field hockey of the same name. According to Jesuit observers, the game was an important healing ritual. Medicine men would prescribe the playing of lacrosse to a sick person, and all the men from the area would gather to play the game on his behalf, no matter what his social rank. A medicine man might even call for a game to cure the perceived malaise of an entire region, in which case the leaders of the surrounding villages would enlist all the available young men, sometimes two or three hundred, to play for fear of a widespread calamity. Ironically, the game was extremely rough, lacking rules regarding personal fouls or improper stick handling; as a result, broken bones were common—the purported curative powers of the game notwithstanding.

The tribes of the southeast, however, appeared to take the game more at face value, calling it the "little brother of war," a reference to the game's occasional role as a war substitute for settling disputes between villages. The Cherokee of North Carolina highlighted the bloody nature of the game by undergoing ritual scratching immediately before playing. In this unusual opening ceremony, a medicine man would drag a comb with teeth made from sharpened turkey bones across the bare arms and chest of each player, creating a crosshatched pattern of bloody lines over the skin. The players considered this bloodletting so important for victory that they would scrape the scabs off with wood chips as they formed to encourage the flow.

Given the overtly physical, even violent, nature of the game, it might appear, as early observers noted, that the game was little more than a vast, semi-organized brawl lacking any sense of sportsmanship. Such a conclusion, however, would be mistaken. The notion that the outcome of the game was determined less by human prowess than by supernatural favor was nearly universal among players and influenced player behavior in two important ways. First, aggressive physical contact was limited to the playing field, and even then only condoned when it furthered the objective of the team, thus limiting personal vendettas. Weapons, for example, were not permitted near the playing field. Further, players were expected to shrug off the sometimes serious injuries they might suffer, setting aside any thought of retaliation in order to avoid appearing childlike. The game also took on a highly ceremonial character. Medicine men performed rituals on the sidelines to promote the success of their respective teams. During the games, players often wore costumes and body paint. Some games were so important, in fact, that various taboos developed concerning the behavior of players in the weeks leading up to them. Cherokee players, for example, avoided eating the meat of rabbits during this period for fear of becoming timid.

The equipment for the game consisted of the lacrosse racket (each player carrying one long racket or two shorter rackets, depending on the tribe) and the game ball. Commercial lacrosse rackets are readily available and are perhaps a more realistic alternative for contemporary reenactment than would be any attempt to make them from scratch given the woodworking skill required. For children, another possibility is to secure an ordinary kitchen sieve to the end of a three-foot length of broomstick. Game balls were generally about the size of modern tennis balls, although the materials from which they were made varied between tribes, some carving them from blocks of wood, others making them from leather pouches stuffed with animal fur. Consequently, the hardness of the ball varied from place to place. For adult reenactors, a commercial lacrosse ball or a baseball would be appropriate. For children, a tennis ball would suffice.

As with all outdoor Native American sports, there were no set dimensions for the size of the field, although in general the playing fields were longer than those used for modern field sports, the goals being anywhere from 100 to 600 yards apart. The goals themselves were generally two wooden poles 6 to 10 feet tall set 3 to 15 feet apart.

Games typically began with two players squaring off in the center of the field, much as in modern hockey. A nonplayer, often a female, would toss the ball into the air and the two opposing players would attempt to knock the ball to a teammate standing a few paces away. Early accounts of the game state that there were sometimes as many as a thousand players per team, but this number is probably inflated considering the hyperbole that often characterized the writings of European observers on the topic of Native American culture. What is clear, however, is that the modern notion of an organized team composed of a finite number of players with rigidly defined roles was foreign to Native American players of the time. Consequently, it is possible that the number of players on the field could be quite large, as there were no second-string players.

Once the ball was in play, there were very few rules except for the basic prohibition on a player touching the ball with his hands, a foul that ap-

Many Native American tribes played lacrosse with a stick in each hand, as this drawing from *Scribner's Monthly* (Vol. 14 May–Oct. 1877) shows. (Smithsonian American Art Museum, Gift of Mrs. Joseph Harrison, Jr.)

parently resulted only in chastisement by fellow players. As the game proceeded, each team attempted to convey the ball down the field and into the goal of the other team, each goal counting as a point, until one team reached the winning number of points to which all agreed in advance.

▦ Snow Snake

Snow snake was a popular outdoor pastime among many North American tribes inhabiting regions with winters cold enough to produce ice and snow. The object of the game was to scoot a specially carved and decorated stick, the "snake," across an icy surface such as a frozen pond or the hard crust atop snow. Whoever scooted his or her snake the farthest was the winner.

While snow snake was quite widespread, custom varied among tribes with respect to the age and gender for whom the game was considered appropriate. Thus, among the Cheyenne and Arapaho in what is now Oklahoma, snow snake appealed primarily to girls. The Chippewa of Minnesota, however, considered snow snake to be a game primarily for young boys. In some tribes, such as the Seneca of New York, adults from different villages competed in organized snow snake tournaments and often wagered on the outcomes.

The materials and designs for the snow snakes also varied greatly among tribes. In some areas, the snow snakes were merely dried reeds pulled from the edge of the frozen pond on which the game was played. Many snow snakes, however, were finely carved from wood such as cedar and sumac, averaging five feet in length but ranging from two to seven feet. There were several basic snow snake body types. One was flat and up-turned at the end much like a modern ski. Another was straight and round with a pointed or egg shaped nose and gradually tapering tail. Yet a third resembled a long wooden spoon with the bowl of the spoon as the head. After making their snow snakes, participants often carved or painted eyes on the heads and stripes down the shaft to resemble snakes.

The playing field for snow snake is any large, flat and icy surface, such as a snowy field over which an ice crust has formed or a frozen pond. Some of the tribes created snow channels through which the snow snakes would travel by dragging logs across the ground. Others added snow ramps so that the snow snakes would jump into the air along the way.

Given the effort that went into the production and decoration of each snow snake, it is apparent that the participants probably spent nearly as much time carving the snake as they did scooting it. For modern players, a painted broomstick or an old cross-country ski is probably a good alternative. The basic move for propelling the snow snake is much like the throwing action required to skip a stone over water. The player stoops and supports the snake head at about knee level with two or three fingers of one hand. Next, the player places the index finger of the other hand against the tail end, holding the snake horizontal with the remaining fingers and thumb of that hand. To propel the snake, the player pushes the tail end of the snake forward sharply in a sliding motion with the index finger.

Using this basic move, the object of snow snake is simply to propel one's snow snake the farthest across the ice from a given point, each participant being allowed from one to three throws to achieve his or her maximum

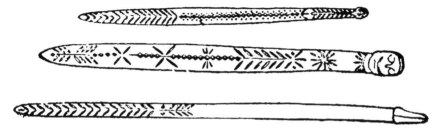

Examples of snow snakes from *Webster's New International Dictionary,* 2nd edition unabridged.

distance. In some versions of the game, the losers forfeited their snow snakes to the winner. The winner would then choose the snakes he or she wanted to keep, throwing the rest away, which resulted in a scramble for them by the losers.

⊞ Target Games

When, in 1585, English artist John White visited Roanoke Island off the coast of what is now North Carolina, he became one of the first Europeans to make eyewitness drawings of the Native American way of life. One of these drawings shows several men engaged in a throwing target game. The object of the game apparently was to pitch grapefruit-sized balls at a square, wooden target perched on top of a tree whose branches have been stripped away, leaving only the bare pole of the trunk.

While the specifics of the Roanoke target game have not survived, several things are clear from the drawing. First, this was no kid's game. Only adult males are playing, and the broken-off stubs of branches are draped with cloth and strings of beads, as was customary with items of value at stake during wagering. Second, the game appears to have been fairly organized, considering the effort required to find and strip a suitable tree and to place the square target on top. This labor-intensive process suggests that the area around the tree was probably dedicated to repeated playing of the game, much like a modern basketball court. Thus, the drawing may be among the earliest depictions of a permanent sports venue in North America.

For contemporary reenactment of the Roanoke target game, players should make a target about one foot square. The target depicted in the White drawing was made by lashing about a dozen foot-long sticks onto two parallel sticks like pickets on a fence, and so, for added authenticity, the modern reenactor may wish to try this method. Otherwise a piece of plywood or even stiff cardboard should suffice. Attach a lanyard at the top, and hang the target on the pole about 10 to 12 feet high. For a pole, a tree whose lowest branches are at least 12 feet from the ground (stripping branches, while authentic, obviously is not recommended), a volleyball, or flagpole will work; care should be taken on a ladder to attach the target.

To attach the target, wrap a bungee cord tightly around the pole and through the lanyard on the target. Softballs are about the size of the balls depicted in the White drawing and should provide a convenient substitute because of their wide availability.

As mentioned above, the rules of the Roanoke target game have been lost. Consequently, reenactment will require some creativity on the part of contemporary players, which is perfectly appropriate considering the spontaneity and flexibility with respect to rules that so often characterized Native American sport in general.

To begin, a good rule might be that all throws must be underhand, as is shown in the White drawing. With the basic throw thus established, play may proceed in one of several ways. Each player may, for example, attempt to achieve the most hits per given number of throws from the same position. For a more complex game, the players may mark several bases in a semicircle around the pole and attempt to hit the target from each of the bases in succession, moving forward only after a successful throw. Finally, the players may each have a predetermined number of balls—say five apiece—and, standing in a semicircle around the pole, attempt to be the first to hit the pole at the signal for all to start throwing.

NATIVE AMERICAN GAMES

▦ Awithlaknannai

Awithlaknannai is a game similar to checkers that was played by the Zuni Indians of New Mexico. The counters in the game are believed to symbolize stones used to kill serpents. The board, which was etched in wood, leather, or on the ground, was made of six adjacent diamonds, with nine counters per player placed on all the points.

Only the center point is left open. Players take turns moving their counters in one of two ways. They can move one of their counters to an adjacent point along a straight line, or jump over and capture an adjacent counter of their opponent if the next space is open. All open jumps must be taken. As in checkers, multiple jumps are permitted. The first player to capture all the opponent's counters is the winner.

▦ Bilboquet (Ring and Pin, Cup and Ball)

If there exists a universal toy, bilboquet is high on the list of candidates. The design is simple: a wooden handle from which hangs a small ball or a ring suspended by a cord. The object of the bilboquet game is to swing the ball or ring up and catch it with the handle.

Like the bow and arrow, this basic design appears in many places around the world. In Europe, for example, where the game was popular in the royal courts, players caught a swinging ball in a hollow or cup at the end of the handle. Among the native inhabitants of North America, the target was typically a ring that the player caught with a skewering motion. Whether the game sprang up independently in regions as geographically diverse as the Arctic, Japan, and Peru or spread via commerce and exploration is open to debate. In North America, the game was both a child's game and, for adults, an opportunity to wager.

In some tribes, ring and pin was known as the "love game" because of its use as an icebreaker during courtship. When a young man of the

Penobscot tribe, for example, sought the affection of a young woman, he might invite her to play a game of ring and pin. The suitor would take his turn first; then, after a certain number of tries, he would pass the toy to her. When her turn was over, she might express her romantic interest in him by asking that the game continue for more rounds. Otherwise, she would hand him back the ring and pin and thank him for the game, at which point the suitor would get the hint, graciously leaving with his pride somewhat intact.

While the basic design of the ring and pin toy was quite simple, there were many modifications from one tribe to the next, some more complicated than others. The wide variety of materials and ring configurations employed should provide a range of possible projects for anyone interested in re-creating the game. At its most rudimentary, the toy was simply a ring tied to a stick.

Keeping score for a game using the basic design was a matter of counting the number of successful catches each player made out of a predetermined number of tries, say 10 tries apiece.

The Mojave, of what is now Arizona, strung on the cord as many as 17 extra rings carved from dried pumpkin shell, securing them with a large knot or button at the end. In this case, the object was to skewer as many rings as possible per try, then add up the total for a given number of tries. In some versions of the game using multiple rings on the string, the rings had progressively higher point values beginning with the ring closest to the handle.

Finally, many tribes added a palm-sized flap of leather to the end of the cord. These flaps typically had a large hole punched in the center surrounded by several smaller holes, each hole being worth varying numbers of points. The flaps of course added an extra degree of difficulty as the player would attempt to poke the stick through the rings and through one of the flap holes in one thrust, thereby scoring the points for both.

Two other versions of the game are noteworthy because they do not use rings as targets for the skewering move. In the first, a ball of grass or bound moose hair was substituted for the ring, and the object was to impale the ball on the end of the sharpened stick. A ball of yarn and a knitting needle would be a logical choice for contemporary reenactment of this version, although considerable caution would be necessary. Second, the Inuit, in what is now Labrador, used the skull of a rabbit as the target, boring several holes in the top of the skull so that a player could catch it by poking the stick into the cranium.

The Inuit from the west coast of the Hudson Bay developed an interesting variation of the game that allowed for multiple players to compete at once. They would hang a flat piece of ivory with a hole in the center from the ceiling of an igloo. At the bottom of the ivory they hung a weight to hold it steady. The players would stand in a circle around the ivory target, each holding a pointed stick. At the signal, all of the players tried to poke the stick through the hole. The first to do so won. Since getting jabbed in the hand as everyone thrust forward was apparently part of the game, dull sticks should be used in a contemporary re-enactment.

⦙⦙⦙ Bowl and Dice

While the familiar, modern six-sided dice were unknown in North America prior to the arrival of Europeans, Native Americans invented a wide array of small, dice-like objects that, when cast upon the ground or shaken in a bowl, produced random patterns determining the outcomes of their various games of chance. Among the most popular were the round, two-sided dice typically made from peach or plum stones used in the game of bowl and dice.

Players shook several of these dice in a bowl and scored points based on the number of dice that landed face up or face down as indicated by the different color painted on each side.

The popularity of bowl and dice raised eyebrows among the Colonists in early-17th-century New England, taught as they were that games of chance were evil, especially when wagering was involved. Native Americans of the period had no such cultural prohibition on gambling. In fact, games of pure chance such as those based on the various types of dice found throughout North America were quite significant to the spiritual life of Native Americans.

In addition to the economic gain possible from the sometimes high stakes, players sought, for however brief a moment, a sense of mastery over the seemingly random aspects of the universe. By winning at a game of chance, therefore, a player moved closer to the great organizing principle responsible for separating day and night, life and death, winter and summer from the chaos. In other words, the winner took a step toward divinity.

Games of bowl and dice frequently became the focal point for festivities involving entire villages, as onlookers hung wagers of valuable items such as animal furs and axes from arbor poles. During play, the onlookers generated so much excitement that the game became known as "hubbub" among the Colonists after the enthusiastic chant of *hub hub hub* that rose from the crowd at each turn. To this day, the term "hubbub" refers to any boisterous activity.

The game requires three basic elements: a large bowl, six dice, and 61 counting sticks for keeping score. The bowl should be deep enough so that the dice do not spill out when jostled around. In addition, it should have a flat surface at the bottom so that the dice do not overlap when they come to rest. A wooden salad bowl or mixing bowl is ideal because many of the native bowls were made of wood. For those interested in authenticity, the dice were usually made of peach or plum pits whose natural oval shapes were rounded and flattened by rubbing on a rock. One side is then charred black or painted to distinguish it from the other side. Six large, identical buttons marked on one side would also work.

For the Penobscot version of the game described below, the players will need 56 round sticks, 4 flat sticks, and 1 crooked stick. There are three phases to the game.

Phase One

The first phase begins with all of the counters in a central pile.

Player A rolls the six dice by shaking the bowl and placing it on the ground. If the roll results in five of the same side face up, player A receives three round sticks and rolls again. A roll of six alike results in one flat stick to player A and another roll.

If a second consecutive roll of five alike is rolled, player A receives nine round sticks and rolls again. A second consecutive roll of six alike results in two flat sticks and another roll.

If a third consecutive roll of five alike is rolled, player A receives one flat stick and the turn is over. A third consecutive roll of six alike results in three flat sticks and the turn is over.

Then player B rolls the dice and the process is repeated, the players alternating turns until all of the counters have been distributed. The crooked stick is awarded last. The winner of the crooked stick also receives two round sticks from the pile of his opponent. The game then proceeds to phase two.

Phase Two

In the second phase, each player begins moving his or her counters into a second pile called the "treasure pile." The object at this point is to move as many sticks as possible into the treasure pile because, in the final phase of the game, each player must forfeit to the other player four round sticks from the first pile for every stick in the treasure pile.

The transfer of sticks into the treasure pile proceeds as follows:

The player whose turn it is next rolls as described above. If that player rolls five alike, he or she may move a round stick into the treasure pile and roll again. For a second consecutive roll of five alike, he or she may move three round sticks into the treasure pile and roll again. For a third consecutive roll of five alike, he or she moves a flat stick into a third pile. This stick is called a "chief." At this point the turn ends.

If the player rolls six alike, he or she moves a flat stick into the third pile as a chief. For a second consecutive roll of six alike, he or she may move two flat sticks into the third pile as chiefs and roll again. For a third consecutive roll of six alike, he or she may move three flat sticks into the third pile as chiefs and the turn is over.

Phase Three

The players alternate turns as described above until one player feels that his or her treasure pile is large enough to bankrupt the other player by causing that player to forfeit all sticks. At this point, the player challenges the other to settle up as follows:

For every stick in a player's treasure pile, the opponent forfeits four round sticks from the first pile.

For every chief in a player's third pile, the opponent forfeits either 4 round sticks from the treasure pile, 1 flat stick from the first pile, or 16 round sticks from the first pile.

Finally, if a player who has been stripped of all of his or her sticks was in possession of the crooked stick, that player gets three final rolls. If that player rolls five or six alike, he or she immediately wins.

⊞ Counting Games

The object of the first counting game is to end up with the smallest odd number of sticks from the central pile. Up to six players sit in a circle. A large handful of sticks is placed uncounted in a heap in the middle of the circle. Proceeding clockwise around the circle, the players take turns picking up a number of sticks. Each player may take as many sticks as he or she wishes per turn. However, on the first round every player must have a turn picking up sticks. If all of the sticks are taken before each player has drawn, then the players who have taken sticks are out and the sticks are returned to the pile. Play then continues with those who did not draw on the first round. If only one person did not draw, that person wins. After the first round, the players continue drawing sticks until all of the sticks are gone.

Each player then divides his or her pile of sticks into groups of 10 and places these groups aside. The player with the smallest odd number of sticks remaining wins. Thus, if one player has 19 sticks and the other has 33, the player with 33 sticks wins; 33 minus two groups of 10 is three, a smaller odd number than nine (19 minus one group of 10).

The object of another counting game is to remember the number of sticks per pile in a sequence of piles. In this two-person children's game, one player divides a bundle of 40 sticks into piles of one to five sticks. The other player then attempts to commit the sequence of piles to memory for a prearranged amount of time—the time, for example, it takes the other player to recite a common rhyme or count to a certain number. When his or her time is up, the player turns away from the piles and attempts to recite numbers of sticks per pile from left or right. For each pile correctly remembered the player scores points equal to the number of sticks in the pile. The counter then arranges the sticks into piles for his or her opponent to remember, and so on until one player achieves the winning number of points to which both have agreed in advance.

The guessing games are reminiscent of hide the ball described earlier, the object being to guess the location of the odd or marked stick in one of two or more piles. In a version played by the Cree of Wyoming, two teams sat facing each other. Beginning at one end of the line, the first player divides a bundle of 25 sticks into two roughly equal bundles under cover of a cloth. He or she then holds a bundle in each hand, and the opposing player must guess which bundle contains the odd number of sticks. A correct guess scores a point for the team and possession of the bundle. If the guess is incorrect, the team in possession remains in possession and scores a point. The bundle is then passed to the next player and the process is repeated until one team achieves the winning number of points to which both teams have agreed in advance.

▦ Hidden Ball

Hidden ball was a guessing game much like the familiar cup and ball of modern carnivals. The object of the game was for one player to locate a stone or bit of wood the other player has hidden in one of four moccasins or wooden tubes.

Despite the simple object, the game was not intended for children. Rather, men were the primary participants, ascribing to the game rich ceremonial and mythological significance. Among the Apache of the area now encompassed by northern New Mexico, for example, the game was associated with a creation myth describing how light and darkness separated to form the first day. According to the myth, the universe was originally dark. Human beings and other creatures that require light grew tired of relying on torches for illumination and wanted daylight to appear. The Bear, the Panther and the Owl, all creatures that prefer darkness, however, objected. After much debate, the two groups agreed to settle the matter by playing hidden ball. The night creatures hid a ball in one of four tubes. Unbeknownst to them, two daylight creatures, the Magpie and the Quail, were able to see where the ball was hidden through the thin wall of the tube. They alerted the humans and, based on this knowledge, the humans won, thus allowing the sun to rise in the east as the night creatures ran for cover. For the Zuni, also of New Mexico, the game represented a contest between the god of wind and the god of water. When played in early spring, therefore, the game became a kind of weather forecasting tool. The amount of rain a village might expect depended on how well the player representing the god of water was performing at various points in the game.

In addition to these mythological overtones, the game was culturally significant because it served as a vehicle for high-stakes gambling. Games might last hours or even days, the competition continuing until one of the players was stripped of his possessions. Meanwhile, a crowd of onlookers might cast large side bets among themselves, thereby involving many more participants than merely the two players.

The equipment for the game consisted of three elements. First, the cup in which the ball was concealed, most often four moccasins or four hollow, wooden tubes an inch and a half in diameter and several inches long with one end plugged. Second, dried beans, pieces of straw, or whittled sticks for keeping score. The number of these counters varied from place to place and also determined how many guessing rounds would take place since the winner of each round would take a number of counters as points until all were gone. A match beginning with around 100 counters was typical. Third, a pebble or ball of carved wood small enough to fit in the tube or under the moccasin. In some versions of the game, the guesser uses a slender rod to select his choice of hiding places.

In the simplest form of the game, two players sit facing each other on a mat on the ground. They place two pairs of moccasins on the mat between them, arranging them in a square.

The players decide who will be first to hide the ball by any one of several methods such as one player attempting to guess in which fist the other has concealed the ball or by flipping a chip of wood or stone. The hider then takes the ball in his or her fist and feigns placing the ball under each of the moccasins, all the while attempting to distract the opponent with misleading comments. When the hider feels that the other player is sufficiently confused, he secretly places the ball under one of the moccasins, obscuring the placement by continuing to put his empty fist under the other moccasins until he is satisfied that his opponent is unaware of the location of the ball. The other player then attempts to guess the location of the ball. If he is correct on the first guess, he receives four points, on the second guess, three points, and so on. That player then becomes the hider and the process is repeated. The player to first accumulate a pre-arranged number of points wins.

A more complicated version of the game involved two teams of four players each. The game begins with each team building a small mound of dirt on opposite ends of an open playing area. Team A, the first team to hide the ball, takes four hollow tubes with plugged ends to its mound and, with two of the team members holding up a blanket to obscure the view of team B, hides a round stone in one of the hollow tubes. Each tube is marked to indicate the point value of that tube, for example 20 points for the first tube, 15 for the second, 10, and 5 for the third and fourth tubes, respectively. Team A then pushes the open ends of the four tubes into the mound so that they are sticking up. When the hiding is complete, team A lowers the blanket and calls a member of team B to cross the central open area and make a guess.

As the guesser approaches, the onlookers favoring team A attempt to distract him by shouting out taunts and misleading hints. The guesser passes his pointer stick over the tubes several times, then makes his guess. If he is correct, the guesser receives as many counters from the bank of 100 and two counters as the point value of the tube. If he is incorrect, he forfeits that number to team A and must try again, forfeiting the point value of each incorrect tube until he finds the ball and wins the point value for the correct tube. At the conclusion of the first guesser's turn, team A calls the next member of team B across as the guesser and the process is repeated until all members of team B have had a turn to guess, at which point, team B brings the tubes back to its mound and becomes the hider. The tubes thus go back and forth until all of the counters have been paid out. When the bank is empty, play continues with each team using its counters to pay or forfeit until one team ends up with all of the counters and thereby wins.

▦ Little Pines

Little pines is a dancing-doll game played by young girls of the Penobscot tribes of the Northeast. The game used anywhere from 6 to 10 dolls made from the tips of evergreen branches such as the Norway or white pine. A strategic stripping away of pine needles creates a skirt, arms, and shawl. The dolls are then balanced and danced on a thin wooden board. A woman sings as she jostles the game board, and the pine sprigs dance and eventually topple. If a pine dancer manages to right itself, then the onlookers exclaim, "She's come back to life!" The last pine dancer to fall from the board is praised for her endurance and dancing skill. The dancers and board are then passed to another to play.

▦ Picaria

This is a tic-tac-toe style game that the Pueblo Indian cultures of the Southwest might have adapted from a similar game learned from Spanish explorers early in the 16th century. The object is to get three in a row by placing counters (small stones, corn kernels, or coins) on the intersecting points of the game board.

Each player gets three counters. The players take turns placing one counter at a time on any vacant point on the board. When all counters have been placed, the players take turns moving one counter one space to any adjacent point. Jumping over a counter is not allowed. The row of three can be made in any direction. The first player to get three in a row is the winner.

▦ Stick Games

The ability of Native Americans to make creative and economical use of the most humble materials around them is perhaps no better illustrated than with the several games played with nothing more than bundles of twigs. These games fall into two basic categories: first, counting games in which the number of sticks in play determines the outcome and, second, guessing games in which one player attempts to guess the position of the odd or marked stick from one of two or more bundles.

As with many Native American pastimes, wagering often played an important part in the enjoyment of the various stick games. At least one tribe, however, the Takulli of British Colombia, told a cautionary tale of what can happen when one's wagering gets out of control. In the legend a young man had such a weakness for stick games that he managed to wager away not only his clothes but his wife and child as well. Outraged by the man's lack of self-control, the village banished him. As the man wandered naked and dejected, he came across a lodge in the forest. The owner of the lodge, an old man, took the young man in, fed and clothed him, and even offered the young man his daughter's hand in marriage.

In time the young man's passion for stick games returned. Seeing this, the old man sent him to the village to win back his possessions, but warned him that upon winning he must discard his sticks and never wager again. The young man returned to the village and won back all of his possessions. The young man, however, disregarded the old man's advice and continued to play. Soon he had again lost all of his possessions and was naked. When he returned to the forest, the old man and the lodge had disappeared.

For the stick games described below, the only equipment necessary is a bundle of sticks. While some tribes polished and decorated the game sticks, others used plain reeds or twigs. For the modern reenactor, a large box of new pencils or even commercial pick-up sticks will do. The number of sticks required depends on the game.

▦ Stone Warrior

When the Spanish began colonizing the area now encompassed by New Mexico in the late 1500s, they apparently brought with them the ancient board game alquerque. While the historical record is not complete, alquerque is the likely source for at least two of the awithlaknannai or "stone warrior" board games played by the native Pueblo tribes. In these games, each player attempts to dominate the board by jumping or surrounding the checker-like game pieces of his or her opponent. Unlike checkers, however, the playing pieces travel along the lines that make up the geometric game board rather than between them, landing on the intersections. Thus, for the descriptions that follow, the word "spaces" refers to these intersections.

The Zuni called one version of stone warrior *kolowisi awithlaknannai*, the *kolowisi* being a mythical serpent, a reference perhaps to the long, diamond-back configuration of the game board. Players typically drew these game boards in the dirt or scratched them onto the flat rooftops of the Pueblo houses. While the board described here has 16 spaces to a side, there were no standard dimensions for the board, and thus the "snake" could be longer or shorter depending on the inclination of the players.

The game begins with the white and black stones arranged in the middle of the board. Each player has one full line of 16 game pieces separated at the center row. In the center row, each player has 7 pieces lined up from either end, with the middle space and the two end spaces left empty. A stone may move in any direction as long as it follows a line, either the straight lines in the middle or the curved lines at the end, and lands on the adjacent empty space. Unless a piece is jumping, and thereby capturing, an opposing piece, a player may only move one space per turn. A player may jump a piece when it is adjacent to his or her piece and the space on the other side of the opponent's piece is empty. As in checkers, a player may string together several jumps if after the first jump the player's piece lands adjacent to another piece vulnerable to capture and so on.

A coin toss may be used to determine who goes first. This player moves one of his or her stones along a line and into one of the three adjacent, empty spaces. The second player then takes his or her turn, either jumping the first player's stone or moving a stone into one of the remaining empty spaces. The players take turns back and forth in this manner, either moving into empty spaces or jumping where possible until one of the players has captured all of the other player's pieces.

Another Zuni stone warrior game involved four players, each sitting at one of the compass points on the game board. In this four-handed version, the players at north and west team against the players at south and east. Each player begins with a playing piece on each of the six empty spaces on his or her side of the board for a total of 12 pieces per team. These pieces were made originally from broken pottery shards ground into one-inch diameter disks and marked on one side with a small hole to distinguish the pieces of each team, one team playing with the pieces hole-side-up and the other hole-side-down. (Interestingly, pottery shard disks like this have been found in prehistoric ruins in the western United States and Mexico, but there is no evidence of the stone warrior game board predating the arrival of the Spanish. The purpose of these disks is not known, although they may have been used as game pieces for a now-lost board game.) For contemporary stone warrior play, different colored buttons are a good substitute.

The object of four-handed stone warrior is for the players of each team to cross the board and occupy the six starting spaces of the player opposite him or her, each team attempting to capture as many of the other team's pieces along the way as possible. The team to place the greatest number of pieces in the starting positions of the other team wins.

Although some of the specific rules are a bit sketchy, a reconstruction of the game might appear as follows: The teams decide which player will go first by coin toss or the like, and thereafter turns proceed in a clockwise direction. The first player advances a piece. The pieces may only move along the diagonal lines (called "trails") one space at a time and may not move backward. Next, the player to his or her left advances a piece and so on, until the pieces, as they traverse the central area of the board, come within capturing range. A piece is captured when it is sandwiched between two of the opposing team's pieces on a diagonal line. The first piece captured by each team is replaced by a larger piece called the "priest of the bow" for the capturing team. This piece has the ability to move one space orthogonally, that is, along the vertical and horizontal lines (called "canyons"), in addition to moving diagonally, but as with the other pieces, it may not move backward.

Thus, the priest of the bow, it was said, had the magical power to fly across the canyons. When a piece reaches the starting position of the opposite player, the piece is safe and remains there for the duration of the game. The team with the most pieces safely across wins.

Apparently, native players were able to distinguish their pieces from those of their teammates, an important distinction due to the fact that north, for example, might inadvertently move west's piece backward relative to west when pushing the piece forward toward south. This problem is solved, however, if each player has a unique color and may only move his or her own pieces.

EUROPEAN IMPORTS

Two very famous episodes that occurred quite early in the history of the Jamestown and Plymouth colonies attest to the powerful role sports played in the lives of the early English settlers. On returning to Jamestown in 1611 after that colony's "starving time," John Smith was amazed to find gaunt men, near death, engaged in lawn bowling inside the fortress. In a similar fashion, on Christmas Day 1621, William Bradford confiscated sporting equipment from idlers playing stoolball when they should have been working (the Pilgrims did not celebrate Christmas). Young men risked starvation and the lash to engage in their favorite pastimes.

Years earlier, in 1565, Spanish soldiers ransacked Fort Caroline, a French settlement near St. Augustine, Florida (the first permanent European city in North America), where they found, among other things, playing cards decorated with chalices and hosts. The soldiers burned them.

Whatever energy was needed to build a colony in the New World, a good portion got channeled or diverted, for good or ill, into sports and games, even though it would take several decades for organized recreation to develop into a regular part of early colonial life.

The Europeans brought a variety of sports and games with them. Some, such as billiards, grew in popularity in taverns and in the homes of the wealthy plantation society. Others, such as bowling, would evolve slightly, while others, such as stoolball would evolve a lot, eventually becoming baseball.

▦ Battledore

Battledore is an early form of badminton played with a flat wooden paddle and a shuttlecock, which is a light projectile originally made of feathers and cork. Battledore was also called shuttlecock. A similar form of the game developed simultaneously in many world cultures at least 2,500 years ago. Greek drawings represent a game almost identical to battledore, and it has been popular in China, Japan, India, and Siam for at least 2,000 years.

Peasants played battledore in Medieval England and by the late 16th century, it had become a popular children's game. In the 17th century, battledore or *jeu de volant* was an upper-class pastime in many European countries. Dutch colonists brought the game to North America in the middle of the 17th century.

Unlike tennis, the most popular ball and racket game of the Renaissance, battledore could be played virtually anywhere, indoors or out, and its equipment was very portable. Thus the game was easy to import to the New World. The paddle is a short-handled wooden bat that resembles a child's hornbook, a thin board of oak, nine inches long by six inches wide, with a short handle. The name likely comes from the French word *batedor* (beater).

Battledore racket and shuttlecock.

Although badminton, which developed in England in the 1870s, would have its own scoring system, battledore was often just a game in which two people volleyed the shuttlecock back and forth to see how many times they could hit it consecutively without letting it hit the ground. In 1830, the Somerset family in England reportedly established a world record of 2,117 consecutive hits.

Modern Ping-Pong paddles and shuttlecocks from badminton sets are serviceable substitutes for anyone wishing to try this game, which can be played in a classroom, gym, across a cafeteria table or even an outdoor bike rack. An entire class can play, with people pairing off and attempting to sustain the longest possible volley.

⚏ Bees

Throughout Colonial and American history, the bee, a social gathering for the completion of a seasonal task, such as corn husking, lot clearing, or apple cutting, was a community building act and also provided opportunities for sporting contests, games, and dances.

Here is how a husking bee might go: the first Saturday in October, the entire corn harvest is dumped on a barn floor and separated into piles. The whole community turns out to pitch in to help turn the dull job of husking all that corn into a festive event.

Corn was a vital staple of the early American diet. Many families survived almost exclusively on foods made from corn, such as corn mush, corn gruel, and corn dumplings. With the exhausting work of harvest nearly complete, the husking bee was looked forward to as a time for good fellowship and fun. Often, townspeople divided into teams and raced against one another to see which team finished husking their pile first. Men and women would sit in alternate seats. When a man found a red ear of corn, he got to kiss the woman sitting next to him. Another common practice was to declare the person who peeled the last ear of corn the winner. So such bees had a social function for young people that might be built on at, say, the harvest moon festival dance.

While the adults worked, the children played. Corn husks were used to make dolls, and kids also played countless games still enjoyed today, including hide and seek, leapfrog, marbles, blindman's buff, I spy, and prisoner's base.

Other types of bees included butchering, logging, stump cutting (often to make stump fences), sugaring, sewing, and the co-op-like sharing of bulk foods, such as when one family obtained a hogshead of brown sugar. Bees remind us of a time when people grew most of their own food and depended on the physical presence of one another to make hard jobs easier, and to give everyone a sense of being part of a community.

▦ Billiards

As early as the last quarter of the 17th century, billiards was being played in North America, a testament to the colonists' demand to recreate as they did in the old country, despite the inconvenience, if not extravagance, of obtaining billiard tables and equipment. Early on, this was a game just for the merchant class of New York and the plantation society of Virginia, who could afford to have local craftsmen fashion tables. Ivory billiard balls were imported from England. Billiards became a popular pastime, along with darts and lawn bowling, at the taverns or "ordinaries" in Virginia.

In his famous diary, William Byrd, a Virginia planter, writes of Sunday mornings spent playing billiards with his cousin because "there seemed to be no more harm in it than in talk."

The American form of pocket billiards, what we call pool today, gained precedence in the mid 19th century, when the word "pool" was synonymous with gambling.

▦ Bowling

Bowling, a game in which a heavy ball is rolled down a long, narrow alley in an effort to knock down pins, has existed in one form or another since ancient times, though its modern, 10-pin variation was chiefly an American invention. The Dutch brought a form of bowling called ninepins or skittles, to the New World in 1623, an image etched 200 years later in what is regarded as the first American short story, Washington Irving's "Rip Van Winkle":

> What seemed particularly odd to Rip was, that though these folks were evidently amusing themselves, yet they maintained the gravest faces, the most mysterious silence, and were, withal, the most melancholy party of pleasure he had ever witnessed. Nothing interrupted the stillness of the scene but the noise of the balls, which, whenever they were rolled, echoed along the mountains like rumbling peals of thunder.

Bowling was very popular in Colonial America, usually as a venue for gambling. According to legend, when Connecticut outlawed "bowling at ninepins" in an effort to stop the gambling element, people merely added a tenth pin, changed the diamond pin configuration of ninepins to a pyramid, and modern bowling was born.

Bowling had been gaining in popularity throughout the Renaissance. In the 1300s, bowling greens began to appear on the estates of wealthy Europeans. The first enclosed bowling center was built in London in 1455. Thirty years later in 1485, the first of many official bans was decreed in England when Edward IV outlawed the "hustling of stones" and other bowling-like sports. In 1555, bowling centers closed because they were being used as places of "unlawful assembly." And there was the famous instance of John Smith returning to Jamestown Colony in 1611 and seeing starving men happily bowling away.

Both the ball and the pins used in 10-pin bowling are larger and heavier than those used in ninepins or any of the sport's variants, which include candlepins, duckpins, and skittles. The invention of the automated pin spotter in the 1940s created the industry and modern sport of bowling, which has become one of the most popular recreational activities in the world. The game is played by both men and women, boys and girls, and is a popular league sport in schools and in communities throughout the United States.

A bowling game is divided into 10 frames consisting of up to two rolls per frame. A "strike" is achieved if all 10 pins are knocked down on a frame's initial throw. If all 10 pins are knocked down on two throws, a "spare" is earned. When a strike is recorded, the player earns 10 points plus the value of the next two throws for that frame. When a spare is recorded, the player receives 10 points plus the value of the next throw for that frame. Thus, the maximum score for any frame is 30 points, making a perfect score 300, or 12 strikes in a row.

The easiest way to participate in bowling is to visit the nearest bowling center. Equipment, including special shoes and bowling balls, as well as instruction and availability of league play are available at most bowling alleys.

▦ Dancing

Dancing is probably the most ubiquitous and universal of all physical activities. Dancing has been a part of every culture and has been used for every type of human expression: solemn religious rites, celebrations, entertainment, and artistic expression. With the exception of the Pilgrims and Puritan sects that banned it, dancing was a part of the lives of every facet of North American society, from Native Americans, to the Europeans who settled here, and the slaves they brought to the New World in chains.

For Europeans, dancing accompanied many social occasions, such as the evenings after muster days or barn raisings, weddings, banquets, and seasonal celebrations. In addition, a ball might follow on the evening of a major sporting event, such as a horse race.

As in Europe, young men of the landed gentry were expected to acquire certain skills, and one of these was dancing. Itinerant dancing teachers would sometimes travel from town to town or plantation to plantation to reach pupils. Whether it was waltzing at a wedding at a Virginia manor house, or a New England country-dance following a husking bee, dancing served many athletic, recreational, and social needs in early America.

⦀ Horse Racing

Of all the sports that have survived to this day, horse racing—the "sport of kings"—was the first to be established in North America. And until the end of the 20th century, when the rise in casinos provided places other than the racetrack to gamble, it was the most popular spectator sport, drawing more fans annually than baseball or football.

Horses were not known in North America until Spanish explorers brought them early in the 16th century. Horse racing is considered the first organized sport because it is the first for which special venues were created, events happened at regular times, prizes were offered, admission fees charged, and the viewing of events was seen as enjoyable entertainment. By the end of the 17th century, conventions of handicapping weight limits on jockeys had been introduced and lawsuits stemming from wagers were on the books.

The first horse race was held in 1665, a year after the British kicked the Dutch out of New Amsterdam and renamed it New York. The first race course, Newmarket (named for the first racecourse in England) was built on Long Island in what is now Garden City. Just as in England, "improving the breed" was stressed as the main justification for holding races. Gambling, however, was also present from the start.

Horse racing occurred throughout the colonies, from Massachusetts to Virginia, with races staged in a variety of ways, according to Nancy Struna in her book *People of Prowess*:

> In New York, the British upper-rank mode of distance racing on a course emerged with the royal governor after 1664, whereas colonists in the Chesapeake favored quarter-mile sprints. Contemporary New Englanders arranged races on roads, village commons, or beaches with horses bred to travel at steady speeds and occasionally with wagons and carts in tow. (76)

Horse racing remained a popular local pastime until the Civil War, after which, with the publication of the *American Stud Book* (1868), the sport became organized on a national level. In just over 20 years, America would boast 314 race courses. In 1894, the American Jockey Club (a regulatory body modeled on one established in England in 1750) was founded to govern the growing sport.

An important footnote on horse racing is that it gave African Americans their first major role in the development of a national sport. Many of the early grooms, trainers, and jockeys were slaves charged with maintenance of the horses.

⦀ Hunting

Hunting in North America began as necessity, grew out of privilege, and later developed into a field sport that is still extremely popular. The

New World teemed with game, but early settlers did little hunting, because venturing out beyond their forts (as was the case with Jamestown), was dangerous. As Native American tribes receded, many early livelihoods depended on hunting and fishing, and thus field sports were interwoven with business pursuits, whether fur trapping, deer hunting, or cod fishing. Hunting and fishing also became one of the most important sources of food, especially given the poor soil of New England and the use of arable land for inedible cash crops, notably tobacco, in the Chesapeake region.

The availability of land to most early settlers also helped solidify hunting's role in daily life. In England, people could hunt only on their own land, which excluded nearly all but the upper classes. In the New World, most people either owned land, or had access to unclaimed or undeeded land, providing near limitless opportunities to hunt deer, rabbits, squirrels, birds, and fowl. In addition, early town governments sometimes offered bounties for the heads or hides of dangerous or livestock-stealing animals, such as bears and wolves.

As militias were established, towns held muster days for training and these events often included shooting contests and prizes. Prowess with a musket or carbine was seen as a necessary skill.

European settlers adapted their approaches from both the dress and hunting techniques of Native Americans. Boots and colored coats gave way to deerskins and moccasins as colonists learned to blend into the immense forests as they stalked their prey.

By the end of the 17th century, colonists were importing quail and duck calls, French hunting hounds, and better horses. Hunting had quickly transcended need to become a sport and remains one to this day.

▦ Rounders

Stoolball, brought to this country from England, would eventually develop into both cricket and baseball. The direct antecedent to baseball, which would be invented in 1845, was a game called rounders, invented in England sometime in the 17th century.

Stoolball involves a pitcher trying to hit a stool with a ball while the batter tries to protect it by batting the ball away. Eventually, additional stools were added that the batter would run to once a ball was hit. It is not clear precisely when stoolball evolved into a game that had multiple bases as its standard, but rounders is cited as "base-ball" as early as 1744 in the publication, *A Little Pretty Pocket-Book*. Clearly, by then, multiple base games were well established.

Rounders takes its name from a batter's having to run around a series of four posts (bases) laid out as a pentagon, to score a run. The batsman stands at a batting square, 28 feet from the front of the bowling square (pitcher's mound). The bowler throws the ball underhand over the batting square, above the batsman's knees and below the batsman's head, what is referred to in baseball as the "strike zone." The batsman is supposed to swing at any pitch in this zone.

Even if the batsman doesn't swing at a legal pitch, or swings and misses, he has to run to the first post. As in baseball, he then tries to proceed to the second, third, and fourth posts. However, the fourth post is not where he started out; it is 28 feet to the left of the batting square.

Rounders has no "foul territory." If the batted ball goes behind the batting square, the batsman can run only as far as the first post until the ball is thrown back into play.

A runner is put out if his or her batted ball is caught on the fly, if a fielder tags them with the ball between posts, or if the post toward which one is running is touched with the ball.

Three consecutive bad pitches entitle a batsman to go directly to the second post; and the team is awarded a penalty "half-rounder." Circling the posts is a "rounder," which scores one point. As in baseball, there are nine players on each team, but each team gets nine outs per inning. Two innings make up a game.

▦ Swimming

The North American continent boasts an amazing number of ocean beaches, freshwater lakes, rivers, ponds, and deltas that provided all those who settled this land abundant opportunity to swim. During the Renaissance, as people in Europe learned that, far from subjecting the body to diseases (a long-held suspicion during the plague-ravaged Middle Ages), exercise in water had many physical and emotional health benefits, swimming became a popular leisure activity. In North America, where colonization progressed from the sea in, swimming took on greater significance as a survival skill.

In his treatise, *The Art of Swimming Rendered Easy*, Benjamin Franklin would call the exercise of swimming "one of the most healthy and agreeable in the world."

Swimming was largely a children's activity during the 17th century, a way to play while enjoying the pristine environment during the warm summer months in places such as Massachusetts Bay or the Chesapeake Bay. But by the turn of the century, once plantation and community life had become well established, swimming became a popular leisure activity among landowners. Virginia plantation owner William Byrd, for example, states in his famous diary that he swam frequently to restore his vigor.

As with many sports, the widespread availability of printed books shaped the activity's development. In 1696, *The Art of Swimming* by a French author named Thevenot first described a type of breaststroke done with the face held out of the water and with an underwater arm recovery, which gave the swimmer stability, even in rough water. Thevenot's work became the standard swimming reference, and the breaststroke was the most popular swimming stroke for centuries.

Most early swimming was done in rivers or bays. Sea or ocean swimming did not become widely popular until late in the 18th century, its first noteworthy proponent being George III, who was king of England when America declared its independence.

SPORTS AND GAMES OF THE INUIT AND ALEUT

Although Inuit peoples can be grouped with all Native Americans, their tradition of games is rich enough and their geography distinct enough to warrant their own section. These are the tribes that constitute the native population of the Arctic and subarctic regions of Greenland, Alaska, Canada, and eastern Siberia. These peoples are separated from the Native American tribes in the United States and Canada by language as well as bodily, geographic, and economic adaptation to the harsh polar regions in which they live. These cultures subsisted almost entirely on caribou, fish, and marine mammals. They made their clothing from fur. Their primary means of transport, the kayak (and the larger umiak) and the dogsled, are still in use today and have grown into extremely popular sports: whitewater and sea-kayaking are engaged in around the world, and dogsledding, from Outward Bound courses to the famous Iditarod endurance race, has risen in popularity.

▦ *Anayumiak* (Ball over the Roof)

Two teams of at least seven players stand on opposite sides of a building. The first team throws a ball over the roof to the opposite team. A player on that team catches the ball and the team runs around the building to throw the ball at members of the first team in an attempt to hit one of them. Any player who is hit must then join the team that hit him or her. Play continues until the other has captured all the players on one team, or until both sides are too tired to continue.

▦ *Angkalutin* (Keep Away)

This is a great game to develop passing skills for sports such as basketball. Two teams attempt to pass the ball back and forth to members on their team while players on the other team attempt to intercept the ball. Each team can have several players, and the game works especially well with teams of two or three. The field of play need not have any boundaries. The object can also vary, such as having to make 10 consecutive passes. Pass counts revert to zero on interceptions.

▦ Caribou Eyes

A group clasps hands and forms a circle around one player who is it. It placed his hands on each of the other players and asked who he was. The answer is always the name of an animal. It would then try to break out of the circle by stepping on the toes of his captors, who would jump nimbly to avoid this. If it succeeded in breaking free, everyone would run after him.

▦ *Hal Hai Jao* (Turn Around Game)

This is another stick game that combines dexterity with luck. The object, as with similar stick games, is to win all of your opponent's sticks. Each player starts with the same number of small sticks. One player goes first: all of the sticks are held in the palm of the hand and are thrown up in the air. When they come down, the player tries to catch as many as possible on the back of the hand, at which point the sticks are thrown up again (off the back of the hand) and caught in a normal fashion. If an odd number of sticks are caught, the player keeps one stick and goes again. If none or an even number are caught, the turn passes to the other player. The player who ends up with all the sticks wins the game.

▦ *Illupik* (Seal Skin Skipping)

This is a form of jump rope that features the *avatuk*, the sealskin float that hunters used to tie the harpoons, tied in the center of a rope. In the absence of a sealskin ball, a small rubber ball tied to a rope with a rag will suffice. Two players hold either end of the rope and swing it over the head of a third player who faces the ball. The player jumps over the rope and after each jump must rotate his or her body a half turn in order to always be facing the ball. The winner is the one who completes the most successive jumps.

▦ Jackstraws

Jackstraws is a skill game played by the Tlingits and other tribes that can be played with any number of players, though it works well one-on-one. Equipment needed to play includes a bunch of slender pieces of wood (jackstraws can be purchased and substitutes might include pencils, pipe cleaners, or drinking straws) and a wooden hook for each player. One player grasps the bundle of sticks between thumb and forefinger of his or her right hand, resting one end on the floor. They are then released so that they fall in a small heap. Each player in turns tries to remove as many straws in succession as possible with their wooden hook without moving

Inuit drawing of sealskin skipping. The illustration is by Sorosilutoo from Cape Dorset on Baffin Island (Government of Canada: Ministry of Indian & Northern Affairs, 1975, #QS-8050-000-BB-A1). (Used with permission of the Elliott Avedon Museum and Archive of Games, University of Waterloo.)

any but the one taken. Each player keeps the straws he removes and the one holding the most at the end is the winner.

▦ *Makpigamimait* (Pole Push)

This is a variation of the tug of war in which players lie on their backs with their feet raised and placed along a wooden stick that is between them. One player puts his feet in the center of the stick while the other places his or her feet on either side of the first player's. The object is to push very hard against the stick in an attempt to push the other player over.

▦ Quoits

This is an Aleut variation of the popular game played in Europe since ancient times. Traditionally, a sealskin with a colored stripe served as the target at which players would toss wooden disks from a sitting or squatting position. A cloth mat with a center stripe can serve as a substitute. Points are scored for rings that hit closest to the stripe. Individuals and two-person teams can play the game.

▦ Seated Tug of War

This is an Athabaskan variation of the common Native American tug of war game, in which one person is pitted against another, the object being to move the other into a standing position. The standard equipment is a set of two strong sticks attached with a short rope: the sticks must be long enough to be gripped with both hands. The players sit on the floor or ground facing each other with the soles of their feet touching. Each person holds one of the sticks firmly in both hands. At a predetermined signal, they pull against each other until one is pulled up.

▦ Shinny

The Eyaks played shinny on the beach. The sticks were naturally curved pieces of wood, and the ball was a roughly rounded wooden block. The size of teams varied, but the sides were more or less evenly matched. The ball is buried in the sand. A player from each team faces off to dig up the ball with their sticks. The teams then try to drive the ball across the opponent's goal line. The field is about two or three hundred yards long. There are no rules, but it is considered wrong to hit an opponent intentionally.

▦ Stick Game (Eyak)

This is a team version of an Eyak guessing game, variations of which are played by many Native American tribes. The game is designed for two teams of between 6 and 14 players. Needed for the game are two sticks small enough to be hidden inside a closed fist. One of the sticks is marked. Also needed is a small pile of tokens (sticks or stones) to serve as counters. These are placed on the ground between the two teams.

The game starts with one team holding the sticks. The players shuffle them about for a few minutes with their hands hidden behind their backs. Then all the players hold out their closed hands in front of them, palms down. One player from the opposing team then tries to guess which hand holds the marked stick.

If the player guesses incorrectly, the player holding the marked stick takes one counter from the pile. If the player guesses correctly, the person concealing the marked stick has to drop out and surrender all of his or her counters. After each guess, the sticks are passed to the opposite team. The number of counters used depends on how long teams want to play. A team has to win all the counters from its opponent and from the pile in the middle to win the game.

▦ Stick Game (*Haidas*)

This is another stick game that can be played by any number of players. The equipment needed includes 40 or 50 round sticks or pieces of wood, five inches long by one-eighth of an inch thick, painted in black and blue rings and polished; one stick that is entirely colored, and one that is entirely plain. Cedar bark and a mat are also required.

Each player has a bunch of sticks (40 or 50) and selects one stick (entirely colored or entirely plain). The player takes a handful of the sticks and hides them under a small pile of cedar bark that he or she keeps nearby. The player divides the sticks into two bunches, wraps them up in the bark, and passes them rapidly from hand to hand and finally moves them around on the ground or the mat on which the players are seated. The opponent watches every move and finally points to the bundle he or she thinks the special stick is hidden in. The player shakes the sticks out of the bark and throws them one by one into the space between the players until it is determined whether the desired stick is in that bundle. If the player has guessed correctly, he or she takes one stick from the opponent's pile. If the player has guessed incorrectly, the player hiding the stick takes one of the other player's sticks. The game continues until one player has won all of the opponent's sticks.

▦ Stones

This simple Aleut game highlights dexterity and is similar in some respects to the catching game jacks, though no ball is used. In stones, a player tosses four small stones into the air with one hand and attempts to catch them all with the same hand before any hit the ground. The winner is the one who first catches all four stones.

▦ Three Jumping Games

In a contest called rabbit jump, a player jumps as far as he or she can with both feet, followed by a hop on one foot and finally a jump with both feet but landing on both hands (somersault), the feet not touching the ground. Finally, the player jumps once more and lands with both feet. The one jumping farthest is the winner. In toe jump, each player stands behind a line, grabbing his or her toes, knees bent, and jumps forward as far as possible without letting go of their toes and maintaining balance. The farthest jump wins. A more physically demanding contest is *peed le ta tuq*, in which players make consecutive jumps from a kneeling to a squatting position (without using the hands) in an effort to outlast their opponents.

▦ Wrestling

Wrestling, among the most universal of all sports, was popular among the Inuit peoples and was practiced in many forms.

On Holman Island, the Inuit there call a similar type of wrestling *una tar tuq*. The intent of this type of wrestling is for two opponents to stand face-

Inuit drawing of wrestlers. The illustration is by Sorosilutoo from Cape Dorset on Baffin Island (Government of Canada: Ministry of Indian & Northern Affairs, 1975, #QS-8050-000-BB-A1). (Used with permission of the Elliott Avedon Museum and Archive of Games, University of Waterloo.)

to-face with their arms around one another and their feet flat on the floor (or ground). The object is for one opponent to lift the other.

Additional Inuit wrestling contests include a type of leg twist wrestling. In this contest, two players lie on their sides facing each other with their feet touching. One foot of each contestant is braced heel to toe against the opponent's opposite foot, while the other foot is hooked around the opponent's opposite foot. Hands are clasped under the knees, and, using only the hooked foot, one opponent attempts to turn the other opponent over.

The Eyaks also wrestled in many forms. The most traditional form was for two players to grab each other and try to throw each other to the ground. In a second form, the wrestlers locked their middle fingers together, each struggling to straighten out the fingers of the opponent. A third form is for two players to sit on the ground with their feet braced together, and they try to pull each other over forward with their arms.

⠿ Yukon Dodge Ball

This is a variation of the game of dodge ball that combines speed and skill and can be played by any number of players. The Athabaskans play using a small caribou or moose-skin ball, which players take turns trying to toss into a hole in the ground. A small wastebasket or box can serve as a substitute. Players make a circle around the basket, and, one by one, each tries to toss the ball into it. If one succeeds, he or she rushes to the basket to retrieve the ball as the others run away. After retrieving the ball, the player tries to throw it at one of the players running away. If the ball hits a player, that player gets one mark against him or her. Two marks and you are out. Play continues until there is only one player left, who is the winner.

▦ OCEANIA

INTRODUCTION

Oceania refers to the myriad of islands (about 10,000) in the central and southern Pacific Ocean, ranging roughly from Australia to Hawaii, including the Malay Archipelago, Melanesia, Micronesia, New Zealand, and Polynesia. It is a large area, covering half a million square miles with a total population today of about 30 million.

During the Renaissance, two voyages of discovery began to bring this region into Western consciousness. In 1513, Spanish conquistador Vasco Nunez de Balboa became the first European to gaze on the vast Pacific Ocean from the North American side, and in 1519–20, Portuguese explorer Ferdinand Magellan sailed across it, going from the tip of South America to Guam in 99 days. The last of Magellan's five ships circumnavigated the globe, proving that a vast, uncharted world of sea and islands separated the New World from Asia.

Exploring these islands, examining their many cultures, societal structures, and the sports and games they played would not begin until the end of the 18th century—long after the Renaissance ended. This does not make it impossible to describe many of the traditional activities native to Oceania—many, such as surfing and boomerang throwing, date back thousands of years—only to ascribe them to the limited time frame of this book.

As is the case with Africa and North America, the lack of written accounts detailing life in this region between 1450 and 1650 forces one to speculate based on very recent writings—most beginning in the late 19th century.

When missionaries and ethnographers began to study daily life in Oceania, many islands of which have been inhabited for over 30,000 years, it was clear that these were cultures of play: evidence of individual and team competition was found in every major island group. In Aboriginal Australia, sports grew from learning the skills necessary for adult life, such as tree climbing, spear throwing, and wrestling. In Polynesia, sporting activities were highly developed and interwoven into each societal level, with a four-month celebration following the harvest called Makahiki that was devoted to sports. During Makahiki, war was forbidden, and athletes competed in boxing, holua sledding, tug of war, surfing, as well as canoe, swimming, and running races.

In addition to sports, ritualized toys and games were common throughout Oceania, and their similarity to those of Native American and African cultures (e.g., the bullroarer, string figures, spinning tops) attests to the universality of how games of chance and modes of play shape and enhance daily life.

The vast Pacific shaped the development of life and culture in Oceania, determining the speed and direction of human movement and how people made a living and shaping peoples' perceptions of the beauty, rhythm, and fury of nature. Above all, the ocean kept these islands isolated until the last 200 years. Oceania's written history may be recent, but its sporting tradition is as old as time.

OCEANIC SPORTS

▦ Boomerang Throwing

The boomerang, a curved throwing stick with skewed ends, is believed to be at least 15,000 years old, making it one of the oldest pieces of sports equipment still used today. It is hard not to think of Australia when you think of the returning boomerang, and indeed the oldest wooden boomerangs (8,000 to 10,000 years old) were discovered in 1974 at Wyrie Swamp in south Australia. But evidence of boomerangs, like the bow and arrow, is widespread, and seems to have developed in ancient Egypt as well as Europe.

A boomerang is held loosely at one end and raised high behind the thrower's ear. The arm is swung forward rapidly and just before the release, the thrower adds spin by flicking the wrist. If thrown correctly, the boomerang sails high in a wide arc and loops back to the thrower. Flights can last several minutes. The world record for maximum time aloft on a single throw is 17 minutes, 6 seconds, set in 1993 with a boomerang made of Kevlar and carbon fiber.

Aboriginal tribes held throwing competitions in which the object was to land the boomerang in a designated target area after completing two or three loops.

Although heavier, nonreturning boomerangs were used in hunting, the returning variety, what we think of today as a boomerang, was thrown for competition and for fun.

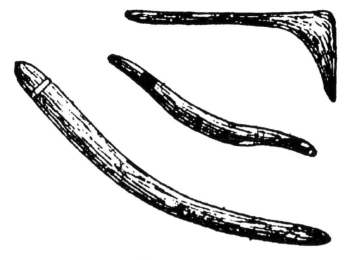

Boomerangs.

A throwing game played today in western Australia is called *kailee,* and the goal is to attain the longest possible boomerang flight before catching it. This is a good activity for class participation. Players line up and throw once each from a specified throwing circle. The area in which the boomerang must be caught successfully can be roughly three times as wide as the throwing circle. Flight durations are timed, and there are five rounds (five throws per participant). The middle time stands as the official time for picking the winner, with ties being broken by players' second-best times.

▦ Football

Various types of football (soccer) were common throughout Oceania. Australian Aborigines played a version without goals or boundaries in which the aim was to keep kicking a ball in the air higher and further than the last person, sort of like ultimate hackey-sack. The types of balls used varied and included kangaroo leather stuffed with animal hair.

A more traditional form of football—one whose object was to kick a ball through an opponent's goal—was played throughout Melanesia, including the islands of Aoba, New Guinea, and the Admiralty Islands. Team sizes always varied but were kept equal. The ball was often a piece of fruit, such as an orange, coconut, or breadfruit.

Football was also played throughout Polynesia, including Hawaii and Tahiti, with balls made from leaves stuffed with grass.

▦ Holua (Land Sledding)

Holua sledding was among the most dangerous and thrilling sports practiced in Hawaii. Competitors shot headfirst down the steep sides of mountains on special sleds capable of deadly speeds. The wooden *papa* (sled) had two narrow runners 10 to 15 feet long with upturned tips and spaced four to five inches apart. A racer held the vehicle by an attached grip, ran to the launching point, and threw himself chest down on the sled, fighting to maintain balance down the grass-lined slope. Courses ranged from a few hundred feet to over two miles. Holua sled tracks were too narrow for side-by-side racing, so the distance determined the winner.

Holua sledding had special significance at the Makahiki festival and was generally a competition reserved for kings and chiefs. Its sheer spectacle and opportunities for gambling made holua sledding popular among all classes.

One of the best preserved holua slides can still be seen on a slope called Pu'u Hinahina backing the Kona Country Club, and an antique holua sled is on display at Hulihe'e Palace in Kailua-Kona.

Another form of sliding was popular among boys and girls as well as adults. Sleds were made of large ti leaves, whose waxy sides were quite slippery. Sliders sat on the wide part of the leaf and steered by clenching and pulling on the top part of the leaf between their legs.

▦ Kangaroo Rat

Kangaroo rat is a game similar in concept to the Native American game of snow snake, which combines strength and technique in hurling an object for distance along the ground. While snow snake involved gliding a specially carved stick over a smooth surface such as a frozen pond, the kangaroo rat is a small piece of wood that is skipped like a stone along the ground. The goal of the game was to achieve the furthest distance or the greatest number of hops.

▦ Keentan (Catch Ball)

Keentan was a ball game popular among Australian Aborigine tribes of Northwest Queensland. Keentan, or catch ball, is a two-team game in which boys and girls participate equally. The rules are simple: one team throws the ball back and forth between its members while members of the opposing team try to intercept it. The ball is thrown high in the air, and interceptions can only be made while the ball is in the air. If a pass is knocked down and touches the ground, or a pass from a teammate is dropped, the other team gets possession of the ball. Players can run anywhere on the field to catch a pass. The game continues until one team is too exhausted to continue. A variation is having the winner be the first team to execute 10 consecutive passes. The game was known as "kangaroo-play" because the jumping players resembled kangaroos.

▦ Maori

Maori is a contest common to New Zealand in which young boys attempt to leap further than anyone else while holding onto a vine. Maori took place over a pond or pool of water with overhanging vines, especially the rata. Participants gripped the vine with fully extended arms, got a running start, bent their knees, and tried to leap as far as possible into the water. The furthest jump won. Maori can be done indoors using a gymnasium climbing rope.

▦ Mungan Mungan

Mungan mungan was an Aboriginal team game played between young boys and men in the Northern Territory of Australia. A white painted stick called a *wormar* representing a young girl is placed in the center of the playing area. The object of the game is for the young boys to try and keep the *wormar* away from the older men by passing it back and forth and evading tackles. The game went until one team quit from exhaustion.

▦ Pit Throwing

This is an Aboriginal throwing game popular among the Kalkadoons of northwestern Queensland in Australia. The object was to throw a stick or bone attached to a piece of twine over a suspended net (one used to catch emus) and into a hole. The game was a test of both skill and accuracy: one had to be strong enough to launch the stick toward the hole without getting it entangled in the net.

This contest can be easily updated and staged in a modern gymnasium with a badminton or volleyball net serving as the net, a large box or recycling bin as the hole, and a stick or small wooden bat serving as the bone. The bin should be placed a few feet behind the center of the net. Players can take turns shooting from the opposite baseline. The first player to land the bone in the bin is the winner. A variation is to play in teams of two or four with players taking a set number of turns, having a successful throw be worth one point, and adding up the final score.

▦ Races

Races in many different venues were popular throughout the Pacific islands. Canoe races often used out-and-back courses of two miles or more.

The sizes of the canoes and outriggers varied and sometimes sails were added to increase speed.

Running races were also popular, and professional Hawaiian runners (Kukini) were known for their great speed and stamina. Races were most often run on the flat sand of the beach at distances of one-half to three-quarters of a mile.

Swimming and surfing were two other favorite racing events. Surfing was more a test of skill than speed, which was dictated by the force of the wave. The ability to stand upon one's board and ride it into shore usually determined the winner.

▦ Reed Darts

Ripening each year during the Makahiki season, sugar cane provided the raw material for one of the festival's most popular events, the *ke'a pua* or "dart of flower stalk" competition. The object of this field event was to throw a sugar cane flower stalk against a small dirt mound or ramp such that it glanced off and, ricocheting upward and away, flew the longest distance.

To make the dart, players cut the roughly two-foot-long flower stalks and lay them out to dry. Once dry, they bound the thick, butt end of the stalk tightly with cord to prevent it from fraying after repeated impacts with the mound. The players then moistened the butt ends of the stalks in their mouths and rubbed them in the dirt. The dirt that clung there added weight to the front end and further blunted it, facilitating the glancing impact necessary for a good ricochet.

When the darts are finished, the players select a small, suitably shaped mound with a smooth dirt face. Standing several paces from the mound, the thrower holds the dart with the right forefinger against the narrow or tail end and the thumb and middle finger on each side of the shaft. The thrower runs several paces, then, with an underhand whipping motion as if skipping a rock over water, throws the dart against the mound at just the right angle so that it careens up and away, a technique that, if executed properly, results in a remarkably high and long trajectory. Whoever achieves the longest flight in a given round won a point, and the player first to achieve ten points won.

In Hawaii, *ke'a pua* was associated strictly with the Makahiki festival because of the flowering season of the sugar cane, but elsewhere in the Pacific, several cultures played a virtually identical game called *teka*, after the general Polynesian word for dart (*ke'a* is the Hawaiian derivative of the word), all year long.

Among the Maori of New Zealand, for example, the game was quite popular, often the occasion for a large social gathering. Here the dart was simply a length of reed, a humble instrument, although one imbued with some measure of supernatural significance. In an interesting cultural echo of the Hawaiian practice of moistening the dart tip with saliva, Maori players spat on the front of the dart tip for good luck and then recited a charm asking that the dart fly like a meteor across the sky before casting it at the dirt mound. The *teka* also figures prominently in a number of Maori myths, all of which share the theme of finding some lost love or thing of value based on where the *teka* lands after a series of throws. In one story, a chief becomes separated from his infant son. Years later, the son, not realizing who his father is, follows a magic dart to his father's door and thereby regains his legacy. Taking the magic element to its logical conclusion, the native inhabitants of the Samoan islands a thousand miles to the northeast of New Zealand claimed that the success of a throw depended on whether the *teka* itself was inherently lucky or unlucky—a fine way to save face after a disappointing throw.

For those wishing to reenact *teka*, the equipment, obviously, is quite simple. A reed or thin, straight stick between two and three feet long will do. The only prerequisite is that the butt end must be both heavy enough to carry the stick in a straight line and blunt enough to avoid catching in the dirt mound. The mound can be made with a shovel, although this might be somewhat dirty and vexing to the grounds keeper; finding a natural, bare knoll is probably best. A propped-up sheet of plywood also will work as a ramp. In any case, some practice will be necessary to develop the proper angle of the pitch.

▦ Spear Throwing

Proficiency at throwing a spear was an essential skill, and thus practice punctuated by competition was common throughout most of Oceania. Competitions included shooting at targets, throwing at moving targets, and throwing for distance. Sometimes actual spears (those used for hunting or in battle) were used. In some places, including Melanesia, pointed reeds or sticks were used. Targets ranged from tree trunks and boughs to a piece of fruit on top of a pole.

In Samoa, men and women both competed in spear-throwing tournaments called *litia*. The spears used were hibiscus sticks over eight feet long. Two competitors—one from each team—threw at once. The side with the most winners won the match.

Spear-throwing games such as the Maori boorna jokee also proliferated. In that game, used to develop skills for battle, young boys took turns standing in the center of the group while the rest threw blunted spears made from reeds or bamboo at him. The players had to avoid the spears by ducking and weaving or blocking them with a small shield.

This activity is easy to re-create with spears made from reeds, thin branches, or dowel rods with foam pads glued to the tips. Small shields can be cut from cardboard.

▦ Spearing the Disc

Spearing the disc was a game common to young boys and men of most Australian tribes. A disc made of thick bark measuring between one and three feet in diameter was rolled across an open space or downhill in front of a line of players, each of whom held a small spear five to eight inches in length. As the disc passed, each one tried to spear it. The winner was the one whose spear hit closest to the center of the disc.

One variation was to replace the disc with two sticks tied together in the form of a cross that was rolled vertically so that it bounced along the ground, representing a bounding wallaby. The line of players tried to knock it down.

This game is easy to re-create using either a hula hoop or a large, round lid. Tennis balls can be used to replace the spears.

▦ Surfing

No one knows exactly where and when surfing began, but it is clear that Hawaiian natives had perfected the sport of *he'e nalu* (wave-sliding) on boards made of wood from the breadfruit tree as early as the 15th century. Hawaii's location in the middle of the immense Pacific put it in the path of the largest and most varied ocean waves on earth, and thus surfing became the most popular traditional sport in Hawaii.

Surfboards were usually cut from tree trunks with stone tools and varied in length from about 9 to 18 feet and were about as wide as a man's chest.

The earliest written account of surfing post-dates the Renaissance by 130 years but nonetheless provides a vivid description of a sport that had not likely changed over the centuries. In 1779, Lieutenant James King, commander of the *Discovery,* completed the narrative portion of Captain Cook's journals after Cook's death and devoted two pages to a description of surfing he witnessed on Kealakekua Bay on the coast of Kona.

> But a diversion the most common is upon the Water, where there is a very great Sea, and surf breaking on the Shore. The Men sometimes 20 or 30 go without the Swell of the Surf, & lay themselves flat upon an oval piece of plan about their Size and breadth, they keep their legs close on top of it, & their Arms are us'd to guide the plank, thye wait the time of the greatest Swell that sets on Shore, & altogether push forward with their Arms to keep on its top, it sends them in with a most astonishing Velocity, & the great art is to guide the plan so as always to keep it in a proper direction on the top of the Swell, & as it alters its direct. If the Swell drives him close to the rocks before he is overtaken by its break, he is much prais'd.

The form and style of surfing King describes is, apart from technical advances in the boards, similar to modern surfing. But the sport took on other forms throughout Oceania. Melanesian surfboards, for example, were quite small, about 12 by 18 inches, and were placed under the chest in the manner of the modern boogie board. This type of surfing was popular with men and women of all ages.

⠿ Tree Climbing

Tree climbing contests were popular among Aboriginal tribes in Australia (especially the tribes of Victoria) and Polynesia (notably Samoa). The ability to climb trees to gather fruit, survey territory, or escape storms was a vital skill in which boys and girls often received special training augmented by competitions. The contest was usually a race to see who could climb up and down a tree the fastest. As skills increased, more challenging trees were selected for contests.

⠿ *Ulumaika* (Pitching Disks)

Ulumaika is the generic term for any one of several traditional Hawaiian games played with flat, round stones roughly the size of small wheels of cheese. Among these are a kind of bowling event in which the object is to roll the *ulumaika* disk through a pair of upright sticks planted in the ground and an indoor game resembling quoits or horseshoes in which players attempt to pitch their disks closest to the edge of a mat on the floor.

Historians believe that the stone *ulumaika* disk developed as a more rugged substitute for disks made from slices of breadfruit, a dietary staple among many Polynesian islands. This theory is bolstered by the fact that in some areas of Hawaii and Samoa children continued to play with breadfruit disks, slicing one and a half inch cross-sections of the round, unripened fruit and trimming the edges to make the disks slightly convex like their stone counterparts. Further, the word '*ulu* means "breadfruit" in Hawaii, and when combined with the word *maika* means "breadfruit pitching disk" even when applied to disks made of stone.

The stone *ulumaika* pitching disks were quite handsomely carved and polished, an undertaking that, considering the lack of iron tools, speaks both to early Hawaiian craftsmanship and a fondness for the game. Fashioned from gray basalt or coral, the expertly rounded *ulumaika* disks used in the bowling game were for the most part slightly convex, the beveling on the edges kept uniform to ensure a straight run. Less often, the bowling *ulumaika* disks were convex only on one side, causing a curved run as they listed slightly on their way. For these one-sided disks, special curved tracks were used, adding an extra challenge to the competition. When reenacting the game, a perfect substitute for the regular or two-sided *ulumaika* is a five-pound barbell weight—not the iron type, but rather the thicker, cheaper kind made of concrete in a plastic shell.

The playing field for bowling *ulumaika* may be any flat, relatively hard surface such as a baseline of a baseball diamond or a length of trail in which the ground has been packed firm. Two stakes pounded into the ground about five inches apart are the goal, and the pitching area is 30 or 40 yards back from that. Scoring may be informal; the winner is the first player to roll his or her disk through the uprights without touching either or the first to score a certain number of successful rolls. The quoits-style *ulumaika* game required a thinner, lighter disc of basalt or slate weighing between two and seven ounces because the object here was to pitch the disk a short distance onto a mat.

▦ Wrestling

As is the case with nearly every world culture, wrestling was immensely popular throughout Oceania, especially in Polynesia. Wrestling matches drew huge audiences, and numerous styles existed, including seated wrestling, pulling hooked fingers, foot pushing, and the standard upright style. Wrestling was also common on the Admiralty Islands and throughout Australia. The Aborigines developed many conventions common to modern wrestling, including boundaries for the match, rules of fair play, and rituals such as the oiling of bodies prior to a match.

OCEANIC PLAY

▦ The Bullroarer

A bullroarer is an Aboriginal noisemaker: a flat piece of wood, about an inch and a half wide and three to six inches long, attached to a piece of string through a hole drilled in one end and tied to another stick 18 to 20 inches long. The longer stick was held in one hand and the bullroarer swung around over one's head, producing a humming or howling sound

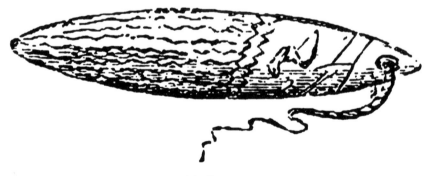

A bullroarer.

that was likened to those of animals or spirits. The instrument also can be made to crack like a whip with a turn of the wrist. Traditionally, the string was made from the sinews of a kangaroo's tail.

Use of the bullroarer varied depending on location: in north central Queensland, men, women, boys, and girls all used the toy. In other areas, it was for men and boys only. On the Bloomfield River, boys were allowed to play with them in public after their first initiation ceremony. In some areas, females were forbidden to view the toy, and it was used to warn women and children away from intruding on men's sacred ceremonies.

Bullroarers were also used among Native American tribes and were believed to cause or cure sickness, bring rain, and promote fertility.

A bullroarer can be made easily using a ruler (many already have a hole in one end) tied to a short stick or baton using a thin leather cord.

▓ Hand Games

Traditionally the Maori have placed great value on the reflexes and agility that make for a fine warrior, inventing a range of games and physical activities designed to promote quickness even in the youngest warrior-to-be. Among these are the *mahi rinaringa* or "hand games," gesture-copying exercises that resemble the familiar playground game of Simon says. The object of these two-person games is to anticipate and simultaneously mimic the next move of one's partner as he or she performs at random a series of standard moves.

While some of the hand games involve a difficult and complicated series of movements, one hand game, called *hei tama tu tama*, is simple enough for beginners, although if done properly it should be quite vigorous and tiring. The game has four basic moves, all of them performed standing: (1) both fists on hips; (2) both fists raised to head level with arms to the sides; (3) right fist raised head level, left fist on hip; and (4) left fist raised head level, right fist on hip.

The game commences with both players facing one another in the first position. As agreed in advance, one player starts as the "caller" and the other the "follower." The caller utters the traditional challenge to play, "*hei tama tu tama*," and the other accepts by calling "*ae*" or "yes." Next, the caller quickly assumes one of the other three positions while chanting "*hei tama tu tama*." At that moment the follower also assumes one of the other three positions, much as in the familiar rock, paper, scissors game.

If the follower fails to match the motion of the caller, the round is a wash and the follower immediately becomes the caller, again chanting "*hei tama tu tama*" and assuming a position for the new follower to match. If the follower matches the caller's motion exactly and without hesitation, he or she wins a point and immediately becomes the caller for the next round. A follower who wins a point in this manner must not hesitate to call out the next movement because the caller can block the point by shouting "*ra*" before the follower gets the next call out. When a caller successfully blocks the point, he or she remains the caller and wins a point. Thus a good game of *hei tama tu tama* should move quite quickly with rapid, cardiovascular-improving gestures as each attempts to thwart the other's point while winning his or her own. The game ends when one of the players reaches the number of points to which the players have agreed in advance.

For those not looking to work up a sweat, a more sedate version of the game called *hipitoi* involves only thumb movements. This game proceeds very much like *hei tama tu tama*, except that the following movements, each of which begins with both fists together at the palms, substitute for the former game's arm movements: (1) both thumbs up; (2) both thumbs down; (3) left thumb up, right thumb down; and (4) right thumb up, left thumb down. The caller chants "*hipitoi*" upon moving, and the follower attempts to match the thumb position. Points are scored or blocked exactly as in *hei tama tu tama*.

▦ *Kilu*

Prior to the arrival of Europeans, traditional Hawaiian society was composed of two distinct groups, the common folk and the aristocracy, or *ali'i*. To promote bonding among the *ali'i*, and to discourage marriage between members of different social classes, the *ali'i* came up with *kilu*, a kind of dating game in which only the *ali'i* participated. The object of this shuffleboard-like game was to scoot an inverted bowl across the floor and hit the wooden marker of the person in whom one had a romantic interest, thereby winning a kiss from that person.

Of course, the *ali'i*, while an exclusive group, could hardly prevent the gods themselves from playing. In Hawaiian mythology, Pele, the goddess of volcanoes and maker of new land, had a dream in which she travels to the neighboring island of Kaua'i and there meets a demigod named Lohi'au. The two fall in love, but Pele's younger sister, Hi'iaka, fearing that Pele might never awaken, rouses her from her happy dream. Pele begs Hi'iaka to go to Kaua'i and bring back Lohi'au. Hi'iaka agrees, but on the condition that Pele guard Hi'iaka's favorite groves and her friend, Hopoe. Satisfied with Pele's assurances, Hi'iaka travels to Kuau'i and finds Lohi'au. As the two are returning, however, they happen upon one of Lohi'au's former lovers. She challenges Lohi'au to a game of *kilu* with the hopes of winning him back. Lohi'au accepts. The resulting delay in Lohi'au's return causes Pele to have a jealous tantrum, her lava flowing down and destroying Hi'aka's grove and friend. Enraged, Hi'iaka seeks revenge by causing Pele to have a vision of Lohi'au and Hi'iaka together as lovers. Consequently, when Lohi'au and Hi'iaka finally arrive, Pele has another tantrum and destroys her love Lohi'au. Clearly the *ali'i* expected happier outcomes.

To play, five men and five women, all *ali'i,* would assemble in the recreation house, a public building set aside for games and amusements, the very place in which, only the night before, men and women of lesser rank might have played *'ume,* the commoners' version of the game. The *ali'i* men would sit at one end of the hall while the women sat at the other, each placing a cone-shaped block of wood in front of them. A *helu 'ai,* or "tally-keeper," represented each team.

Before a round, the two tally-keepers met in the middle of the room. In a low voice one of the tally-keepers would say the name of a player he or she represented, and the other tally-keeper, based on the knowledge of the romantic desires of the players, would respond, likewise in a low voice, with the name of one of his or her players. The two tally-keepers then return to their respective sides and hand the aforementioned players each a bowl, called a *kilu,* made from half a coconut.

Once the male player received his *kilu,* he would turn it upside-down and, sliding it across the floor, attempt to hit the wood block in front of the female who had the other *kilu.* If he was successful, he crossed over to the female player for his prize, a *hongi,* that is, the Polynesian greeting of pressing noses together. After the male had his turn, the female would attempt to hit his block with the *kilu,* her accuracy more or less dependent on her interest in him.

▦ Knucklebones

Knucklebones, familiar to American children as the playground game of jacks, is an ancient and widely distributed pastime throughout the world. The game takes its name in the West from the practice in ancient Greece of casting the dice-like knucklebones from a leg of mutton on the ground for gambling or divination.

From this practice a game emerged whose object was to throw a small pebble into the air and scoop up a number of the knucklebones laid out on the ground in various configurations while the pebble is still in the air. Elsewhere, instead of knucklebones, the game pieces might be small pebbles, nuts, berries or whatever materials are available, in which case the game is sometimes called "jackstones."

While the game has been played by a variety of cultures from the Greeks to modern Eskimos, the Maori of New Zealand seem to have a special affinity for the game, many tribes inventing their own distinctive versions of the game for children and adults.

In general, the Maori knucklebone games proceed in a series of progressively difficult movements, each of which must be successfully completed before the player may progress to the next. The Ngai Tahu tribe of

New Zealand's South Island play an eight-movement knucklebone game with five stones called *koruru*. The movements proceed as follows:

1. Arrange four stones on the ground in two pairs. Then, tossing a fifth stone into the air with the right hand, snatch up one pair and catch the fifth stone before it lands. While keeping hold of the first pair, throw the fifth stone back into the air and snatch the remaining pair, catching the fifth stone before it lands without dropping the first pair.

2. Arrange four stones in a small square on the ground. Tossing one of the four stones into the air, snatch up the remaining three and catch the fourth before it lands. This move must be completed twice successfully before proceeding to the third move.

3. Arrange four stones in a small square on the ground. Tossing a fifth stone into the air, snatch up the four stones and catch the fifth before it lands.

4. Hold four stones in one hand and throw one into the air, catching it with the same hand. Repeat. Then repeat movement number one.

5. Arrange four stones in a small square. Tossing a fifth stone into the air, move one of the four stones into the center of the square. Catch the fifth stone before it lands and repeat until all four stones are in a pile in the center. Throw the fifth stone into the air and snatch all four stones, catching the fifth stone before it lands.

6. Hold all five stones. Toss one into the air and arrange the remaining four in a square on the ground, catching the fifth before it lands.

7. Throw all five stones and catch them on the back of the same hand.

8. Place one stone on the ground and toss the other four in the air. Snatch up the first stone and, with the same hand, catch the rest before they hit the ground.

While knucklebones is often thought of as a children's game, it is not uncommon among the Maori for adults to compete either one on one or in family or village teams of two to ten players. For competition between two players, one player goes first (as agreed in advance) and works his or her way through the movements until a mistake occurs. At that point, the other player takes a turn, likewise progressing through the movements until a mistake occurs. Then the first player picks up where he or she left off, and so on until one of the players completes all of the movements and thereby wins.

For team play, the members of each team begin the movements simultaneously at a signal. Any player who makes a mistake must either return to the beginning movement or attempt the unsuccessful movement again until successful, as agreed in advance. The first team whose members complete all of the movements wins.

▦ *Mumu*

Children and young adults in Papua, New Guinea, are fond of identification games along the lines of blind man's buff. *Mumu* (smoke) is one such game in which one player with closed eyes tries to catch and identify one of the players encircling him or her. The player chosen to be it stands in the center of the circle and closes his or her eyes. The other players dart in and try to gently touch the player on the head. If the player in the center can grab someone, he or she must identify the person without opening her eyes. If successful, that player goes into the center for the next round. A nearly identical game is blind man. In this variation, the player in the center is blindfolded but is given a few seconds to view the order in which people are standing. After the blindfold is put on, the circle moves a few steps to the right or left. The player then moves to touch and identify a player just as in *mumu*.

⊞ String Figures

String figures (e.g., cat's cradle, Jacob's ladder) are games in which shapes are built by winding and weaving long pieces of string through the fingers in moves of increasing complexity that sometimes require two people. String figures predate history and are among the most universal pastimes. Their use in ritual, storytelling, and as mnemonic devices for such things as recitations of lineage gave string figures greater significance in the nonliterate islands of Oceania. A good deal of history and culture could be woven into this intricate form of play.

The shape of the figure might re-create the building of a house, as in the *naum* figure of the Maori people of New Zealand; it could be adapted from a region's flora and fauna, as in the palm tree figure from Torres Strait, or in the crane from Fiji, for which a picture and directions follow.

1. Place the string on each hand so that the string runs across the palm in front of the index, middle and ring fingers, but behind the thumb and little finger, across to the other hand.

2. From above pass right thumb behind left hand palmer loop and return to position, rotating thumb towards you as you do so.

3. Pass left thumb from below into left little finger loop and return with the near string.

4. Insert index fingers into thumb loops from below and return with far strings; release little fingers.

5. Transfer index loops to little fingers.

6. Insert index fingers from below into thumb loops and return with far thumb strings.

7. Navajo thumbs and release little-finger loops.

8. Pass little fingers towards you under transverse far index string, then over the oblique strings which cross the far index string, and pick up the transverse string in the middle of the figure on the backs of the fingers and return to position.

9. Pass thumbs under far index strings and return with these strings on their backs.

10. Navajo thumbs, and release index loops.
11. Take up on tips of index fingers the oblique strings that form the bases of the triangular spaces under the thumbs, pressing the thumbs against the index fingers to hold the strings secure. This makes A Crane.

> Hornell, James. *String Figures from Fiji and Western Polynesia.* Bernice P. Bishop Museum, Bulletin No. 39, Honolulu, 1927

▦ Top Spinning

Throughout Oceania, children and adults loved to spin tops. Tops could be manufactured for the purpose (usually out of baked clay) and made from small pebbles, nuts, shells, and fruits, by piercing with a twig and then spinning on any flat surface.

The people of Cape Bedford in Queensland made tops by pushing a small splinter through a flattened disk of beeswax. The Cooper Creek (Australia) people molded clay tops around small wooden pegs.

The Murray Island people in Torres Strait made tops out of stone, with a hole drilled through for a stick. They sometimes weighed nine pounds. The stone was 5 to 10 inches in diameter, and the stick was 7 to 15 inches long. The tops were intricately painted. During competitions, onlookers sang special songs while the contestants spun their tops on pieces of melon skin. Some could spin for more than half an hour.

The women of Lake Eyre baked tops made from flattening one side of a spinning ball and inserting a small wooden peg. They would then spin them inside wooden bowls, sometimes separately, and sometimes all at once. The person whose top spun the longest won.

The people of the Lower Tully Valley in Queensland, Australia, made a spinning top, called an *ngor-go,* by threading a string through two holes drilled into one side of a dried gourd. The thumbs were inserted at either end of the wide loop and the string twisted by spinning the ball. When the hands are pulled apart, the string unwinds, spinning the ball. Then the tension is quickly released, allowing the spinning ball to twist the string again. The ball can be kept spinning indefinitely like a yo-yo.

In addition to tops, spinning balls were also favorite toys throughout Oceania. Balls were usually made from mixtures of clay, lime, ash, or sand; they were rolled smooth and then baked hard. Players might spin two balls at once, the winner being the one whose ball spun the longest.

OCEANIC GAMES

▦ *Konane*

When Captain John Cook became the first European to set foot on Hawaii in 1784, he found the native Hawaiians playing an already ancient board game called *konane*. Played on a grid with sometimes over 200 black and white pieces, the object of this two-player capturing game is to force one's opponent into a position such that there are no longer any moves in which he or she can jump, and thereby capture, an enemy piece.

There were no official dimensions for a *konane* board; games with grids of varying sizes carved in slabs of lava or native wood have been found at archeological sites throughout the island. A 10-by-11 square grid with 110 intersections or points is a good, not-too-unwieldy size with which to start, although the game can be made longer and more challenging without affecting the basic style of play simply by increasing the size of the grid. Boards with up to 238 points were not uncommon; the games on them, when played by the elder men of a village, sometimes lasted from morning to sunset.

The game pieces are simply round black and white stones much like checkers. The best ones, according to tradition, are found at the beach of Haloa near Ninole in Hawaii, where the surf has ground bits of black basalt and white coral into polished game pieces. Black and white buttons the size of pennies will certainly work.

The rules of the game are very simple. On a grid of 110 points, each player begins with 55 game pieces. Facing one another the long way over the board, the players arrange the pieces alternating black and white in each row until the board is filled. Two adjacent black and white pieces in the center of the board (sixth rank, columns five and six) are removed, leaving two empty points. (Traditionally, the initial empty spaces of some wooden *konane* boards were marked with inlaid human molars, their crowns flush with the surface of the board, an adornment, however, that might be somewhat difficult to replicate unless one is friends with an oral surgeon.) White moves first. To move, one must always jump, and thereby capture, an enemy piece.

The jumping capture may occur when an enemy piece occupies a point immediately adjacent (in any direction) to the capturing piece and the space on the opposite side of the enemy piece is empty; the capturing piece jumps over the enemy, landing on the opposite side, and the enemy is removed. Jumping captures may be linked together in one move, as in checkers, if there is an enemy piece vulnerable to capture adjacent to the space on which the capturing piece lands. Linked captures are not mandatory, however. The capturing piece may stop after the initial capture if the player so chooses. Each player takes turns jumping and capturing the pieces of the other until one of the players is left in a position in which he or she is unable to jump and capture an enemy piece. At that point the other player wins.

⠿ Lulu

Lulu is a Hawaiian dice game played with four dice in which the object is to be the first player to achieve 100 points by adding up the value of rolls on each turn. Hawaiian dice were made from round, two-sided pieces of igneous (formed from cooling lava) rock that were smoothed and then painted. One side was blank, and the other side contained one, two, three, or four dots to indicate its value.

Four discs were used to play lulu. Players shook the dice in both hands and tossed them on the ground, receiving the total value of those that fell face up, for a maximum of 10 points per turn. Any that fell face down were rolled by the next player and added to his or her score.

You can make dice by marking small, round stones with a white X and then adding one, two, three, and four dots to the pieces with red paint. In a pinch, you could use Scrabble tiles (which are blank on one side) for letters worth one to four points, respectively.

▦ Mu Torrere

The only indigenous board game of the Maori culture, *mu torrere* is a two-player strategy game played on an eight-point star. The object of the game is to box in one's opponent such that he or she has no free spaces in which to move.

The game is most closely associated with the Ngati Porou tribe of New Zealand's North Island. Here the players make their *mu torrere* game boards on an as-needed basis from local materials, either scratching them in the dirt, drawing them with charcoal on flat pieces of wood, or etching them on the green inner bark of the totara plant so that, as the bark dries, the designs darken, the curling sheets of bark held flat by sticks tied at either end.

Because the Maori also refer to the European game of draughts as *mu*, an apparent transliteration of the English word "move," there is some thought that *mu torrere* is an early colonial import, perhaps a variant of draughts. Several factors weigh against this theory, however. First, the two games bear no resemblance to one another, except, of course, for the unhelpful observation that in both games pieces move around a pattern on a game board. Otherwise, the two games have nothing in common, the manner of movement and ultimate objective of each being quite different. Second, the Maori readily adopted draughts into their small repertory of board games. Their enthusiasm for draughts, and the extent to which the game has survived unchanged since its introduction, suggests that *mu torrere* did not descend from draughts, evolving away from its European roots to satisfy the cultural preferences of the Maori. In other words, the two games are from two distinct families, one European, the other Maori. The *mu* was probably added to *torrere* as a prefix sometime after the introduction of draughts.

To play, draw a game board on a piece of paper by making an eight-pointed star with equidistant points at north, south, east, and west, with one point in between to make eight. Connect the points with lines to a circle in the middle of the star, known as the *putahi*. Next, find eight game pieces, four black and four white. Pebbles or bits of wood will do as long as each player's pieces are distinctive.

One player places his or her game pieces on the four points on one side of the board, and the second player places the remaining pieces on the remaining four points so that the pieces face each other with the center the only unoccupied space. White moves first, and the players alternate thereafter. A player may move a piece into the center (*putahi*) or onto an adjacent, unoccupied point of the star. Pieces may not share a point or the *putahi*, nor may pieces jump over other pieces. There is no capturing in this game. The object of the game is to arrange one's pieces such that the opponent has no free adjacent spaces in which to move. In order to avoid blocking in a player in the opening move for an immediate, unfair win (white moving three into the *putahi* on the first move, for example, would result in no legal moves for black and the game would end prematurely) during the first two moves of the game, only the pieces on points one, four, five, and eight may move. After that, there are no restrictions on movement except for those stated above. The first player without a legal move loses.

⊞ BIBLIOGRAPHY

Achebe, Chinua. *Things Fall Apart.* New York: Fawcett Crest, 1959.

Anderson, James M. *Daily Life during the Spanish Inquisition.* Westport, CT: Greenwood Press, 2002.

Ashe, Arthur, Jr. *A Hard Road to Glory: A History of the African-American Athlete 1619–1918.* New York: Warner Books, 1988.

Baker, William J. *Sports in the Western World.* Totowa, NJ: Rowman and Littlefield, 1982.

Baker, William J., and James A. Mangan (editors). *Sport in Africa: Essays in Social History.* New York: African Publishing (Holms & Meier), 1987.

Bell, R. C. *Board and Table Games from Many Civilizations.* New York: Dover Books, 1979.

Brasch, Rudolph. *How Did Sport Begin? A Look at the Origins of Man at Play.* New York: David McKay, 1970.

Bryant, A.T. *The Zulu People.* Pietermaritzburg: Shuter and Shooter, 1949.

Byrd, William. *The Diary and Life of William Byrd of Virginia.* Edited by Kenneth A. Lockridge. London: 1987.

Castiglione, Baldassare. *The Book of the Courtier* (a new translation by Charles Singleton). New York: Doubleday, 1959.

Cohen, Elizabeth S., and Thomas V. Cohen. *Daily Life in Renaissance Italy.* Westport, CT: Greenwood Press, 2001.

Corbett, Doris, et al. *Unique Games & Sports around the World.* Westport, CT: Greenwood Press, 2001.

Cordesm, Kathleen A. "Sport of the Aztec and Maya Indians." North American Society for Sport History, Proceedings and Newsletter, Columbus, Ohio, 1979.

Cullin, Stewart. *Games of the North American Indians.* New York: Dover, 1975.

Duran, Fray Diego. *Book of the Gods and Rites and the Ancient Calendar.* Translated by Fernando Horcasitas and Doris Heyden. Norman: University of Oklahoma Press, 1977.

Ferguson, Wallace K. *The Renaissance.* New York: Holt, Rinehart, and Winston, 1940.

Ferguson, Wallace K. *The Renaissance—Six Essays.* New York: Harper Torch Books, 1953.

Hale, J.R. *The Civilization of Europe in the Renaissance.* New York: Simon & Schuster, 1995.

Hoby, Sir Thomas. *The Courtyer of Count Baldessar Castilio.* London: Wyllyam Sereres, 1561. Reprinted London: David Nutt, 1900.

Huizinga, J. *The Waning of the Middle Ages.* New York: Doubleday, 1954.

Khuri, Fuad I. *Tents and Pyramids: Games and Ideology in Arab Culture from Backgammon to Autocratic Rule.* London: Saqi Books, 1990.

Levinson, David, and Karen Christensen (editors). *Encyclopedia of World Sport.* Denver: ABC-CLIO, 1996.

Mathys, Fritz K. "The Ritual Character of Ball Games in Ancient Mexico." *Olympic Review* 221 (1986): 173–76.

Mathys, Fritz K. "Shakespeare and Sport." *Olympic Review* 285 (1991): 344–47.

Morgan, Ted. *Wilderness at Dawn: The Settling of the North American Continent.* New York: Simon & Schuster, 1993.

Parlett, David. *The Oxford History of Board Games.* New York: Oxford University Press, 1999.

Pettegree, Andrew. *Europe in the Sixteenth Century.* Oxford: Blackwell, 2002.

Rowse, A.L. *The Elizabethan Renaissance,* Volume 1: *The Life of the Society.* New York: Scribner, 1971.

Russell, Bertrand. *A History of Western Philosophy.* New York: Simon & Schuster, 1945.

Singman, Jeffrey L. *Daily Life in Elizabethan England.* Westport, CT: Greenwood Press, 1995.

Spears, Betty, and Richard A. Swanson. *History of Sport and Physical Education in the United States.* Madison, WI: Brown & Benchmark, 1978.

Spears, Betty. "Chinese Sport during the Ming Dynasty." North American Society for Sport History, Proceedings and Newsletter, Columbus, Ohio, 1984.

Stow, George. *Native Races of South Africa.* London: Swan and Sornenschein, 1905.

Struna, Nancy L. *People of Prowess: Sport, Labor, and Leisure in Early Anglo-America.* Urbana and Chicago: University of Illinois Press, 1996.

de Vaca, Cabeza. *Cabeza de Vaca's Adventures in the Unknown Interior of America.* University of New Mexico Press, 1983.

Wagner, Eric. *Sport in Asia and Africa: A Comparative Handbook.* Westport, CT: Greenwood Press, 1989.

Weir, Alison. *Henry VIII: The King and His Court.* New York: Ballantine Books, 2001.

Wilkins, Sally. *Sports and Games of Medieval Cultures.* Westport, CT: Greenwood Press, 2001.

Williams, Penry. *Life in Tudor England.* New York: Putnam, 1973.

Zimmerman, Susan, and Ronald E.F. Weissman. *Urban Life in the Renaissance.* Dover: University of Delaware Press, 1989.

▦ INDEX

About the Author

ANDREW LEIBS is a noted expert on sports and disability. He is the author of *A Field Guide for the Sight-Impaired Reader* and is editor of Greenwood's "Sports and Games through History" series. *Sports and Games of the Renaissance* is his second book. The National Sportscasters and Sportswriters Association named Leibs New Hampshire Sportswriter of the Year in 1997 for his work at the *Manchester Union Leader*. He has written on sports and disability for numerous publications, including the *Boston Globe* and the *San Francisco Examiner* and has presented at national conferences. He lives in Portsmouth, New Hampshire.